THE CONSTITUTION

Singapore's Constitution was hastily drafted after her secession from the Federation of Malaysia in 1965. In the subsequent 50 years, the Constitution has been amended many times to evolve a Constitution like no other in the world. Outwardly, Singapore has a Westminster-type constitutional democracy, with an elected legislature, fundamental liberties and safeguards to ensure the independence of the judiciary. On closer inspection, the Constitution displays many innovative and unusual characteristics. Most notable among them are the various types of Members of Parliament that have been introduced since the mid-1980s, the office of the Elected President and the fact that there is no constitutional right to property. This volume seeks to explain the nature and context of these constitutional innovations in the context of a pluralistic, multi-ethnic state obsessed with public order and security. The volatile racial mix of Singapore, with its majority Chinese population nestled in a largely Malay/Islamic world, compels the state to search for ethnic management solutions through the Constitution to guarantee to the Malays and other ethnic minorities their status in the polity. In addition, it examines how the concept of the rule of law is perceived by the strong centrist state governed by a political party that has been in power since 1959 and continues to hold almost hegemonic power.

Constitutional Systems of the World
General Editors: Peter Leyland, Andrew Harding
and Benjamin L Berger
Associate Editors: Grégoire Webber and Rosalind Dixon

In the era of globalisation, issues of constitutional law and good governance are being seen increasingly as vital issues in all types of society. Since the end of the Cold War, there have been dramatic developments in democratic and legal reform, and post-conflict societies are also in the throes of reconstructing their governance systems. Even societies already firmly based on constitutional governance and the rule of law have undergone constitutional change and experimentation with new forms of governance; and their constitutional systems are increasingly subjected to comparative analysis and transplantation. Constitutional texts for practically every country in the world are now easily available on the internet. However, texts which enable one to understand the true context, purposes, interpretation and incidents of a constitutional system are much harder to locate, and are often extremely detailed and descriptive. This series seeks to provide scholars and students with accessible introductions to the constitutional systems of the world, supplying both a road map for the novice and, at the same time, a deeper understanding of the key historical, political and legal events which have shaped the constitutional landscape of each country. Each book in this series deals with a single country, or a group of countries with a common constitutional history, and each author is an expert in their field.

Published volumes

The Constitution of the United Kingdom; The Constitution of the United States; The Constitution of Vietnam; The Constitution of South Africa; The Constitution of Japan; The Constitution of Germany; The Constitution of Finland; The Constitution of Australia; The Constitution of the Republic of Austria; The Constitution of the Russian Federation; The Constitutional System of Thailand; The Constitution of Malaysia; The Constitution of China; The Constitution of Indonesia; The Constitution of France; The Constitution of Spain; The Constitution of Mexico; The Constitution of Canada

Link to series website
http://www.hartpub.co.uk/series/csw

The Constitution of Singapore

A Contextual Analysis

Kevin YL Tan

·HART·
PUBLISHING
OXFORD AND PORTLAND, OREGON
2015

Published in the United Kingdom by Hart Publishing Ltd
16C Worcester Place, Oxford, OX1 2JW
Telephone: +44 (0)1865 517530
Fax: +44 (0)1865 510710
E-mail: mail@hartpub.co.uk
Website: http://www.hartpub.co.uk

Published in North America (US and Canada) by
Hart Publishing
c/o International Specialized Book Services
920 NE 58th Avenue, Suite 300
Portland, OR 97213-3786
USA
Tel: +1 503 287 3093 or toll-free: (1) 800 944 6190
Fax: +1 503 280 8832
E-mail: orders@isbs.com
Website: http://www.isbs.com

© Kevin YL Tan 2015

Hart Publishing is an imprint of Bloomsbury Publishing plc.

British Library Cataloguing in Publication Data
Data Available

ISBN: 978-1-84946-396-6

Typeset by Compuscript Ltd, Shannon
Printed and bound in Great Britain by
CPI Group (UK) Ltd, Croydon CR0 4YY

Contents

Table of Cases

Table of Legislation

Sri Lanka

Straits Settlements

United Kingdom

Introduction

General – Towards Independence and Three Imperatives – Organisation of the Book

I. GENERAL

SINGAPORE IS AN unlikely country and an even more unlikely nation. It is small, with a land area of about 716 sq km although it was originally much smaller. Through decades of massive land reclamation, its original 580 sq km was increased to its current size. Situated at the tip of the Malay peninsula, it is an essentially Chinese city-state sitting in the middle of a Malay-Muslim region, with Malaysia to its north and Indonesia to its south. With absolutely no natural resources, it is difficult to imagine that Singapore is a thriving metropolis with a population of 5.4 million and a Gross National Product of over US$280 million making it one of the richest countries in the world. Singapore's population is made up of Chinese (74%), Malays (13%), Indians (9.1%) and other minorities (3.9%). Its population is also multi-religious, with 42.5% Buddhists, 13% Muslim, 8.5% Taoists, 4% Hindus, 4.8% Catholics and 9.8% non-Catholic Christians.

Singapore's economic success stemmed initially from its excellent location. It was the desperate search by the British for a foothold 'in the Eastward' to break the Dutch monopoly on the spice trade, that led them to the island. Declaring it a free port, the British immediately succeeded in attracting numerous erstwhile traders from the region to the island which was blessed with a deep harbour and ample fresh water supplies. Singapore was a British colony from 1824 to 1963, and during this time, grew from a small village to become one of Britain's most important possessions and significant military bases. English law was officially introduced to Singapore through the Second Charter of

Justice in 1826 and this provided the basic legal framework enabling the merchants to conduct their businesses and trade, assured that their rights could be enforced by the courts.

While English justice provided the backdrop to a flourishing mercantile community, the settlement's institutions were overtly colonial in structure. Even after the Straits Settlements (which included Singapore, Malacca and Penang) was transferred to the Colonial Office in 1867 and when it was given its own Legislative Council, there was no provision for democratic representation on the Council. True, the Governor tried his best to include the Settlements' leading merchants and community leaders, but this was driven by a practical, rather than democratic impulse. These leaders were needed to help the Governor keep everyone in check, and to smooth things over if relationships became strained.

This state of affairs persisted for some 80 years. The placidity of the general population and tolerance of British rule was due largely to the fact that many of the early traders, especially those who came from China and India, were sojourners who never imagined sinking roots in Singapore. This was where they made their fortunes, not where they eventually retired. The same could be said for most of the European traders. It was only after the Japanese Occupation (1942–45) that a spirit of nationalism and self-determination was awoken among its long-term residents. This was when ideas of representations, democracy, fairness and equality of the races became important and crept into everyday discussions about the future.

II. TOWARDS INDEPENDENCE AND THREE IMPERATIVES

The tentative steps towards independence from the 1950s onwards heightened political consciousness and expanded constitutional discourse and dialogue, and by the time Singapore was ready for self-government, the general public was caught up in a constitutional maelstrom whether they knew it or not. The People's Action Party's (PAP's) success at the 1959 General Election set things in motion immediately. Because the PAP has been in power for so long, we cannot understand the trajectory of Singapore's constitutional development without knowing the three key imperatives of the PAP's outlook: (a) economic growth first; (b) managing ethnicity; and (c) political dominance. Law was important but was not of itself normatively valuable. It would be deployed as a tool in service of these wider imperatives.

A. Economic Growth

The first imperative is the primacy of economic growth. Without economic growth, the lives and lots of Singaporeans cannot be improved and before long, the PAP will lose its legitimacy to rule. To push economic growth along, the PAP could not afford to leave things to the 'invisible hand' of the market. As Goh Keng Swee, Singapore's former Deputy Prime Minister and chief economic architect explained:

> Taking an overall view of Singapore's economic policy, we can see how radically it differed from the laissez-faire policies of the colonial era. These had led Singapore to a dead end, with little economic growth, massive unemployment, wretched housing, and inadequate education. We had to try a more activist and interventionist approach.[1]

Law, the legal system and politics were thus harnessed to fire the engines of economic development. The developmental imperative meant that human rights, while important, had to take a back seat to other pressing concerns. The labour unrests between 1954 and 1963 were debilitating: a total of 2,866,355 man-days were lost as a result of 697 strikes involving 183,022 workers.[2] To fix this problem, labour had to be disciplined. Reflecting on that early period of Singapore's political economy, Goh Keng Swee remarked:

> The greatest difficulty we faced was in industrial relations. How to break the vicious cycle of trade union militancy and poor economic performance? We were fortunate that part of the solution was contributed by the Malaysian Government during the two years of merger, when we were a constituent state.

---

[1] Goh Keng Swee, 'A Socialist Economy that Works' in CV Devan Nair (ed), *Socialism That Works ... The Singapore Way* (Singapore, Federal Publications, 1976) 77–85, at 84.

[2] These figures were gleaned from WG Huff, *The Economic Growth of Singapore: Trade and Development in the Twentieth Century* (Cambridge, Cambridge University Press, 1995), at 295.

Most of the militant trade unions were under the control of the underground Communist Party of Malaya and operated under the leadership of open United Front leaders. As trade union activities were legal, it was not possible for the Singapore Government to arrest them. Nor was it of any use to plead with them to moderate their activities in the national interest.[3]

To counter the radical left-wing's dominance of the labour movement, the PAP Government turned to the law. One of the first things it did after coming to power in 1959 was to pass the Trade Unions (Amendment) Bill to empower the Registrar of Trade Unions to refuse registration of any trade union. Appeals against the Registrar's decision lay to the Minister for Labour whose decision was final. With these powers firmly in hand, the PAP Government disbanded and deregistered numerous small splinter unions. In 1960, the government introduced the Trade Unions Bill to further tighten its hold on the labour movement and to create a unified trade union body. Under the bill, all unions seeking registration had to have a minimum of 250 members, belong to one of the thirteen categories enumerated in the law, and affiliated to an 'association of unions' (in this case the Trades Union Congress). However, the bill was ultimately allowed to lapse when relations between the left-wing union leaders and the PAP crumbled. By this time, it was clearly not in the PAP's interests to have a strong unified labour movement moving against its economic imperatives.

In 1961, the Singapore Trades Union Congress (STUC)—the umbrella association of all trade unions—was itself proscribed by the government and deregistered. Following the security blitz, Operation Coldstore—made possible by the draconian Internal Security Act— over 120 trade union and political leaders, including all the top leaders of the opposition Barisan Sosialis were detained and the power of the unions was broken. By the time of Singapore's independence in 1965, the PAP Government 'did not have to deal with a union movement that was substantially divided ideologically and which included a radical union with its own parent political party'.[4]

---

[3] Goh Keng Swee, 'Transformation of Singapore's Economy, 1960–1985' in L Low (ed), *Wealth of East Asian Nations* (Singapore, Marshall Cavendish Academic, 2004) 23–33, at 26.

[4] R Vasil, 'Trade Unions' in K Singh Sandhu & P Wheatley (eds), *Management of Success: The Moulding of Modern Singapore* (Singapore, Institute of Southeast Asian Studies, 1989) 144–70, at 154.

Three other major changes to labour legislation completed the PAP Government's efforts to tame the trade unions. The first was the Trade Unions (Amendment) Bill introduced on 24 June 1967. It amended the Trade Unions Ordinance and provided that employees of any statutory board—or body specified by the Minister for Labour—could not be a member of any union unless that union's membership was restricted only to the employees of that board or body. This change was targeted at reducing the influence of the Amalgamated Union of Public Employees (AUPE) which was the largest common union organisation of public employees. Shortly after the bill's enactment, the Minister for Labour directed employees of three statutory boards—the Singapore Telephone Board, the Housing and Development Board and the Public Utilities Board—to leave the AUPE and form their own separate unions. As far as the PAP Government was concerned, the rights of workers and unions were subjugated to the imperatives of economic development:

> To them, compulsions of economic advancement and racial harmony made it imperative that the government control all instruments and centres of power, and as a corollary that no foci of power, such as unions and business and industry, be allowed to become too strong.[5]

B. Managing Ethnicity

The fact that Singapore is a predominantly Chinese society in a Malay-Muslim world heightens sensitivities regarding race. These sensitivities go back a long way, to when the British adopted a divide and conquer strategy when managing the colonial polity. A remarkable thing was that from the 1950s, Singapore politicians eschewed the organisation of political forces around ethnicity even though this was a pattern assiduously cultivated in the Malay States, just north of Singapore. All the early political parties were multi-racial in orientation—the Malayan Democratic Union, the Progressive Party, the Labour Party etc. This multi-racialism was in some ways socially entrenched when David Marshall, a Sephardic Jew (one of the smallest minorities in Singapore), became Chief Minister in 1955. Marshall was at pains to ensure that his

---

[5] ibid, at 157.

Council of Ministers was made up of ministers from all different races. It comprised Chinese, Malays, Eurasians and even a European. This pattern of political appointments was carried on by the PAP when it came to power. Unfortunately, racial tensions heightened when Singapore became a constituent state of the Federation of Malaysia which constitutionally privileged the Malays. Quotas for jobs and educations were imposed on the basis of race in all the states of Malaysia except Singapore which, under the Federal Constitution, retained control over education and labour. This 'disparity' created a tension between the Malays and Chinese in Singapore when the former called for similar privileges.

When Singapore seceded from the Federation in 1965, immediate steps were taken to ensure that the Malays and all other ethnic minorities in Singapore were not discriminated against. This precipitated the appointment of the Wee Chong Jin Constitutional Commission to 'receive and consider representations on how the rights of the racial, linguistic and religious minorities can be adequately safeguarded in the Constitution' as well as to ensure no legislation would be discriminatory against any racial, linguistic or religious minority in its practical application. As we shall see, the Commission recommended the establishment of a body known as the Council of State to scrutinise legislation to ensure it is not discriminatory in application. This was later embedded in the Constitution as the Presidential Council for Minority Rights.

The Constitution was once again called upon to manage ethnic minority interests in 1988 with the creation of the Group Representation Constituency (GRC) scheme. This constitutional innovation was designed to ensure that no matter which political party takes power, Singapore's Parliament would always feature a racially balanced slate of members.

At about the time the GRC scheme was introduced, the government also introduced the Ethnic Integration Policy for public housing to ensure that racial enclaves did not form in certain public housing estates. Citing the example of Bedok town, the Minister for National Development pointed out that 'if present trends continue, the proportion of Malays will reach 30% by 1991 and will exceed 40% in 10 years' time'.[6] The policy called for the limiting of the number of Chinese, or

---

[6] S Dhanabalan, Statement, 'Better Racial Mix in HDB Housing Estates' *Singapore Parliamentary Debates Official Reports,* 16 Feb 1989, vol 52, col 651.

Malay or Indian households in each block of flats as well as within a neighbourhood. The plan was thus to roughly replicate a microcosm of Singapore's demographic mix within each block of flats and each housing estate. While no constitutional amendment was made to effect this policy, it arguably contradicts Article 12(2) of the Constitution, which provides, among other things, that there shall be no discrimination on the ground only of 'race'.

C. Political Dominance

The imperative of political dominance is not unusual but in the case of the PAP stems from its belief that no other party can possibly run Singapore properly. This belief is buttressed by the fact that since 1968 there has not been an effective opposition in Singapore. Even after the 2011 General Election when the opposition Workers' Party made its greatest inroads into Parliament, it commands all of eight seats and is not seen as a viable alternative to the PAP. This obsession with political dominance took hold after the opposition Barisan Sosialis abandoned Parliament in 1966 and refused to contest the 1968 General Election. With a hegemonic hold on political party from 1968 to 1981, the PAP began to take electoral victory and dominance for granted and was unafraid to use the myriad legal arsenal at its disposal to thwart its opponents. For example, the GRC system, which was designed to ensure minimal ethnic minority representation in Parliament, was enlarged to not only allow the team to manage larger towns, but also to make it more difficult for their erstwhile political opponents to partake in and win elections in these enlarged constituencies. Draconian legislation like the Internal Security Act and the Sedition Act remain on the statute book and act as powerful deterrents to would-be opponents of the party.

III. ORGANISATION OF THIS BOOK

This book is organised into eight main chapters. The first chapter provides an overview of the development of Singapore's Constitution. In many ways, this development was typical of the transition that took place when colonies moved towards self-government and independence, and with the departing colonial powers handing over power to a favoured political elite. The story of Singapore's post-independence development is rather less typical. A brief interlude as a constituent state of the Federation of Malaysia was followed by four decades of modifications and adaptations that brought about a uniquely autochthonous version of its Westminster-based constitutional model. Major modifications were made to the parliamentary system of government, a topic which is covered in greater depth in chapter three; as well as to the presidency, which I deal with in chapter six.

Chapter two is a discursive essay that provides a background to how constitutionalism is understood and practised in the Singaporean context. In particular, I discuss the three key concepts of constitutional supremacy, the rule of law and democracy and constitutional culture, and how they impact the operation of constitutionalism within the Singapore polity. Chapter three provides a fairly in-depth explanation for the development of three major innovations in the Singapore electoral system—the Non-Constituency Member of Parliament, the Group Representation Constituency and the Nominated Member of Parliament. These are uniquely Singaporean innovations designed to provide alternative voices in Parliament as well as to guarantee a modicum of ethnic minority representation in the House.

The law-making process is the subject of chapter four. Because the ruling PAP has exercised almost total dominance in Parliament, the law-making process is augmented with endorsement procedures involving the Presidential Council for Minority Rights and the elected President. The next two chapters focus on the executive branch of government and the elected presidency. Like most other Westminster-based systems of government, real power in the state lies with the Prime Minister and his Cabinet, and not the President. Chapter five looks at the unique features of Singapore's Cabinet, the rationale for Ministers being the highest paid in the world, and the role of the Attorney-General. Chapter six takes a detailed look at one of the most problematic and controversial institutions in Singapore—the elected presidency—its rationale, effectiveness and problems. The judiciary is dealt with in chapter seven while chapter eight looks at the protection of human rights under the Constitution. In particular, we look at specific challenges—the lack of property rights, the power of the executive to preventively detain persons without trial, and the protection of minority rights—and consider the contexts in which they manifest and operate. The concluding chapter nine attempts to tie together the various strands of arguments made throughout the book under the rubric of three persistent recurring themes—regime dominance, economic development and the management of ethnicity and religion.

1

A Brief Constitutional History

Introduction – The Straits Settlements Period – The Japanese
Occupation – The Colony of Singapore – The Rendel Constitution –
Constitutional Talks and Self-government – Merger and
Separation – Post-1965 Developments – Conclusion

I. INTRODUCTION

ALTHOUGH SINGAPORE ATTAINED independence in
1965, its constitutional history stretches back further than that.
To understand the nature of the Singapore state, its relation
with its neighbour, Malaysia, and the constitutional structure it now
possesses, we need to go back to 1819, the year the British first arrived
on the island.

II. THE STRAITS SETTLEMENTS PERIOD (1819–1942)

A. The Founding of Modern Singapore

English settlement in Singapore came about as a result of the
Anglo-Dutch trade rivalry in what we now call Southeast Asia. The
English were latecomers to the region and had only successfully established settlements in Penang and Bencoolen (in the south of Sumatra)
while the Dutch, who had a dominating presence in the region since
the seventeenth century, had ports throughout what is now the
Indonesian archipelago. Sir Thomas Stamford Raffles, the bright, ambitious Lieutenant-Governor of Bencoolen—against the orders of his
immediate superior, Governor John Bannerman in Penang—sneaked
out of Penang in the middle of the night of 19 January 1819, arriving

on the island of Singapore on 29 January 1819. Discovering that the Dutch had yet to settle the island, he immediately signed a preliminary agreement with Abdul Rahman, the Temenggong or 'public security chief' of the Johor empire. On 6 February 1819, Raffles signed a Treaty of Friendship and Alliance with Tengku Hussein, the man the British recognised as the Sultan of Johor,[1] and owner of the island. With this treaty, and in consideration of an annual recompense of 3000 Spanish dollars, the British East India Company established a trading post at Singapore and Raffles declared it a 'free port'.

On 19 November 1824—following the signing of the Anglo-Dutch Treaty or Treaty of London in March 1824—the British East India Company signed a treaty of cession with Sultan Hussein and Temenggong Abdul Rahman to 'cede in full sovereignty and property to the Honourable the English East India Company, their heirs and successors for ever, the Island of Singapore'.

B. Early Administration of the Straits Settlements

As Singapore had only several hundred inhabitants at the time the British first landed, they treated the island as *terra nullius*. From 1819 till 1824, the status of Singapore as a British port was often cast in doubt owing to incessant Dutch claims on the island. This was settled by the Treaty of London in 1824 under which the British surrendered their settlement in Bencoolen to the Dutch in exchange for the Dutch colony of Malacca. The Dutch also relinquished any claim they had on the island of Singapore. In 1825, the territories of Singapore, Malacca and the old British settlement of Penang were amalgamated as the Straits Settlements and with the ratification of the Treaty of Cession by the British Parliament the following year, was administered as part of the Presidency of Bengal in Calcutta, India.

---

[1] Although Tengku Hussein was the elder of the two sons of the late Sultan Mahmud III of Johor, his brother Abdul Rahman (not to be confused with the Temenggong) was installed Sultan of Johor while Hussein was away, getting married in Pahang. Capitalising on this succession dispute, Raffles brought Tengku Hussein to Singapore from Tanjong Pinang (in what is now Batam Island), recognised him as Sultan of Johor (under whose jurisdiction Singapore lay) and proceeded to sign the treaty with him.

Between 1819 and 1827, the British administered an elementary version of English law through the Resident's Court and by relying on leaders of the various 'native populations' to resolve disputes within their respective communities. Raffles himself promulgated a set of regulations in 1823[2] and although clearly illegal, these appeared to have been enforced until 1827.

Legal chaos prevailed until 1827 when the Second Charter of Justice, dated 27 November 1826, arrived, establishing the Court of Judicature for Prince of Wales Island (Penang), Malacca and Singapore[3] and brought English common law into the three territories.[4] Under the Charter, a Recorder, based in Penang, was to travel on circuit. His court was charged to 'give and pass judgment and sentence according to justice and right' (English common law). Owing to severe budgetary constraints and the lack of an institutional infrastructure, the first few decades of judicial administration were fraught with administrative and financial problems. It was very difficult to be governed from afar. Having no law-making capability of its own, the Straits Settlements was reduced to petitioning Calcutta every time laws were needed. Furthermore, the Second Charter of Justice failed to provide the Court of Judicature with admiralty jurisdiction, with the result that pirates arrested in territorial waters had to be sent to Calcutta for trial.

C. Becoming a Colony Proper

On 1 April 1867, after much local agitation for greater autonomy and control, the Straits Settlements became a Crown Colony and was placed under London's direct control. It was granted a colonial constitution[5]

---

[2] See 'Raffles' Singapore Regulations—1823', reprinted in (1968) 10 *Malaya Law Review* 248, with an introduction by MB Hooker.

[3] See James William Norton Kyshe's *A Judicial History of the Straits Settlements 1786–1890*, which was originally published as the Preface of his four-volume work *Cases Heard and Determined in Her Majesty's Supreme Court of the Straits Settlements, 1808–1890*, reprinted with an introduction by MB Hooker in (1969) 11(1) *Malaya Law Review*.

[4] On the Second Charter of Justice and its significance, see ABL Phang, *From Foundation to Legacy: The Second Charter of Justice* (Singapore, Singapore Academy of Law, 2006).

[5] Letters Patent dated 4 February 1867.

under which the Straits Settlements had its own Governor, Legislative Council and Supreme Court. Legislative authority was vested in the Legislative Council (Legco) which had two classes of members: the official members and the unofficial members, with the former taking precedence over the latter. The 'official' members included the Colonial Secretary, the Attorney-General, the Financial Secretary, the Officer Commanding the Troops and the Resident Councillors. The 'unofficial' members were non-government appointees drawn from among the leaders of the mercantile and ethnic communities.

There were always more official members than unofficial members and the Governor—the first of which was Sir Harry Ord—held a casting vote. In 1867, the Legco consisted of the Governor, the Chief Justice, the Officer Commanding the Troops, the Lieutenant-Governor of Penang, the Colonial Secretary, the Attorney-General, the Colonial Engineer and four unofficial Europeans. By 1871, the Lieutenant-Governor of Malacca, the Judge of Penang, the Treasurer, the Auditor-General and two more unofficial members were added to the Council.

By 1832, Singapore had surpassed Penang in importance and the seat of government had moved permanently to Singapore. In 1868, the Court of Judicature was abolished and replaced by the Straits Settlements Supreme Court presided over by the Chief Justice with two puisne judges, one for Penang and another for Singapore and Malacca. In 1877, an Executive Council was introduced to advise the Governor.[6] Thereafter, the structure of government remained largely unchanged until World War II.

In the interim 65 years, the only noteworthy changes were the increase in the number of unofficial members of the Legislative Council. In the 1920s, two unofficial members of the Legislative Council were nominated to sit on the Executive Council and the Legislative Council was enlarged to comprise 26 members, with equal numbers of unofficials and officials. The Governor retained his casting vote. The Penang and Singapore European chambers of commerce could each nominate one unofficial whilst the Governor nominated the rest on a racial basis: five Europeans including one each from Penang and Malacca; three Chinese British subjects, one Malay, one Indian and one Eurasian. It is worth noting that this idea of ethnic representation through the legislative

---

[6] Kyshe, *A Judicial History of the Straits Settlements 1786–1890* (n 3).

chamber had its origins in a memorandum submitted by the Straits Settlements (Singapore) Association in 1920, and continues in modified fashion in the current constitutional order.[7]

III. THE JAPANESE OCCUPATION (1942–45)

The structure of the Straits Settlements Constitution remained almost intact until the Japanese invaded Singapore in February 1942.[8] At first, there was much confusion as to who had proper legislative authority. Several government or military bodies had power to make laws. At the top was the Supreme Command of the Southern Army Headquarters, then came the 25th Army Headquarters, the Military Administration Department and then the Malai Military Administration Headquarters and the City Government of *Tokubetu-si*. Most of these bodies issued streams of regulations, laws and notices through the *Tokubetu-si* without adhering to the normal chain of command. Often these laws and regulations were contradictory but the problem usually resolved itself since the body higher up the hierarchy always prevailed. All existing courts ceased to function and a Military Court of Justice of the Nippon Army was established by a Decree.

On 27 May 1942, the civil courts were re-opened and all former laws British laws were administered so long as they did not interfere with the Military Administration. At the apex of this judicial administration was the Syonan Supreme Court or the *Syonan Koto-Hoin* which opened on 29 May 1942. Although a Court of Appeal was constituted, it never sat. Perhaps the most remarkable thing about the application of law during the Japanese Occupation was the fact that on a day-to-day basis, English law continued to be applied in the courts. There was no major disruption in the continuity of colonial law, making it much easier for the British to re-establish their legal authority in the post-1945 era.

---

[7] See ch 3, on Group Representation Constituencies at II.B.

[8] See generally, Goh Kok Leong, 'Legal History of the Japanese Occupation in Singapore' (1981) 1 *Malaya Law Journal* xx.

IV. THE COLONY OF SINGAPORE (1946–58)

The Japanese surrendered in September 1945 and Singapore came under military rule. The British Military Administration (BMA)[9]— established by Proclamation of the Supreme Allied Commander for Southeast Asia, Lord Louis Mountbatten—lasted from September 1945 to April 1946. Under Proclamation No 1 of 1945,[10] all laws and customs existing prior to the Japanese Occupation were brought back into force. At the same time, the BMA was given 'full judicial, legislative, executive and administrative powers and responsibilities' over Malaya. A Chief Civil Affairs Officer was appointed, and he was assisted by two deputies—one for Malaya and the other for Singapore.

Civilian government was restored on 1 April 1946. By this time, the old Straits Settlements had been disbanded and abolished. The United Kingdom Parliament disbanded the old colony as the territories of Malacca and Penang were to be amalgamated into the new Malayan Union (alongside the old Federated and Unfederated Malay States).[11] Singapore became a Crown Colony with its own constitution.[12] The Constitution preserved the Governor's veto and reserved powers over legislation and set up an advisory Executive Council comprising six officials and four nominated unofficials. The Legco comprised four ex-officio members, seven officials and up to four nominated unofficials, and nine elected members.

These provisions were intended as stop-gap measures and were heavily criticised for their lack of local representation. By 24 April 1946, the new Governor, Sir Franklin Gimson convened a committee to 'make recommendations as to the nature of the provision required for regulating the election of members of the Singapore Legislative Council'. The committee—popularly known as the Reconstitution Committee— submitted its recommendations in September 1946. Among other things, it recommended a revamped Legco comprising four ex-officio members, five officials, four nominated unofficials, three chamber of

[9] See M Rudner, 'The Organization of the British Military Administration in Malaya: 1946–48' (1968) 9(1) *Journal of Southeast Asian History* 95–106.

[10] Proclamation No 1, *BMA Gazette*, vol 1, no 1.

[11] Straits Settlements (Repeal) Act 1946.

[12] Singapore Colony Order-in-Council 1946 (SI 464/1946).

commerce representatives (representing the Singapore, Chinese and Indian Chambers of Commerce) and six popularly elected members.[13] The new constitution came into effect on 1 March 1948[14] and elections were held for the first time on 20 March 1948. Most of the seats in the first election were won by the Progressive Party, which dominated Singapore politics until the mid-1950s. The judicial structure and hierarchy of courts remained unchanged. In place of the Straits Settlements Supreme Court was the Supreme Court of the Colony of Singapore with its own Chief Justice. Final appeals, as in the pre-War years, lay to the Judicial Committee of the Privy Council in London.

V. THE RENDEL CONSTITUTION

From 1948 to 1953, Singapore's constitutional development was slow. The people of Singapore were more concerned with rebuilding their lives after the War, and the British Government was occupied by events in the Malayan Union and later, the Federation of Malaya, as well as with communist front activities. In 1950, the Progressive Party demanded and obtained three additional elected seats in the Council,[15] and the change was implemented in time for the triennial elections in 1951 in which the Progressive Party won six of the nine seats.

To widen political participation, more changes in the Constitution were necessary. To this end, a Constitutional Commission, comprising colonial officials and several local notables, and headed by Sir George Rendel (a former Bank of England Governor), was set up in 1953. The Rendel Commission was asked to conduct 'a comprehensive review of the Constitution', by now in operation for five years. Why so? The Commission issued its report in February 1954[16] and recommended automatic registration of voters and a new Legislative Assembly of 32 members. Of these 32 members, 25 would be elected unofficial

---

[13] See *Report of the Committee for the Reconstitution of the Singapore Legislative Council*, reproduced in *Annual Report of Singapore for 1 April to 31 December 1946*, app A, at 17–25.

[14] See Order-in-Council dated 24 Feb 1948 (SI 341/1948).

[15] Legislative Council Elections (Amendment) Ordinance No 13 of 1951.

[16] See *Report of the Constitutional Commission Singapore* (Singapore, Government Printer, 1954).

members, 3 ex-officio official members holding ministerial posts, and 4 would be nominated unofficial members. The Commission also recommended the creation of a Council of Ministers comprising three ex-officio official members and six elected members appointed by the Governor on the recommendation of the 'Leader of the House', who would be the leader of the largest party in the Assembly or of a coalition of parties assured of majority support. The government accepted most of these recommendations.

These recommendations were implemented under the 1955 Constitution and 79 candidates contested the 25 seats at the general elections that followed. The Labour Front, led by David Marshall won 10 seats; the Progressive Party 4 seats; the People's Action Party 3 seats; the Singapore Alliance 3 seats and the Democratic Party 2 seats. Marshall became Singapore's first Chief Minister and formed a coalition government with the Singapore Alliance.

Marshall's government took office in one of the most tumultuous periods of Singapore history. Attacked by militant pro-communist unions, Marshall was unable to do much to stem the incessant stream of strikes all over the island since responsibility for internal security lay in the hands of the British. Marshall was, however, more successful in his attacks against the British colonial system. Just months into his term of office, he fomented a constitutional crisis by demanding the right to appoint four assistant ministers to his Council of Ministers. The Rendel Constitution did not clearly define the ambit of the Chief Minister's power and Governor Sir Robert Black insisted that Marshall had no such power of appointment. When Black refused, Marshall immediately threatened to resign unless Singapore was given immediate self-government.

The Colonial Office was appalled by Marshall's demands but feared that his resignation would pave the way for more radical and irresponsible government or a possible communist takeover. The Governor was therefore instructed to act on the Chief Minister's advice and the British agreed to hold constitutional talks the following year to discuss self-government for the Colony. Under the Rendel Constitution, the portfolios of Finance, Administration and Internal Security and Law remained in the hands of the British and appeared to local politicians to be major impediments to the development of self-government.

VI. CONSTITUTIONAL TALKS AND SELF-GOVERNMENT
(1956–58)

In 1956, a 13-member all-party delegation representing all the parties in Singapore's Legislative Assembly held constitutional talks in London with officials of the Colonial Office. In London, Marshall demanded full internal self-government by 1 April 1957. He wanted control of internal security, but was prepared to leave foreign policy and external defence in British hands provided Singapore had a veto on defence and rights of consultation on foreign affairs. The British rejected his proposal, insisting that they retain absolute control over defence and foreign affairs and that their High Commissioner have the casting vote in a proposed Internal Security Council. Marshall refused to concede this point and the talks broke down. Having promised the people of Singapore 'independence', Marshall resigned on his return and Lim Yew Hock replaced him as Chief Minister.

Lim, a tough-talking veteran labour leader, proved much more adept at dealing with militant trade unionists than Marshall. He had no scruples about using the draconian preventive detention laws at his disposal, and the number of strikes and industrial disturbances dropped dramatically. The British felt assured and were prepared to work with Lim and in March 1957, invited a second all-party delegation to London to renew discussions on self-government. This time, the British agreed that in the seven-member Internal Security Council, Britain and Singapore would each have three representatives; whilst the seventh member would be appointed by the soon-to-be independent Federation of Malaya. The delegation accepted these terms and in 1958, a third all-party mission went to London to settle the final terms for the new constitution.[17]

On 1 August 1958, the British Parliament passed the State of Singapore Act, which converted the Colony into a self-governing state. By the Singapore (Constitution) Order-in-Council 1958, the post of Governor was abolished and the office of the Yang di-Pertuan Negara

---

[17] See Singapore (Constitution) Order-in-Council 1958, SI 1956 of 1958; see also O Hood Phillips, 'The Constitution of the State of Singapore' (1960) *Public Law* 50; and LA Sheridan, 'Singapore's New Constitution' (1959) *Malayan Law Journal* xxv.

(Head of State) was established. The Yang di-Pertuan Negara would appoint as Prime Minister the person most likely to command the authority of the Assembly and the ministers were also appointed on the Prime Minister's advice. The new Legislative Assembly had 51 elected members, and the party winning the majority of seats in the Assembly would be invited to form the government. The Westminster Cabinet system, under which members of the Cabinet were drawn from members of the legislature, was operationalised with the portfolios of Foreign Affairs and Defence in the hands of the British. At the same time, the structure of the judiciary was left very much intact, with the Chief Justice being appointed by the Yang di-Pertuan Negara on the Prime Minister's advice. In the 1959 General Elections, the People's Action Party (PAP) won 43 out of the 51 seats and its secretary-general Lee Kuan Yew, became Singapore's first Prime Minister.

The PAP had been established on 21 November 1954. It comprised two main groups of nationalist politicians—the self-styled English-educated moderate group led by Lee Kuan Yew, and the left-wing pro-communist group led by Lim Chin Siong and Fong Swee Suan. In many ways, the PAP was a marriage of convenience born out of political expediency. The English-educated group were able to debate with the British on their own terms and were trusted by the British to the extent that they represented a non-communist alternative in the eventual handover of power in Singapore. However, they were among Singapore's intellectual, economic and social elites and thus did not have the mass support that the Chinese-educated left-wing group commanded. The latter held sway over the Chinese Middle School students, blue-collar workers and the trade unions and had a well-oiled machinery to mobilise the masses to collective action. However, the British were staunchly anti-communist—having proscribed the Malayan Communist Party in 1948—and would never hand over the reins of power to a communist government. At the same time, the English-educated group could never hope to attain power through the ballot box without the support of their left-wing colleagues. Each segment of the PAP's leadership hoped to capitalise on the other's strengths and advantages and the only commonality they shared was their determination to rid Singapore of the British.

VII. MERGER AND SEPARATION (1963–65)[18]

A. The 'Battle for Merger'

Although Singapore attained self-governing status in 1959, it was not yet independent. The British did not expect that a political entity as small as Singapore, with no hinterland or natural resources of its own, could exist as an independent state. Besides, the British, with their military and naval bases on the island, had too much at stake to risk it being governed by an independent pro-communist government. Independence, when granted, had always been seen within the context of a much larger entity. Having created the Federation of Malaya in 1948, the British determined that Singapore would only gain its independence as a constituent state of the Federation of Malaya. For that reason, the PAP Government sought merger with the Federation of Malaya as a matter of urgency. The PAP's pro-communist elements opposed this plan as they feared being preventively detained by the Federation of Malaya's fiercely anti-communist government under the powerful Internal Security Act 1960.

The campaign for merger led to a split between the PAP moderates and their left-wing colleagues who crossed the floor. Thirteen erstwhile PAP Assemblymen were expelled from the party and went on to establish the opposition Barisan Sosialis (Socialist Front) with Lim Chin Siong as its secretary-general. After much prevarication, Malaya's Prime Minister, Tunku Abdul Rahman ('the Tunku') agreed to the merger plan. Under the Malaysia Agreement, North Borneo, Sarawak and Singapore were incorporated into the Federation of Malaya to form the Federation of Malaysia. Singapore left control over foreign affairs, defence and internal security to the central government but maintained considerable powers over finance, labour and education. She was allocated 15 of the 127 seats in the new federal legislature and retained her

---

[18] On Singapore's constitutional position in Malaysia, see HE Groves, *The Constitution of Malaysia* (Singapore, Malaysia Publications Ltd, 1964); and Tan Tai Yong, *Creating Greater Malaysia: Decolonisation and the Politics of Merger* (Singapore, Institute of Southeast Asian Studies, 2008).

own executive government and legislative assembly.[19] The day-to-day administration of Singapore was the responsibility of the executive government and Singapore was to pay 40 per cent of her income from taxes to the Federal Government. A new State Constitution[20] was granted to Singapore to effect this change in status.[21]

B. The Rift between Singapore and the Federation

Singapore did not last long in the Federation. A number of economic and political reasons conspired to cause Singapore to secede from the Federation in 1965. Most of the problems between Singapore and Kuala Lumpur stemmed from differing perceptions about the nature of the new Malaysian state and the degree of political participation and engagement resulting therefrom. The Tunku saw Singapore's inclusion as the twelfth state of the Federation as nothing more than a new entity being included on terms already established by the Federal Government. The status quo, with its special privileges for Malays and the primacy of the United Malays Nationalist Organisation (UMNO)—the Federation's Malay political party that dominated the political scene—would remain. Lee and his PAP comrades, on the other hand viewed the creation of Malaysia as the inauguration of a new state altogether, a state which was fair game in the political and economic stakes, entitling them to extend PAP influence into the peninsula.

There are several reasons for Singapore's exit from the hard-fought union with the Federation. The first reason was economic. The economic terms of Singapore's entry into Malaysia were not hammered out till the last minute. The Federation expected a substantial financial contribution from the Singapore Government to federal finance and loans from the Singapore Government to aid in the development of the Sabah and Sarawak territories. The more it could extract from Singapore, the lighter the burden would be to the Federal Government.

---

[19] See A Ibrahim, 'The Position of Singapore in Malaysia' [1964] *Malayan Law Journal* cxi.
[20] See Malaysia: The Sabah, Sarawak and Singapore (State Constitutions) Order-in-Council 1963 (SI 1493/1963).
[21] See LA Sheridan, 'Constitutional Problems of Malaysia' (1964) 13 *International & Comparative Law Quarterly* 1349; E Sadka, 'Singapore and the Federation: Problems of Merger' (1962) 1(11) *Asian Survey* 17–25.

High on Singapore's agenda was the establishment of a common market. The island's industrialisation programme dictated that it establish large enough markets for its manufactured goods within the Federation, a move which was received far less enthusiastically by the Federation politicians who were keen to compete in the industrial sector against Singapore.[22]

Singapore viewed its entry in Malaysia as a necessity for economic survival. A tiny and densely populated island totally bereft of natural resources, populated mainly by Chinese immigrants in a Malay geo-political environment could not realistically expect to survive. In this respect, merger was Singapore's salvation, especially with the prospect of a common market for Singapore's manufactured goods. Although most of these issues were resolved in June 1963, the question of Singapore's contribution to federal and development finance became major bones of contention between the Singapore and Federal Governments.

The second factor contributing to Singapore's secession lay in the vastly different personalities and approaches adopted by the politicians on both sides of the Causeway. Lee's PAP adopted an open and aggressive style appealing directly to the voter while the Tunku's Alliance preferred a more conciliatory approach, with 'the airing of differences behind closed doors, in more confidential and secretive surroundings'.[23] Open confrontation and defiance of the Federal Government was a means by which the PAP demonstrated to its electorate that it bargained for and secured the best possible terms of merger for them. The PAP's approach was even more offensive to Kuala Lumpur since its leaders viewed Singapore as being more important than the other states in the union. The Singapore leaders were simply not prepared to play a 'quiet subordinate role within a Malaya-dominated federal structure'.[24]

Finally, the PAP's attempt to supplant the Malayan Chinese Association (MCA) as a partner in the Alliance led to full-scale political warfare between the two Chinese-dominated parties. Initially, there was an agreement between the Tunku and Lee Kuan Yew that the PAP

[22] See MN Sopiee, *From Malayan Union to Singapore Separation: Political Unification in the Malaysia Region 1945–65* (Kuala Lumpur, Penerbit Universiti Malaya, 1976), at 184.
[23] ibid, at 184.
[24] ibid, at 185.

would not contest elections on the mainland, and that UMNO would not interfere in Singapore's elections. However, the MCA, UMNO's junior partner in the Alliance saw no need to honour this accord. In May 1963, the MCA President, Tan Siew Sin,[25] openly expressed his party's interest in Singapore by stating that the MCA had a 'duty to perform in Singapore' and that it was Singapore's 'only hope for future stability and progress'.[26] That same month, two MCA senators, TH Tan and Khaw Kai Boh, visited Singapore to recruit business support for the MCA. Thereafter, relations between the MCA and the PAP soured and a series of acrimonious exchanges resulted. Lee called the MCA intervention the 'root cause' of the problem with Kuala Lumpur. As far as Lee was concerned, the MCA had breached his unwritten understanding with the Alliance in localising their respective parties' influence. Lee also saw the MCA's move as an attempt to set him on a collision course with the Tunku. In retaliation, the PAP began openly challenging the MCA's ability to win votes for the Alliance and positioned itself as the most viable alternative to the MCA to carry the votes in urban areas.

The fact that the Singapore Alliance—which comprised the Singapore branches of the Alliance in Malaya: UMNO, MCA and the Malayan Indian Congress (MIC)—failed to win a single seat in the 1963 Singapore General Election gave the PAP a false sense of its ability to penetrate mainland politics. In an ill-conceived move, the party decided to campaign in the April 1964 Federal and General Elections with disastrous results. The Tunku came out in open support of its coalition partner and of the nine seats the PAP contested, it lost all but one, the sole seat being captured by CV Devan Nair in the Bungsar constituency.[27] For about 10 weeks after the elections, the animosity between the Singapore Government and the Federal Government abated, but this was just the calm before the storm. In July 1964, communal riots broke out in Singapore.

[25] Tan Siew Sin is the son of Sir Tan Cheng Lock, founder and President of the MCA. He is also the cousin of Singapore's Finance Minister, Goh Keng Swee.
[26] See *The Straits Times* 23 May 1963.
[27] For a detailed account of this election, see KJ Ratnam and RS Milne, *The Malaysian Parliamentary Election of 1964* (Kuala Lumpur, University of Malaya Press, 1969).

C. The 1964 Racial Riots

The 1957 Federal Constitution entrenched special rights for the indigenous people of the land: the Malays or *bumiputras* (literally translated, 'Sons of the Soil'). When Singapore entered the Federation, the Malays on the island had hoped that these special rights and privileges would apply to them equally as well. This was not to be. Singapore's 1963 State Constitution required the Government of Singapore 'constantly to care for the interests of the racial and religious minorities in the State',[28] and to recognise 'the special position of the Malays, who are the indigenous people of the State' and thus 'protect, safeguard, support, foster and promote their political, educational, religious, economic, social and cultural interests and the Malay language'.[29] These constitutional requirements were not, however, interpreted by the PAP leaders to mean the reservation of special posts or positions for the Malays or racial quotas either for entry into education or public service, or even in the granting of licences or permits of any sort. Indeed, Prime Minister Lee was at pains to make this point quite clear in his negotiations with the Federal Government before Malaysia came into being. The official interpretation coincided with Lee's even though it was not constitutionally entrenched.[30]

However, this did not deter the extremist elements or 'ultras' as Lee called them,[31] from capitalising on the inconsistency in the application of a federal constitutional provision. Why, they asked, did it not mean the same thing in Singapore? The ultras in Singapore UMNO, led by its secretary-general Syed Ja'afar Albar, and the *Utusan Melayu*, a Malay newspaper printed in the Jawi script, capitalised on this apparent discrepancy, charging the PAP with depriving the Malays of their constitutional rights and privileges. As Leifer put it:

> Malaysia had not brought the Malays of Singapore the special privileges enjoyed by their co-religionists on the mainland. Although the Singapore

---

[28] See The Sabah, Sarawak and Singapore (State Constitutions) Order-in-Council 1963 (SI 1493/1963), Art 89(1).

[29] ibid, Art 89(2).

[30] See 'Progress Report Of Constitutional Provisions for Singapore in Federation of Malaysia in Accordance with White Paper Cmd. 33 of 1961 (Statement by the Prime Minister)', *Singapore Legislative Assembly Official Reports* 5 Apr 1963, vol 20, cols 30–32.

[31] The term 'ultras' was first used in GP Means, *Malayan Government and Politics in Transition*, PhD dissertation (Seattle, University of Washington, 1960). Lee picked it up after reading Means' dissertation from cover to cover.

constitution recognised the special position of the Malays, the Malaysia Agreement stipulated that special privileges enjoyed by the Malays in the former Federation of Malaya should not extend to Singapore ...

Whatever expectations existed were stimulated by the Malay language newspapers, in particular, *Utusan Melayu*, whose motto is 'To fight for religion, race and homeland.' Besides constant harping on the depressed economic state of Malays in Singapore, for which there was some justification, it reiterated that Malays were being persecuted by the PAP government led by 'step father' Lee Kuan Yew against whom continual abuse was directed. Reference was also made to 'the PAP's social revolution for the destruction of our race.'[32]

To clarify the Singapore Government's position on Malay rights, the Minister for Social Affairs, Othman Wok, sent an invitation to 114 Malay organisations to meet him with the Prime Minister on 19 July. Unfortunately, this move produced a 'hostile reaction'[33] from the UMNO leaders in Singapore who were left out of the meeting. They in turn called for a Malay convention on 12 July which was attended by a crowd of some 12,000 people. Albar, who addressed the crowd, claimed that the Malays now lived in worse conditions than under the Japanese. A Malay National Action Committee was set up at the convention, with responsibility for matters affecting the welfare of the Malays in Singapore.[34] The Prime Minister's meeting on 19 July was attended by over 1000 Malays from 101 of the 104 organisations invited.[35] Lee again reiterated his meritocratic policy: there would be no special rights for Malays, no job quotas, no special licences and no land reservation. Members of the week-old Action Committee left the meeting unconvinced and dissatisfied even though Lee promised that every effort would be made by his government to train and equip the Malays to compete with non-Malays in finding jobs. Singapore Senator Ahmad Haji Taff, chairman of the Action Committee, called it an insult to the Malays.

---

[32] See M Leifer, 'Singapore in Malaysia: The Politics of Federation' (1965) 6 *Journal of Southeast Asian History* 54–70, at 63–64.

[33] ibid, at 64.

[34] ibid.

[35] See R Clutterbuck, *Conflict and Violence in Singapore and Malaysia 1945–1983* (Singapore, Graham Brash, 1984), at 320.

The following day, 20 July, leaflets bearing the heading 'Singapore Malay Action Committee' were circulated in Singapore. They claimed that the Chinese in Singapore had drawn up a plan to kill the Malays, and that 'Before Malay blood flows in Singapore, it is best to flood the state with Chinese blood'. The next day, during a procession in which 25,000 people gathered to celebrate the Prophet Mohamed's birthday, communal rioting broke out. A curfew was imposed till the following morning, but as fighting broke out in various parts of the island, the curfew was reimposed. As terrorist expert Major General Richard Clutterbuck recounts:

> On 21 July there was a demonstration by Malays protesting that, since Singapore was now part of the Federation, their same Constitutional privileges should apply. Exchanges of taunts and insults with Chinese bystanders on the streets developed into fighting in which two people were killed and over 100 injured. A curfew was imposed from 9.30 pm to 6 am but rioting continued next day and the curfew was re-imposed.
>
> Next day the curfew was extended all day except for two periods, 5.30-10 am and 3.30-6 pm to enable people to get to and from work. There was, however, another major Malay procession to celebrate the Prophet's Birthday. In pursuance of their Confrontation with Malaysia, a number of Indonesians had clandestinely entered Singapore in small boats or by parachute and some of these had attempted to arouse the religious zeal of the more fanatical Malays. At the same time the violence of the two previous days had brought out the Chinese Secret Society gangs. There were widespread riots in 12 separate districts and police fired tear gas. The riots continued for 5 days during which 22 people were killed and 454 injured, 256 arrested for unlawful assembly and rioting and another 1,579 for curfew-breaking. The curfew was gradually relaxed but kept in force at night (8 pm to 5 am) until Sunday, 2 August.[36]

All parties in the Alliance and the PAP appealed for calm and for a while their feuding stopped. Everyone was concerned to preserve racial harmony. Nonetheless, in September, a second communal riot broke out in Singapore when a Malay trishaw-rider was stabbed to death in Geylang. The rioting lasted five days and nights during which 12 people were killed and over 109 injured, 240 arrested for rioting and over 1000

---

[36] ibid, at 320–21.

for curfew-breaking.[37] To calm the situation down, a meeting between the Alliance and the PAP leaders was set up for 29 September 1964. Following the meeting, the PAP's chairman, Toh Chin Chye, told the press that the parties had agreed a two-year truce and that they would not raise 'any sensitive issues regarding the respective positions of the communities in Malaysia' and that 'party differences will be relegated into the background'. Before long, the truce was broken when, on 25 October, Mohamed Khir Johari, the Malaysian Minister for Agriculture and Cooperatives and chairman of the Singapore Alliance, reorganised the Singapore Alliance and announced that he was 'confident that in the next general election in Singapore in 1967, the Singapore Alliance will win enough votes to form the next government'. Shortly afterwards, Toh Chin Chye told *The Straits Times* that the PAP would be 'reorientated and reorganised so that we can get at Malaya'. From that point on, relations between the Singapore Government and the Federation Government went on a steadily downhill path so much so that Malaysian Finance Minister Tan Siew Sin likened it to a marriage gone so sour that the couple 'could not even agree on who should use the bathroom first'.

A combination of attacks from the 'ultras' and Tan Siew Sin and his MCA contributed significantly to the serious deterioration of the situation. By February 1965, the verbal conflict between the PAP and the Alliance escalated further, and by May that year, what had started out as a dispute between a state government and its federal colleagues became extremely polarised on the issue of race. At UMNO's 18th general assembly on 15 May, a resolution was unanimously passed demanding the arrest and detention of Lee Kuan Yew. By 22 July, the situation seemed irretrievable and the Tunku, convalescing in France, received a cable from his Deputy Prime Minister, Tun Razak saying that the senior members of the Cabinet were in full agreement with him that Singapore should go its own way.[38] Tun Razak was told to 'proceed with the necessary legal chores and the amendments to the constitution' and Razak

---

[37] ibid, at 321. It has been suggested that this riot was instigated by Indonesian agents. See Sopiee, *From Malayan Union to Singapore Separation* (n 22), at 195, and J Drysdale, *Singapore: Struggle for Success* (Singapore, Times Books International, 1984), at 364.

[38] See *The Sunday Times* 15 Aug 1965.

replied that he would convene Parliament on 9 August to 'go through the readings of an amending bill on a certificate of urgency'.[39]

The Tunku returned to Kuala Lumpur on 5 August. On 6 August, Goh Keng Swee and other Singapore leaders were informed about the Tunku's decision to separate and Lee, who was holidaying in the Cameron Highlands, hurried to Kuala Lumpur. Lee and Goh informed the Tunku that Toh Chin Chye and Rajaratnam (Culture Minister) were unwilling to sign the separation agreement and they asked the Tunku to write Toh a brief note. In this now historic letter, the Tunku told Toh that 'in the interest of our friendship and security and peace of Malaysia as a whole, there is absolutely no other way out' and if he did not accept the agreement, the situation might go out of control. Toh accepted. In the meantime, the British High Commissioner, Lord Head, had not been told of this momentous decision, and when he found out, he went searching for the Tunku to try to save the situation. The Tunku could not be found till 3 am when Lord Head found him hiding in a friend's penthouse. By that time, it was too late, a Royal Malaysian Air Force jet had been sent to Singapore on 7 August to secure the rest of the Cabinet's signatures to the Separation Agreement and returned to Kuala Lumpur on 8 August. The next day, Parliament was summoned at 9.30 am and the Alliance members were told to vote for the bill to ensure a two-thirds majority necessary for a constitutional amendment. At 10.00 am, when division was sounded, Singapore became an independent, sovereign state.

VIII. POST-1965 DEVELOPMENTS

A. The Aftermath of Independence

Singapore attained independence on 9 August 1965 but without a new constitution. In passing the Malaysia (Singapore Amendment) Act the Malaysian Parliament relinquished control over Singapore, paving the way for its independence. The Malaysian statute did not bestow the new state with a new constitution, leaving the way clear for Singapore to craft a constitution of its own. In the aftermath of independence, Prime

---

[39] ibid.

Minister Lee Kuan Yew promised Singaporeans that a new constitution would be drafted and even despatched Law Minister EW Barker to secure the help of Australia and New Zealand in this undertaking.[40] By the time Singapore was admitted as the 117th member of the United Nations on 21 September 1965, the constitution-drafting process had yet to begin. By December, the Singapore Government decided against drafting a new constitution. Instead, a makeshift constitution would be cobbled together with the Constitution of the State of Singapore 1963 as its foundation. The Republic of Singapore Independence Act was passed by Parliament on 22 December 1965 to import into Singapore, certain provisions of the Malaysian Federal Constitution, most notably the fundamental liberties provisions. In 1980, these three documents were consolidated into one after the Attorney-General was empowered to issue a Reprint of the Constitution. The 1980 Reprint of the Constitution of the Republic of Singapore, incorporated all amendments to 31 March 1980.

B. The Wee Chong Jin Commission

Given the sensitivities engendered by the racial riots of 1964, the new Singapore Government was especially concerned with the protection of minority rights and interests. To this end, a Constitutional Commission (only Singapore's second), headed by then Chief Justice Wee Chong Jin, was set up in December 1965. It was charged with seeing how these interests could be safeguarded. The Commission issued its report in 1966 and made a number of important recommendations:[41]

a. Constitutional provisions relating to fundamental liberties, the judiciary, the legislature, general elections, minority rights and the special position of Malays, and the amendment procedures themselves should be entrenched. This was to be done by making these provisions amendable

---

[40] KYL Tan, 'State and Institution Building Through the Singapore Constitution 1965–2005' in Li-ann Thio & KYL Tan, *Evolution of a Revolution: Forty Years of the Singapore Constitution* (London, Routledge-Cavendish, 2009) 50–78, at 53.
[41] See *Report of the Constitutional Commission* (Singapore, Government Printer, 1966).

only if the amendment secured a vote of two-thirds majority in Parliament and a two-thirds majority at a national referendum.

b. Creation of a Council of State whose main function would be to 'consider all proposed legislation, except all Supply Bills or a Bill presented on a Certificate of Urgency, and to report thereon to Parliament'. The Council would be a purely advisory body and would not be part of the legislature. It would offer Parliament 'serious and weighty advice' on impending legislation and its effects on racial, linguistic, religious or cultural minorities.

c. Creation of the office of an Ombudsman or Parliamentary Commissioner for Administration to ensure 'that civil servants carry out their administrative duties according to law so that citizens may feel that, apart from the ministerial responsibility for the acts of civil servants which is a feature of our parliamentary system in Singapore, there is also an independent check on the acts and decisions of civil servants'.

d. Entrenching of judicial offices to maintain the independence of the judiciary and a more appropriate method of appointing members of the Public Service Commission.

Following a brief debate, Parliament rejected most of these recommendations and only pursued the Council of State proposals which were sent to select committee. This body was later enacted as the Presidential Council.[42]

As constituted under the 1969 constitutional amendments, the Presidential Council comprised a chairman, 10 permanent members and 10 non-permanent members appointed by the President on the advice of the Cabinet. Its general function was 'to consider and report on such matters affecting any racial or religious communities in Singapore as may be referred to the Council by Government', while its particular function was 'to draw attention to any Bill to any subsidiary legislation if that Bill or subsidiary legislation is in the opinion of the Council a differentiating measure or otherwise inconsistent with the fundamental liberties of the subject'. It is significant that Parliament rejected the Wee Chong Jin Commission's recommendation for the Presidential Council to comprise only non-politicians. Parliament thought that such a recommendation was unrealistic as it was the politicians who were closest to

---

[42] See Thio Su Mien, 'The Presidential Council' (1969) 1 *Singapore Law Review* 2.

the ground and could understand inter-ethnic issues best. Thus, the first 10 permanent members appointed were all members of the ruling PAP Government. Today, it is a combination of current and former Cabinet members of the PAP.

C. Changes to the Judiciary

Singapore's judicial structure was altered by its merger with Malaysia. The 1955 Courts Ordinance—the last Ordinance to refer back to the jurisdiction of the English High Court—was replaced by the Courts of Judicature Act 1964. Under this Act, the High Court of Malaysia in Singapore replaced the old Supreme Court of the Colony of Singapore. Under this new system, the Singapore branch of the Malaysian High Court was part of the larger national system of courts that included the two sister High Courts of Malaya and Borneo. At the top of the hierarchy was the Federal Court.

At independence, Singapore's Parliament decided to retain the Federal Court as the intermediate appellate court in its judicial hierarchy, and the Judicial Committee of the Privy Council as its final appellate court. No reasons were offered for this decision save that 'it would be in the interest of the administration of justice if this were to remain so'.[43] Some years later, Law Minister EW Barker revealed that the courts were 'left to carry on within the legal framework that had been laid down when we were part of the Federation of Malaysia' because the momentous changes brought by Singapore's independence 'claimed priority over other changes'.[44] As such, the Singapore High Court remained part of the Federal Court structure and between 1966 and 1969, one enjoyed the unusual spectre of the Federal Court sitting in Singapore. This situation was remedied only in 1969 with the passing of the Constitution (Amendment) Act 1969 and the Supreme Court of Judicature Act 1969.[45] This amendment was necessary to constitute the Singapore judiciary because the 1963 State Constitution did not provide

---

[43] Prime Minister Lee Kuan Yew, on moving the Constitution (Amendment) Bill, *Singapore Parliamentary Debates Reports* 22 Dec 1965, vol 24, col 442.

[44] Speech of EW Barker, Debate on President's Address, *Report of Singapore Parliamentary Debates* 15 May 1968, vol 27, col 284.

[45] Act No 24 of 1969.

for a separate state judiciary and all matters involving the judiciary were dealt with at federal level. The amending Act also made the Judicial Committee of Her Britannic Majesty's Privy Council Singapore's final court of appeal.

The shortage of High Court judges led to two significant changes in the Constitution which effectively undermine judicial independence. The first was the 1971 amendment to Article 94 to permit the appointment of *supernumerary judges* and the second, the creation of the post of Judicial Commissioner. In the first instance, judges of the Supreme Court who were compelled by the Constitution to retire at the age of 65 were permitted to stay on as 'contract judges', usually for terms of between one to three years. While these judges had the same rights and privileges as all other judges, they lacked security of tenure. In 1979, another scheme was created to entice more senior practitioners to take up appointments on the Bench.[46] Judicial Commissioners were appointed for between six months and three years and at the end of their stint were allowed to return to private practice. Like supernumerary judges, Judicial Commissioners have no security of tenure. To compound the situation, Article 94(5) allows the appointment of Judicial Commissioners 'to hear and determine a specified case only'. This last provision, which must surely violate the judicial power of the Supreme Court, has never been used nor challenged.

In 1989, the Constitution was amended to restrict appeals to the Privy Council. Appeals would only proceed to the Privy Council if both parties to the litigation agreed prior to their Court of Appeal hearing (in civil cases); or where the death penalty was involved and there was no unanimity amongst the judges in the Court of Criminal Appeal. In 1993, all appeals to the Privy Council were abolished,[47] and a constitutional amendment was passed to constitute a permanent Court of Appeal and to create a new class of judges known as Justices of Appeal who would rank above puisne judges and sit on appeals in the new court.

At the time of independence, the PAP Government decided that appeals to the Privy Council would be retained for practical and strategic

---

[46] The first Judicial Commissioner to be appointed under this scheme was Chan Sek Keong, the former managing partner of the firm Shook Lin & Bok. Chan subsequently became a puisne judge, Attorney-General of Singapore and was, in April 2006, appointed Chief Justice of Singapore.

[47] Judicial Committee (Repeal) Act 1994 (No 2 of 1994).

reasons. The government was anxious to assure would-be foreign investors that their rights would be duly enforced and that unlike the courts of some other developing states, the Singapore courts would steadfastly apply the law without fear or favour. By having the Privy Council as the court of last resort, these investors would be assured that ultimately, their cases could be heard by a 'British court' whose credentials were impeccable and unimpeachable.

The Court of Appeal is presided over by the Chief Justice as the Court's President. In September 1994, a new Article 100 was inserted into the Constitution, establishing a *Special Tribunal* consisting of not less than three judges of the Supreme Court. The President may refer to this tribunal 'for its opinion any question as to the effect of any provision' of the Constitution. The tribunal is under a duty 'consider and answer the question so referred as soon as may be and in any case not more than 60 days after the date of such reference'.[48]

This amendment was not only significant, but also foretold things to come. The then Deputy Prime Minister, Lee Hsien Loong pointed out that unlike in Malaysia, the 'Singapore Constitution does not have any provisions for referring questions of interpretation of the Constitution to the Courts for an advisory ruling'. Lee explained that having such a tribunal will be useful in resolving interpretation of the complex provisions of the elected presidency scheme, and that an issue with respect to the interpretation of Article 22H relating to the President's veto powers had already arisen. This Special Tribunal determined its first reference in early 1995 in *Constitutional Reference No 1 of 1995*.[49]

D. Entrenching Singapore's Sovereignty

One of the first amendments made to the Constitution after independence was to its amendment procedure. While a two-thirds majority in Parliament was previously required to effect a constitutional amendment, this was changed to a simple majority at the time of independence.

---

[48] Constitution of the Republic of Singapore, Art 100(2).
[49] [1995] 2 SLR 201. See Thio Li-ann, 'Working Out the Presidency: The Rites of Passage' [1995] *Singapore Journal of Legal Studies* 509; for a rebuttal to Thio, see Chan Sek Keong, 'Working Out the Presidency: No Passage of Rites—In Defence of the Opinion of the Constitutional Tribunal' [1996] *Singapore Journal of Legal Studies* 1.

This change was prompted by the PAP's concern that it might not muster the required two-thirds majority to change the Constitution should the need arise. This made for an extremely flexible constitution that could be changed in exactly the same way as any other ordinary legislation.

In 1967, a right-wing political party, the National Party of Singapore, was established with the aim of working 'for the eventual re-unification of Singapore with Malaysian on the basis of equal footing'. Given the ease with which the Constitution could be amended, it would have been easy for Singapore to re-join the Federation. In 1971, an attempt was made to revive the National Party and the government moved to amend the Constitution to protect Singapore's sovereign status.[50] A new Part III was added to preclude any surrender or transfer of Singapore's sovereignty by merger, federation or otherwise, unless it was supported by at least two-thirds of the electorate during a national referendum. The amendment also prohibits the relinquishing of control over the Singapore Police Force and/or the Singapore Armed Forces, under the same terms. The two-third majority for constitutional amendments other than for provisions in Part III was restored in 1979.

E. Changes to the Parliamentary System

From 1968 to 1981, the PAP occupied every single seat in Parliament. This was, in no small way aided by the fact that in 1966, the leading opposition party, the Barisan Sosialis (Socialist Front), decided to abandon Parliament and take the fight to the streets. One by one, the Barisan Assemblymen resigned, allowing the PAP to capture all the seats they vacated. The Barisan Sosialis also refused to take part in the 1968 General Election, leaving the field open for the PAP to win all the seats. The PAP's dominance of Singapore politics from 1968 to 1980 resulted from a combination of good governance, ability to deliver the economic goods and a non-ideological approach to politics. Adopting an ideology of 'pragmatism', the PAP readily adopted any idea or policy that would work, making it extremely difficult for opposition parties to make ideological inroads on the political front.

---

[50] 'Riff-raff who want to try their luck' *The Straits Times* 30 Aug 1972, at 5.

Invariably, there remained pockets of dissent and unhappiness and eventually this would be manifested through the ballot box. In 1981, veteran Workers' Party secretary-general JB Jeyaretnam defeated the PAP's candidate in the Anson constituency by-elections and broke the PAP's stranglehold on power. To quell demands for more opposition members in Parliament, a constitutional amendment was passed in 1984 to 'ensure the representation in Parliament of a minimum number of Members from a political party or parties not forming the government'.

Under this scheme, the six best 'losers' in the general elections (on the basis of percentage votes cast) would be invited to Parliament as Non-Constituency Members of Parliament (NCMPs). NCMPs have all rights and privileges as regular MPs but cannot vote on bills to amend the Constitution, supply or money bills or on a motion of no confidence in the government.[51] In the 1984 General Elections, two opposition members were directly elected to Parliament. It was thus decided that only one NCMP seat would be offered but there were no takers for this offer. The first NCMP was veteran opposition leader Lee Siew Choh (1917–2002) who stood on the Workers' Party ticket alongside Francis Seow and Mohd Khalit Baboo in Eunos GRC in the 1988 General Election. Defeated by PAP team by just 1279 votes, the Workers' Party was invited to nominate one member of that team as NCMP. Lee was its nominee.

One of the most important constitutional amendments took place just before the 1988 General Elections. This amendment introduced the Group Representation Constituency or GRC. Under this new scheme, three single-member constituencies would be clustered into one Group Representation Constituency. Each GRC would have at least one candidate from a minority race, ie Malay or Indian or other (non-Chinese) race. The amendment was prompted by the government's observation that there was a 'voting trend which showed young voters preferring candidates who were best suited to their own needs without being sufficiently aware of the need to return a racially balanced slate of candidates'. This amendment was intended to entrench the multi-racial component of politics in Singapore's Constitution.[52]

---

[51] See VS Winslow, 'Creating A Utopian Parliament' (1984) 28 *Malayan Law Review* 268.

[52] See EKB Tan, 'Multiracialism Engineered: The Limits of Electoral and Spatial Integration in Singapore' (2005) 4(4) *Ethnopolitics* 413–28.

The GRC scheme was expanded in each subsequent general election. In 1991, the number of MPs in a GRC was increased from three to four. The reason offered was that as the populations grew in these constituencies, the workload for MPs grew correspondingly and it would need more MPs to help shoulder the burden. In 1996, it was increased from four to between four and six members. In the 1997 General Election that followed, Singapore was divided into 15 GRCs of between four and six members each and nine single-seat wards. While all the single-seat wards were contested, only six GRCs were contested.[53] In the 2013 General Election, there were a total of 12 SMCs and 15 GRCs. All but one GRC was contested.

In 1990, the Constitution was amended to introduce yet another class of Member of Parliament—the Nominated Member of Parliament (NMP). The government felt that there should be alternative views on policies, different from those espoused by the political parties represented in Parliament and that this would best be achieved by nominating non-political persons to serve as NMPs. The first two Nominated MPs, Dr Maurice Choo and Mr Leong Chee Whye, were sworn into office. Originally, the maximum number of NMPs allowed under the Constitution was six, but this was increased to nine in a 1997 constitutional amendment.

F. The Elected President

In his National Day Rally speech in 1984, Prime Minister Lee Kuan Yew mooted the idea of transforming the office of President into an elected one. What prompted this radical suggestion was his fear of a 'freak election' result that would bring to power a profligate non-PAP Government:

> From the politics of poverty in the 1950s and 60s, we have moved to the politics of progress; from the politics of desperation, to the politics of hope; from the politics of squatters, to the politics of owners. You have more at stake than ever before.

---

[53] For a critique of these changes, see KYL Tan, 'Constitutional Implications of the 1991 Singapore General Election' (1992) 13 *Singapore Law Review* 1; and KYL Tan, 'Is Singapore's Electoral System In Need of Reform' (1997) 14 *Commentary* 109–17.

If you vote in rogues or opportunists, or incompetent or impractical men, the value of your flats and of your savings will shrink. It has become your business to ensure that the people elected to Parliament are capable and honest so that your flats will increase in value and your CPF will grow.

... The danger is that there is nothing to prevent a future government from running through these reserves ... In one five-year spending spree, Singapore can be rendered prostrate and bankrupt.[54]

Lee's fears were not unfounded. In the General Election of December that year, the ruling PAP suffered a 12.6 per cent drop in popular vote, recording a popular majority of 64.8 per cent. Lee was furious and suggested that he needed to look again at the one-man-one vote system to prevent a 'freak result'.[55]

It is necessary to try and put some safeguards into the way in which people use their votes to bargain, to coerce, to push, to jostle and get what they want without running the risk of losing the services of the government, because on day, by mistake, they will lose the services of the government.[56]

Had there been another 14 per cent vote swing, Lee warned, 'You tell me whether you're going to go home tonight and sleep well?'[57] To safeguard Singapore's reserves, a large part of which is made up of Singaporeans' Central Provident Fund savings, Lee said that the government was 'working out a blocking mechanism whereby the President can block the spending of any reserve which the government in office has not itself accumulated'.[58]

The object of this proposal was to protect Singapore's foreign reserves against a profligate government. Under Singapore's Westminster system of government, an elected government had virtually unlimited power over taxation and spending. The first White Paper proposing the elected presidency scheme appeared in 1988. This was followed by a second White Paper in 1990. After much debate, the Constitution was amended in 1991 to provide for a popularly elected Head of State. The purpose was to institutionally safeguard Singapore's massive foreign reserves

---

[54] 'Protection plan: To help you keep what you have' *The Straits Times* 20 Aug 1984, at 1.
[55] 'Critical three to six months' *Straits Times* 31 Dec 1984, at 1.
[56] 'PM replies to voters' signal' *Straits Times* 24 Dec 1984, at 1.
[57] ibid.
[58] Ee Boon Lee, 'Big changes likely after polls' *Singapore Monitor* 20 Aug 1984, at 1.

and the integrity of its civil service from a profligate and populist government. Under this complicated scheme (which we shall deal with in chapter three), the popularly elected President would hold the 'second key' to the reserves and have veto power on the appointment of top civil servants. At the same time, the amendments gave the elected President veto powers over the continued preventive detention of prisoners and the issuing of prohibition orders against extremist religious proselytes.

There are several notable features of the new presidency:

a. provisions relating to the elected presidency cannot be amended without the President's concurrence unless it is supported at a referendum by a two-thirds majority;

b. the qualifications for candidacy are extremely stringent with a three-man Presidential Elections Committee determining who is or is not eligible to run for President;

c. the Constitution requires any candidate wishing to run for office to be non-partisan in that he or she cannot be a member of any political party; and

d. under the Presidential Elections Act, if there was only one candidate for the elections, there would be no need for formal elections and that candidate would be deemed elected as President.

The first presidential elections were held on 29 August 1993. Ong Teng Cheong, a former Deputy Prime Minister, chairman of the PAP and long-time trade union leader and politician, defeated retired banker and former Accountant-General Chua Kim Yeow to become Singapore's first elected President. A series of amendments have been made to the elected presidency provisions in the last decade. These are dealt with in greater detail in chapter three.

G. Amendment to Citizenship Laws

In 1985, an amendment was passed to consolidate the provisions relating to citizenship under the Constitution. Under the new Article 135, the government is empowered to deprive a citizen of Singapore of his citizenship if he 'voluntarily claimed and exercised any rights ... available to him under the law of any country' or if he has 'applied to authorities of a place outside Singapore for the issue or renewal of a passport or used a passport issued by such authorities as a travel document'. A major change to the citizenship provisions was the inclusion of a new ground for deprivation, ie where a citizen has been 'ordinarily resident outside Singapore for a continuous period of 10 years'. In 2004, the citizenship provisions were again amended to allow citizenship by descent to be conferred on children of Singapore women.

IX. CONCLUSION

Singapore's post-independence constitutional development was in large part driven by the imperatives of state and institution building.[59] In the first 40 years of its existence, the Singapore state has focused on strengthening the hand of government and good governance, rather than on constitutional niceties and individual liberties. Most of the institutional changes made between 1965 and 1979 were directly related to Singapore's departure from the Federation of Malaysia. However, changes made to the parliamentary system of government in the 1980s were designed not only to entrench minority ethnic representation in the legislature but also to entrench the PAP in power. In the case of the elected presidency in 1991, the PAP Government was so driven by the nightmare of a non PAP-type party being swept into power, that it created a PAP-type strong man in the form of the President to act as a check against such a government which, it was convinced, would be profligate.

Singapore's Parliament has always viewed 'law' formalistically, often adopting a Diceyan notion of the *rule of law* in that everything should be done in accordance with the law; a purely positivist perspective. Law is an instrument of the state, to be used by its leaders to be moulded and shaped to further what they perceive to be the state's best interests. Law is not an autonomous limiting factor. As Jothie Rajah observed, 'though the state claims the liberalism of the "rule of law", its instrumentalist legalism is more properly labelled "rule by law"'.[60] In that sense, as one

---

[59] KYL Tan, 'State and Institution Building Through the Singapore Constitution 1965–2005' in Li-ann Thio & KYL Tan, *Evolution of a Revolution: Forty Years of the Singapore Constitution* (London, Routledge-Cavendish, 2009) 50–78.

[60] J Rajah, *Authoritarian Rule of Law: Legislation, Discourse and Legitimacy in Singapore* (New York, Cambridge University Press, 2010), at 3–4.

scholar has remarked, it is 'an idea of rule *through* law rather than rule *of* law'.

Ideally, a constitution must organise, separate and control the arbitrary exercise of power. Given the political realities of a single-party dominant system of government in Singapore, the limiting powers of the Constitution are weak indeed. Other than the sovereignty provisions under Part III and the elected President provisions—which require a two-thirds majority in a national referendum—everything and anything in the Constitution is amendable by a two-thirds majority in Parliament. This special majority has been easily obtained since 1968 when the PAP secured an almost hegemonic grip on power. The party system with its Whip-enforced discipline was inherited from the British, and lovingly cherished by the PAP. This allows the ruling party to change the Constitution almost at will and the ease with which the amendments are constantly made erodes its sanctity as the *supreme* law and its legitimacy as the nation's legal beacon of light.

Notwithstanding its self-proclamation as the state's *supreme law* many Singaporeans probably view it with little more awe or respect than any other piece of legislation; maybe less. Indeed, if Singaporeans are looking to their Constitution to help control and limit government, they will come away disappointed for they will discover that control on government is not achieved through the haloed words of a sanctified and revered national document or the activist intervention of the courts. Checks on government power can, ultimately, only come from the people themselves, through the ballot box.

FURTHER READING

R Clutterbuck, *Conflict and Violence in Singapore and Malaysia 1945–1983* (Singapore, Graham Brash, 1984).

J Drysdale, *Singapore: Struggle for Success* (Singapore, Times Books International, 1984).

RH Hickling, 'The Origins of Constitutional Government in Singapore' in his *Essays in Singapore Law* (Kuala Lumpur, Peladuk Publications, 1992) 1–51.

M Leifer, 'Singapore in Malaysia: The Politics of Federation' (1965) 6 *Journal of Southeast Asian History* 54–70.

J Rajah, *Authoritarian Rule of Law: Legislation, Discourse and Legitimacy in Singapore* (New York, Cambridge University Press, 2010).

LA Sheridan, 'From the Federation of Malaya to Malaysia' (1965) 14 *Journal du Droit International* 543.

———, 'Constitutional and Legal Implications and Problems in the Separation of Singapore from Malaysia' (1966) 1 *Fiat Justitia* 47.

KYL Tan, 'A Short Legal and Constitutional History of Singapore' in KYL Tan (ed), *The Singapore Legal System*, 2nd edn (Singapore, Singapore University Press, 1999) 26–66.

———, 'State and Institution Building Through the Singapore Constitution 1965–2005' in Li-ann Thio & KYL Tan, *Evolution of a Revolution: Forty Years of the Singapore Constitution* (London, Routledge-Cavendish, 2009) 50–78.

——— & Lam Peng Er (eds), *Managing Political Change in Singapore: The Elected Presidency* (London, Routledge, 1997).

Tan Tai Yong, *Creating Greater Malaysia: Decolonisation and the Politics of Merger* (Singapore, Institute of Southeast Asian Studies, 2008).

CM Turnbull, *A History of Modern Singapore: 1819–2005* (Singapore, NUS Press, 2009).

Yeo Kim Wah, *Political Development in Singapore 1945–1955* (Singapore, Singapore University Press, 1973).

WEBSITE

http://statutes.agc.gov.sg/aol/home.w3p (Full text of the Constitution)

2

Constitutionalism in Singapore

Introduction – The Constitution as Supreme Law – Separation of
Powers – Constitutionalism and the Rule of Law – Constitutional
Culture

I. INTRODUCTION

MOST DEFINITIONS OF 'constitutionalism' tend to be
tautologous. The venerable *Oxford English Dictionary* offers
two meanings: 'a constitutional system of government' and
'adherence to constitutional principles'. The smaller *Longman Dictionary
of Contemporary English* fares slightly better: 'a set of basic laws and principles that a country or organization is governed by' and the *New Oxford
Companion to Law* is a little more specific: it 'posits that the powers of
government must be structured and limited by a binding constitution
incorporating certain basic principles if the protection of values like
human liberty and dignity is to be assured'.[1]

One of the best working definitions was offered by the late Professor
Stanley de Smith in a public lecture entitled 'Constitutionalism in the
Commonwealth Today', given on 28 August 1962 at the University of
Singapore during the First Southeast Asian Regional Conference on
Legal Education.[2] 'To me' de Smith said,

> constitutionalism in its formal sense means the principle that the exercise of
> political power shall be bounded by rules, rules which determine the validity
> of legislative and executive action by prescribing the procedure according to
> which it must be performed or by delimiting its permissible content.[3]

---

[1] T Daintith, 'Constitutionalism' in P Cane & J Conaghan (eds), *The New Oxford
Companion to Law* (Oxford, Oxford University Press, 2008), at 209.
[2] SA de Smith, 'Constitutionalism in the Commonwealth Today' (1962) 4(2)
Malaya Law Review 205.
[3] ibid.

More importantly,

> Constitutionalism becomes a living reality to the extent that these rules curb the arbitrariness of discretion and are in fact observed by the wielders of political power, and to the extent that within the forbidden zones upon which authority may not trespass there is significant room for the enjoyment of individual liberty.

> To be more specific, I am very willing to concede that constitutionalism is practised in a country where the government is genuinely accountable to an entity or organ distinct from itself, where elections are freely held on a wide franchise at frequent intervals, where political groups are free to organise and to campaign in between as well as immediately before elections with a view to presenting themselves as an alternative government, and where there are effective legal guarantees of basic civil liberties enforced by an independent judiciary; and I am not easily persuaded to identify constitutionalism in a country where any of those conditions is lacking.[4]

Broken down into its constituent parts, *constitutionalism* would require the presence of a constitution or basic document that legally sets out the powers and jurisdictions of the various branches of government; the judicial control of executive action; guarantee of fundamental liberties; and free and fair elections. Several ingredients must exist for these elements of constitutionalism to function properly. First, the Constitution must have status as the supreme law of the land if it is to be the basic legal document; all laws inconsistent with the Constitution must be invalid. Second, there must exist an effective separation of powers among the legislature, executive and judiciary, with the judiciary vested with power to pronounce on the constitutionality of statutes. Third, for all of this to work, the *rule of law* must exist as an overriding concept.

II. THE CONSTITUTION AS SUPREME LAW

A. The Amendment Regime

Although Great Britain remains one of the few countries in the world with no written constitution, almost every one of its former colonies—

---

[4] ibid, at 205–06.

including Singapore—has a written constitution. Written constitutions differ significantly from unwritten ones in that their validity and supremacy emanate from the people directly, rather than through Parliament. As pointed out by the American constitutional law scholar Edward Corwin many years ago, in the:

> *written Constitution*, higher law at last attained a form which made possible the attribution to it of an entirely new sort of validity, the validity of a statute emanating from the sovereign people. Once the binding force of higher law was transferred to this new basis, the notion of the sovereignty of the ordinary legislative organ disappeared automatically, since that cannot be a sovereign law-making body which is subordinate to another law-making body.[5]

The Constitution is thus a higher law that cannot be easily supplanted by an ordinary act of the legislature. As observed by Chief Justice Chan Sek Keong in *Mohammad Faizal bin Sabtu v PP*, constitutional supremacy mandates the courts to 'declare an Act of the Singapore parliament invalid for inconsistency with the Singapore Constitution and, hence, null and void'.[6] However, a constitution is not supreme merely because it declares itself to be such, as does Article 4 of the Singapore Constitution, which reads:

4. This Constitution is the supreme law of the Republic of Singapore and any law enacted by the Legislature after the commencement of this Constitution which is inconsistent with this Constitution shall, to the extent of the inconsistency, be void.

The Constitution is supreme because its provisions are more firmly entrenched than provisions under ordinary law. Generally speaking, constitutional amendments can only be effected only through special or super majorities. In Singapore, this has not always been the case. When Singapore became independent in 1965, Parliament changed the Constitution so that amendments could be effected by a simple majority. This was because the People's Action Party (PAP) Government, having won 37 of the 51 seats in the 1963 Legislative Assembly election, commanded what it regarded as a 'risky' 72 per cent of the vote in the Assembly. If the PAP lost just four more seats—either through

---

[5] ES Corwin, 'The "Higher Law" Background of American Constitutional Law' (1929) 42(3) *Harvard Law Review* 365, at 409.
[6] [2012] 4 SLR 947, at 958.

by-elections or defections within the party—it would lose the two-thirds majority needed to amend the Constitution at will.

The two-thirds majority was restored in 1979 after the party considered that all amendments that were necessitated by Singapore's exit from the Federation of Malaysia had been made. It also helped that in 1966, the Barisan Sosialis, the PAP's biggest opponent in Parliament, decided to abandon the parliamentary process and take its struggle to the streets. In 1968, the Barisan refused to contest the general election and thus allowed the PAP to win every single seat in that election and every other election till 1980. Thus, by 1979, the PAP was securely in control of Parliament and could happily restore the two-thirds majority required for constitutional amendments.

The current constitutional amendment regime in Singapore is extremely complex. Most provisions in the Constitution may be amended by a two-thirds majority in Parliament as provided in Article 5(2):

> 5(2)   A Bill seeking to amend any provision in this Constitution shall not
> be passed by Parliament unless it has been supported on Second and
> Third Readings by the votes of not less than two-thirds of the total
> number of the Members thereof.

There are, however, two exceptions to this general rule. The first is found in Part III of the Constitution, which deals with the surrender of Singapore's sovereignty and armed forces. In 1972, Article 8 of the Constitution was inserted to ensure that Part III cannot be amended unless it is supported by two-thirds of the voters in a national referendum:

> 8(1)   A Bill for making an amendment to this Part shall not be passed by
> Parliament unless it has been supported, at a national referendum,
> by not less than two-thirds of the total number of votes cast by the
> electors registered under the Parliamentary Elections Act (Cap. 218).

The second exception was inserted in 1991 when massive changes were made to the Constitution to introduce the elected presidency scheme. Many of these changes are extremely technical in nature. For our purposes, we need only concentrate on the amendment procedures under Articles 5A and 5(2A).

Article 5A provides that the President may withhold his assent to the passage of any law that 'provides, directly or indirectly, for the circumvention or curtailment of the discretionary powers conferred upon the President by this Constitution'. The question as to what constitutes the 'circumvention or curtailment of the discretionary powers conferred upon the President' by the Constitution, may be referred to a Special Tribunal under Article 100.

Where the Tribunal rules that the bill does not affect the President's discretionary power, he is 'deemed to have assented to the Bill' on the day of its opinion. But where the Tribunal rules that the bill does in fact affect the President's discretionary powers, the Prime Minister may direct that the bill 'be submitted to the electors for a national referendum'[7] and where a two-thirds majority of votes is secured in such a referendum, the President is 'deemed to have assented to the Bill on the day immediately after the publication in the *Gazette* of the results of the national referendum'.[8] If the President fails to assent to any bill or refer it to the Special Tribunal, he is 'deemed to have assented to the Bill on the day immediately following the expiration of the said 30 days'.[9]

Under Article 5(2A), the President has discretion to refuse to concur with any bill that would amend any provision in:

a. Part IV of the Constitution relating to fundamental liberties;
b. Article 65 or 66—provisions relating to the prorogation and dissolution of Parliament, and the conduct of general elections;
c. any provision in Chapter I of Part V relating to the office and powers of the President; or
d. Article 93A, which sets out the jurisdiction to determine questions as to the validity of presidential elections; and
e. any provision of the Constitution which authorises the President to act in his discretion.

The scheme demonstrates Parliament's anxiety to entrench the office of the elected presidency, thus making it almost a permanent fixture in the Constitution, just like Singapore's sovereign status. This move is puzzling given that no other institution of government under the Constitution is so tightly entrenched. Technically speaking, Parliament could resolve, by a two-thirds majority, to abolish itself or the judiciary, but not the presidency.

To complicate matters, Articles 5(2A) and 5A have not been brought into force even though they were passed in 1991. The fact that these two

---

[7] Constitution of the Republic of Singapore, Art 5A(4).
[8] ibid, Art 5A(5).
[9] ibid, Art 5A(6).

provisions have been held in abeyance means that the various changes made to refine the elected presidency scheme since 1991 were passed by Parliament without the need for the President to exercise his discretionary powers. Two Nominated Members of Parliament—in 2007 and 2014— questioned the government on why these two provisions remain in abeyance after so many years. On both occasions, two successive Law Ministers stated that as the 1991 changes to the Constitution were so complex and novel, more time was needed to fine-tune the system. The government was also asked why the provisions relating to the entrenchment of fundamental liberties and of elections could not be brought into force first, while the government continued tweaking the financial provisions. To this, the reply was that Article 5(2A) 'should operate as an integrated package' and as such, could not be 'staggered'. While it is not difficult to see the logic that more time was required to fine-tune the financial provisions, the 'integrated package' argument is much harder to fathom.

B. Can the Constitution be Impliedly Amended?

Two related questions arise here: first, can a constitution with no entrenchment provision be amended by the enactment of an ordinary law in Parliament; and second, can any bill that does not declare itself to be a constitution amendment bill, effectively alter the Constitution if it is passed by the requisite majority in Parliament. These are not purely academic issues since the situations could well have arisen in Singapore. As mentioned above, the amendment procedure of Singapore's 1963 State Constitution was reduced from a two-thirds majority to a simple majority between 1965 and 1979. As such, a constitutional amendment could easily have been effected by the same procedure as that of ordinary legislation.

At the same time, Singapore's Parliament has, since 1968, been overwhelmingly dominated by the PAP; between 1968 and 1981, the PAP held *all* the seats in Parliament, and following the 2011 General Election, it commands 80 of the 87 elected seats.[10] This represents

---

[10] After 2011, Singapore's Parliament comprises 99 Members of Parliament. However, the three Non-constituency MPs and nine Nominated MPs are left out of the computation since they are not entitled to vote on bills to amend the Constitution.

almost 92 per cent of the seats in Parliament, making the two-thirds majority very easy to secure in any instance.

In 1966, the Constitutional Commission headed by Chief Justice Wee Chong Jin recommended that a bill to alter the Constitution should not be passed unless it expressed declared itself to be a constitutional amendment bill:

> 76 The first method is a provision in the Constitution that a Bill for an Act of Parliament altering the Constitution shall not be passed by Parliament unless it is expressed to be one for amendment of the Constitution and contains no other provision. Although it is the weakest form of constitutional entrenchment, it nevertheless provides a useful safeguard in that it protects the Constitution from amendment by implication. We think this method will also have some practical value in that it would specifically draw the attention of Members of Parliament and the public to the fact that the a government in office proposes to alter the supreme law of the Republic.[11]

This recommendation was not implemented and there remains a question as to how easy it will be to impliedly amend the Constitution. While the use of super majorities has acted as a check in most jurisdictions, the PAP's overwhelming command of Parliament renders such a check illusory. Save for Part III of the Constitution, Parliament can amend any other part of Singapore's Constitution at will whether explicitly or implicitly. Political reality, rather than institutional design, has thus rendered Singapore's Constitution a highly flexible one.

The PAP's overwhelming majority may well lull Parliament into a complacent mood when passing legislation, including constitutional amendments. As a recent controversy in Parliament revealed, a bill could be inadvertently passed without the requisite quorum of members. In July 2014, Nominated MP Eugene Tan interrupted parliamentary proceedings twice to point out to the Deputy Speaker that Parliament lacked a quorum (a quarter of its members) to proceed with the passage of two bills before the House. The Deputy Speaker had to ring the division bell to summon the remainder of the members, who filed into the Chamber to resume their seats. Tan had previously pointed out the lack of a quorum on two previous occasions in 2012.

---

[11] *Report of the Constitutional Commission* (Singapore, Government Printing Office, 1966), at para 76.

C. The Basic Features Doctrine

Provided Parliament abides by the strict procedures laid out under the Constitution, can it amend the Constitution so completely as to make it a totally different document? Indeed, are there parts of the Constitution that cannot be amended at all? Can Parliament, for example, vote to dissolve itself forever and hand over the entirety of its power to a dictator? Put simply, are there limits to amending the Constitution?

These questions lead us to the controversial 'Basic Features Doctrine' which originated from a series of Indian Supreme Court decisions starting with *Shankari Prasad v Union of India*[12] and culminating in the monumental decision of *Kesavananda v The State of Kerala*.[13] *Kesavananda's* case was argued before a full bench of 13 judges, and in a judgment so lengthy it merited the issue of a separate volume of law reports, the basic features doctrine was upheld by a bare majority of 7-6. In his leading majority judgment, Chief Justice Sikri opined that every provision in the Constitution could be amended provided that its 'basic foundation and structure' remains the same. He went on further to identify five characteristics of the Indian Constitution's basic structure: (a) supremacy of the Constitution; (b) Republic and democratic forms of government; (c) secular character of the Constitution; (d) separation of powers between the legislative, executive and judicial branches of government; and (e) federal character of the Constitution. Six of his fellow judges agreed with him but each of them had a different idea as to what constituted the 'basic features' of the Indian Constitution. In his leading dissenting judgment, Justice Ray argued that if the power of amendment did not contain any limitation, any attempt by the court to lay down limits on the amending power was tantamount to laying down a new constitution.

The basic features doctrine has been argued in the local courts and expressly pleaded and discussed in two Singapore cases. The first was *Teo Soh Lung v Minister for Home Affairs & Ors*[14] where Justice FA Chua held that the framers of Singapore's Constitution did not intend to limit the power of amendment and that the courts would be usurping

---

[12] AIR 1951 SC 455.
[13] AIR 1973 SC 1461.
[14] [1989] 1 SLR(R) 461; [1989] SGHC 108 (High Court, Singapore).

Parliament's legislative function if they imposed any limitation on the legislature's power to amend the Constitution:

> If the framers of the Singapore Constitution had intended limitations on the power of amendment, they would have expressly provided for such limitations. But Art 5 of the Constitution does not put any limitation on the amending power.

> If the courts have the power to impose limitations on the Legislature's power of constitutional amendments, they would be usurping Parliament's legislative function contrary to Art 58 of the Constitution. Article 5 expressly provides that any provisions of the Constitution can be amended by a two-thirds majority in Parliament.[15]

Justice Chua went further, adding:

> I am of the view that the Kesavananda doctrine is not applicable to our Constitution. Considering the differences in the making of the Indian and our Constitution, it cannot be said that our Parliament's power to amend our Constitution is limited in the same way as the Indian Parliament's power to amend the Indian Constitution. In any case, in my judgment, none of the amendments complained of has destroyed the basic structure of the Constitution.[16]

The second case was *Cheng Vincent v Minister for Home Affairs & Ors.*[17] Justice Lai Kew Chai concurred with Justice FA Chua's judgment in *Teo Soh Lung* and held that:

> [T]he well known *Kesavananda* doctrine enunciated by the Supreme Court of India, which would have implied a limitation on the legislative powers of Parliament under art 58 to legislate or under art 5 to amend if the legislation or amendment would alter the basic structure of the Constitution, is not the law in Singapore.[18]

Despite the Singapore judiciary's rejection of the *Kesavananda* doctrine, the courts have nevertheless stated that the doctrine of the separation of powers is part of the 'basic structure' of the Singapore Constitution. In *Mohammad Faizal bin Sabtu v PP*,[19] Chief Justice Chan Sek Keong held that the 'principle of separation of powers, whether conceived as

---

[15] ibid, at 475.
[16] ibid, at 479.
[17] [1990] 1 SLR(R) 38.
[18] ibid, at 52.
[19] [2012] 4 SLR 947.

a sharing or a division of sovereign power between these three organs of state, is therefore part of the basic structure of the Singapore Constitution'.[20]

III. SEPARATION OF POWERS

The separation of powers doctrine has existed since the time of the ancient Greeks but received its most eloquent elucidation in a book by French nobleman and scholar Baron de Montesquieu entitled *Les esprits des Lois* or *The Spirit of the Laws*. Montesquieu believed that to secure freedom and liberty of the individual, it was best to create a government in which power was balanced among its three branches: the legislature, the executive and the judges. These branches of government should have equal but different powers so that one branch can check and balance the others. Montesquieu felt that if all the legislative, executive and judicial power were to repose in the same person, the individual's liberty was in peril. Even if two of these powers were placed in the hands of one branch of government, there can be no liberty. Montesquieu's ideas found their greatest manifestation in the American Constitution.

As a former British colony, Singapore inherited the UK's Westminster model of government in which the separation of powers between the legislative and executive branches of government is not significant. Members of the executive (the Prime Minister and his Cabinet) are drawn directly from the legislative branch (Parliament). At the same time, the party system, with its strict party discipline, makes it difficult for Parliament to hold the executive accountable for its actions especially if the ruling party commands a huge majority in Parliament. Where no party commands an overwhelming majority in Parliament or indeed, no majority at all, this check and balance mechanism would be much more effective. Former English Lord Chancellor, Lord Hailsham observed that the government's powers in Parliament are 'now largely in the hands of the government machine, so that the government controls Parliament and not Parliament the Government' and that we effectively live 'under an elective dictatorship'.[21]

---

[20]　ibid, at 957.
[21]　Lord Hailsham, 'Elective Dictatorship' *The Listener* 21 Oct 1976, at 496–500.

Regardless of its efficacy as a check and balance device, the separation of powers doctrine is an intrinsic part of the Singapore Constitution. As Chief Justice Chan Sek Keong observed in *Mohammad Faizal bin Sabtu v PP*:

> The specific form of words used in Art 4 reinforces the principle that the Singapore parliament may not enact a law, and the Singapore government may not do an act, which is inconsistent with the principle of separation of powers to the extent to which that principle is embodied in the Singapore Constitution.[22]

Chan CJ's approach to the separation of powers is based squarely on a structural understanding of what a Westminster-style *written* constitution requires rather than on some vague notion of what the basic features of the Constitution are. Unlike its British antecedent, the Singapore Constitution is a written document and thus reigns supreme as a legal document that sets out how powers are distributed across the various branches. And as all branches of government are governed by the Constitution, it is the courts who are the final arbiters of what the law requires and when the limits of the law have been broken.

IV. CONSTITUTIONALISM AND THE RULE OF LAW

Fundamental to the operation of constitutionalism and its underlying logic and theoretical foundations is the *rule of law*,[23] the idea that everything should be done in accordance with law and that no person is above the law and that the law applies equally to all.[24] This notion of the rule of law, first propounded by British jurist Albert Venn Dicey in his *Lectures Introductory to the Study of the Law of the Constitution* in 1885, has in recent years, been described as a 'thin' version of the concept as it merely addresses the formal, positivist aspect of the rule of law. Jurists

---

[22] [2012] 4 SLR 947, at 958.

[23] For a detailed consideration of the debates on this subject, see Thio Li-ann, *A Treatise on Singapore Constitutional Law* (Singapore, Academy Publishing, 2012), at 164–96; and Thio Li-ann, 'Between Apology and Apogee, Autochthony: The "Rule of Law" and Beyond the Rules of Law in Singapore' [2012] *Singapore Journal of Legal Studies* 269–97.

[24] AV Dicey, *An Introduction to the Study of the Law of the Constitution*, 10th edn (London, Macmillan, 1959), at 202.

have called for a more substantive or 'thick' reading of the rule of law doctrine in which other normative content is included. In the words of Professor Robert Summers:

> A substantive theory is characterized mainly by the greater substantive content it incorporates. Thus it incorporates to some degree one or more of the following: rules securing minimum social welfare, ie, the 'welfare state', rules securing some variety of the market economy, rules protecting at least some basic human rights, and rules institutionalizing democratic governance.[25]

Exactly what content is embedded in such a substantial or 'thick' conception of the rule of law depends on the ideology of those advocating its adoption. And because of the amorphous nature of its content, a thick conception of the rule of law has long been seen as problematic and has thus been rejected by the Singapore Government.

In one of the earliest serious debates on the concept, Non-Constituency MP JB Jeyaretnam argued that 'an Act of Parliament can violate the Rule of Law' and the 'question is whether that law itself violates the Rule of Law as understood through the centuries'.[26] He then proceeded to list instances in which the rule of law had been violated: (a) detention without trial; (b) failure by law enforcement officers to inform those arrested of the charge for which the arrest was effected; (c) denial of the right of arrested persons to legal counsel; (d) denial of bail by courts without adequate reasons; (e) denial of freedom of speech and assembly; (f) denial of reasons for executive decisions and shutting out appeals to the court; and (g) power given to the Housing and Development Board to throw out lessees or tenants without having to take them to court. In raising these issues, Jeyaretnam clearly had in mind more than a procedural notion of the rule of law.

The PAP's members who responded to Jeyaretnam—all of whom were legally trained—took a decidedly procedural and Diceyan stance. For example, Minister of State for Law, Ho Peng Kee retorted:

> [T]he Rule of Law refers to the supremacy of law, as opposed to the arbitrary exercise of power. The other key tenet is that everyone is equal before the law. The concept also includes the notions of the transparency, openness

---

[25] RS Summers, 'A Formal Theory of the Rule of Law' (1993) 6(2) *Ratio Juris* 127, at 135.

[26] Debate on 'Rule of Law' *Singapore Parliamentary Debates Official Reports* 24 Nov 1999, vol 71, col 576.

and prospective application of our laws, observation of the principles of natural justice, independence of the Judiciary and judicial review of administrative action.[27]

Chin Tet Yung, a PAP MP, who was at the time Dean of the Faculty of Law at the National University of Singapore, stated that in Singapore, all 'laws are prospective, stable, properly and constitutionally enacted' and that their application, 'should be guided by clear and general rules, that is, avoiding any personal bias or favour, treating equal cases equally, making decisions rationally and in the public interest, and in accordance with the written laws of the land'. This procedural perspective was reiterated in a speech given by Law Minister S Jayakumar at the International Bar Association's Rule of Law Symposium:

> The concept of the Rule of Law, per se, does not address the substantive content of laws. Hence it does not guarantee that only good laws are enacted or that bad laws will be repealed. It also does not specify the process of enacting laws or specify the balance that should be struck between the rights and interests of the individual and the rights and interests of the society as a whole.
>
> It is not possible to have a universal prescription when applying the Rule of Law. These issues have to be determined according to the social, cultural and political values of each society.[28]

One abiding theme articulated by the Singapore Government is the important role of the rule of law in *good governance*. 'In modern society', Jayakumar stated, 'the value of Rule of Law is that it is essential for good governance'.[29] This point was made again by K Shanmugam, Jayakumar's successor as Law Minister in a speech at the New York State Bar Association International Section's seasonal meeting in Singapore in 2009 where he argued that four conditions were necessary for good governance: (a) rule of law; (b) stability; (c) security from external threats; and (d) a high quality public service.[30]

---

[27] ibid, at col 592.

[28] S Jayakumar, 'The Meaning and Importance of the Rule of Law', keynote address at the International Bar Association Rule of Law Symposium, 19 Oct 2007, available at: www.mlaw.gov.sg/news/speeches/keynote-address-by-dpm-prof-s-jayakumar-at-the-iba-rule-of-law-symposium.html, at paras 2–6.

[29] ibid, at para 2.

[30] K Shanmugam, Speech at the New York State Bar Association Rule of Law Plenary Session, 28 Oct 2009, available at: www.mlaw.gov.sg/news/speeches/

Speaking of the judiciary's approach to interpreting the rule of law at a major Rule of Law Symposium organised by the Singapore Academy of Law and the law faculties of the National University of Singapore and the Singapore Management University in February 2012, Chief Justice Chan Sek Keong defended the independence of the judiciary as an upholder of the rule of law and concluded:

> One of the greatest global challenges today is how to provide good government to people all over the world. It is the role of the Judiciary which claims the ultimate capacity to decide what the law is and to apply the law impartially and equally to all. No powers are above the law and no person or institution is beyond the reach of the courts. The Judiciary has the duty to check all unlawful legislative or executive acts, but it also has the responsibility not to interfere with or obstruct the lawful policies of an elected government. … It is only in so doing that the Judiciary upholds the 'rule of law' in the interest of good government and the welfare and happiness of the people.[31]

The position taken by the Singapore Government and judiciary is essentially positivist and procedural—a thin conception of the rule of law. For the government, this is a practical approach since there is no universal agreement on the substantive content of the rule of law. Moreover, the PAP politicians take a strictly Burkean view of the role of elected representatives, believing that once elected into Parliament, a government must do what it believes is right and best and, when necessary, make tough and unpopular decisions. The standards it sets, the mores it keeps and the laws it enacts will all be subject to the people's scrutiny through the ballot box. For the PAP, the rule of law is not to be studied and analysed *in vacuo* but should be understood in a programmatic fashion, promoting good governance and economic and social progress for Singapore.

The judiciary, on the other hand, adopts a procedural approach to interpreting the rule of law for two reasons: first because it fears overstepping its judicial function by 'legislating' substantive rules where there are none; and second because it also believes that the rule of law should serve the 'interest of good government and the welfare and happiness

---

speech-by-minister-for-law-k-shanmugam-at-the-new-york-state-bar-association-rule-of-law-plenary.html, at paras 14–18.

[31] Chan Sek Keong, 'The Courts and the "Rule of Law" in Singapore' [2012] *Singapore Journal of Legal Studies* 209–31.

of the people'. This attitude is manifested in the courts adopting what Harlow and Rawlings call the 'green-light' view of administrative law:

'Green-light' views of administrative law do not see the courts as the first line of defence against administrative abuses of power: instead, control can and should come internally from Parliament and the Executive itself in upholding high standards of public administration and policy. In other words, seek good government through the political process and public avenues rather than redress bad government through the courts. On a greenlight approach, the courts play a supporting role by articulating clear rules and principles by which the Government may abide by and conform to the rule of law.[32]

Ultimately, as Chief Justice Chan Sek Keong observed, in an extra-judicial speech:

The role of the courts is to give litigants their rights, but at the same time the courts should play a supporting role in promoting good governance by articulating clear rules and principles by which the Government can conform to the rule of law. As an institution of the State, it is the duty of the Judiciary to work for the common good in dispensing justice. This is where empathy is called for rather than angst or worse, cynicism, about the judicial process.[33]

These debates about the meaning of the rule of law were largely ignored by the public at large. It was the lawyers and academics who spent most time discussing the merits or pitfalls of the respective arguments. No empirical survey has been commissioned to study the attitudes of the general public towards law generally. Even so, it may be surmised from anecdotal evidence that the general population is less anxious about possible meanings a thick conception of the rule of law may contain, and far more concerned with its procedural aspects. People expect that the government should abide by its own laws; that criminal laws are not retrospective in nature; that laws are clearly known and certain and that all persons are treated equally before the law. This practical approach to the rule of law stems in large part from Singapore's mercantile history. In a Weberian sense, the capitalist system that made Singapore prosperous and successful as an entrepot trading centre was premised on parties knowing what the law is (certainty) and knowing that their rights will be enforced by the courts.

---

[32] Chan Sek Keong, 'Judicial Review—From Angst to Empathy' (2010) 22 *Singapore Academy of Law Journal* 469, at 480.
[33] ibid, at 485.

V. CONSTITUTIONAL CULTURE

Singapore does not have a long constitutional history but over the last half century has developed fragments of a distinct constitutional culture. 'Constitutional culture' refers to the agglomeration of beliefs and attitudes that the people, judges, lawyers and the state hold towards the Constitution and constitutional law in general. Naturally, what may be said about such beliefs and attitudes is necessarily anecdotal and speculative since nothing short of an in-depth, widespread qualitative survey will be necessary to address the topic more systematically.

Several key factors have played an important role in the evolution of Singapore's brand of constitutionalism. The first influence is its history. Modern Singapore was, for over 140 years, a British colony, administered under English law and by institutions steeped in the British tradition. As we saw in chapter one, Singapore's institutions of government developed along British lines, albeit under colonial control. Its courts mirrored their counterparts in England and in other parts of the empire, and its judges and lawyers were all trained in the common law and in the Inns of Court in the mother country. Indeed, there was no local law school in Singapore until 1957 when the Department of Law at the University of Malaya was established. The continuous application of English common law principles, by English-trained judges and lawyers, and the retention of the same system of courts beyond independence embedded in its key legal actors a common law legal culture.

The second factor affecting Singapore's legal culture has been its post-independence economic, social and political challenges. While the common law formed the backdrop against which these challenges were to be met, Singapore's political leaders were prepared to adopt measures that went against the grain of the common law tradition. In the words of Law Minister K Shanmugam:

> [T]he precepts of the law, and of the Rule of Law, must be applied with hard-nosed practicality. There is no use having beautiful laws, embodying the noblest ideals, only to do something else in practice. Elegant constitutions can be easily had, and are not hard to find. What matters is how the laws apply in practice. The truest test of the success of the law, the Rule of Law, lies in the benefits it produces for society and individuals.[34]

---

[34] K Shanmugam, 'The Rule of Law in Singapore' [2012] *Singapore Journal of Legal Studies* 357, at 356.

Institutionally, this was done through the many amendments made to the legislative system and with the introduction of the elected presidency. In terms of substantive laws, the PAP Government took the view that Parliament should have the flexibility to take difficult and unpopular decisions that temporarily marginalised established constitutional principles.

One example of this was the right to property. When Singapore became independent and became part of the Federation of Malaysia in 1963, all persons enjoyed the right to property by virtue of Article 13 of the Federal Constitution. When Singapore left Malaysia in 1965, the government intentionally omitted the right to property clause in the Constitution as it was about to embark on a massive public housing and industrialisation programme that would involve the state compulsorily acquiring large chunks of private property. The national interest, as perceived by the ruling party, and backed by the majority of the population, enabled the PAP Government to literally bulldoze its way through these programmes that resulted in a highly successful public housing programme under the Housing and Development Board, and a productive industrialisation programme under the Jurong Town Corporation.

Constitutional rights are thus not sacrosanct, and can be adjusted to suit the circumstances of the times. So, between 1966—when the Land Acquisition Act[35] was passed—and 2007, owners of land that had been compulsorily acquired by the government received compensation pegged at market values of a predetermined date. While this predetermined date had been amended several times, the compensation could never keep up with the rising market values of property in Singapore. Naturally, this was a source of great unhappiness and discontent among those whose property had been compulsorily acquired. However, by 2007, the government took the position that since its main housing and industrialisation programmes were complete, compensation would no longer be pegged at any predetermined date but instead according to prevailing market value.[36] The constitutional right to property,[37] which Singaporeans had from 1963 to 1965, has not been restored but the net effect for landowners is now the same as it was in the pre-1966 era.

---

[35] Act No 41 of 1966.
[36] ibid, s 33(1)(a), as amended by the Land Acquisition (Amendment) Act, Act 19 of 2007.
[37] See ch 8, at section V.

This attitude—of practicality and pragmatism in favour of the 'greater good' of the community—has embedded itself into the constitutional culture of Singapore. The kinds of checks and balances that find favour in countries like the United States are not regarded as de rigueur by Singapore's leaders, who favour the check and balance of the ballot box instead. Legitimacy for the Singapore Government is garnered less from its adherence to constitutional and legal forms than from its track record as a good government. It favours what Carl J Friedrich calls 'performance legitimacy'.[38]

Once elected into office, the government of the day should be allowed wide latitude to do a proper job and to work in the best interests of the community. This attitude towards constitutionalism—at least insofar as checks and balances are concerned—stems from the PAP's view of the 'good politician'. With echoes of Plato's philosopher-kings and Confucius' honourable men, the PAP has long felt that only the best and brightest should govern, and once in office, he should be left to do his job properly without fear or favour, and not having to bend to the fickle whims of popularism. This vision of government was articulated in the *Shared Values* White Paper issued in 1991 as follows:

> The concept of *government by honourable men* '君子' *(junzi)*, who have a duty to do right for the people, and who have the trust and respect of the population, fits us better than the Western idea that a government should be given as limited powers as possible, and should always be treated with suspicion unless proven otherwise.[39]

The *Shared Values* White Paper was the result of an attempt by the government to develop a national ideology based on common values that could be shared by all and which would preserve the heritage of the different communities in Singapore. The exercise commenced in 1988 and culminated in a White Paper which was presented to Parliament on 5 January 1991 and which was followed by a nation-wide debate. The five 'Shared Values' adopted by Parliament are: (a) nation before community and society above self; (b) family as the basic unit of society;

---

[38] See CJ Friedrich, *Limited Government: A Comparison* (New Jersey, Prentice-Hall, 1974), at 110.

[39] *White Paper on Shared Values* (Cmd 1, 1991), at para 41.

(c) community support and respect for the individual; (d) consensus and not conflict; and (e) racial and religious harmony.[40]

While the White Paper may have received widespread attention at the time it was formulated and debated, it is pretty much forgotten today and is seldom referred to by public actors. That said, it seriously reflects the operational ethos of the PAP and its outlook on how the state should be governed. It is a communitarian outlook that is much more concerned with the majority and the whole, rather than the individual.

The Singaporean public has not had much of an opportunity to develop its own unique constitutional ethos. This is partly due to the fact that it had practically no part to play in Singapore's constitution-making. When Singapore became independent as part of the Federation of Malaysia in 1963, its constitution was ready-made and packaged by the Colonial Office and local politicians as part of the Malaysia Agreement,[41] and when Singapore seceded from the Federation in 1965, it was Parliament that cobbled together the documents that would make up Singapore's Constitution. At no time was constitution-making a plebisciterian effort involving the masses. In any case, much of Singapore's population was not terribly interested in constitution-making to begin with, being far more concerned with bread-and-butter, day-to-day matters of survival. As a result, Singaporeans reacted to constitutional changes rather than participated in them. Changes to the Constitution and local institutions were effected top-down by the government of the day. The impact of this trajectory is that Singaporeans do not have a natural affinity with the Constitution or the values it embraces. For many people, the Constitution is a distant document and reactions to the Constitution often tend to be reactions against the government. This appears to be changing. In more recent years, largely due to the greater publicity given to high-profile constitutional law cases as well as greater articulation of constitutional principles in Parliament, the Constitution has become the starting point for much of public discourse.

This culture is changing as more and more people learn about the Constitution through various sources, especially the internet. Members

---

[40] For a discussion on the impact and operation of the Shared Values, see Thio Li-ann, *A Treatise on Singapore Constitutional Law* (n 23), at 104–20.

[41] See the Sabah, Sarawak and Singapore (State Constitutions) Order-in-Council 1963 (SI 1493/1963).

of Parliament, especially Nominated MPs like legal academics Walter Woon and Thio Li-ann, have also articulated constitutional concerns publicly in the legislature, and consequentially, raising the public's awareness. At the same time, more constitutional challenges have been brought in the Singapore courts and the ensuing publicity given to the issues has educated the public further and led to a higher level of consciousness about constitutional rights and issues. The willingness of the government and the judiciary to engage in constitutional discussions in recent years—through symposia, speeches and dialogues—has also led to an attitudinal change in the way lawyers and students view the Constitution.

FURTHER READING

Chan Sek Keong, 'Judicial Review—From Angst to Empathy' (2010) 22 *Singapore Academy of Law Journal* 469.

——, 'The Courts and the "Rule of Law" in Singapore' [2012] *Singapore Journal of Legal Studies* 209–31.

SA de Smith, 'Constitutionalism in the Commonwealth Today' (1962) 4(2) *Malaya Law Review* 205.

AV Dicey, *An Introduction to the Study of the Law of the Constitution*, 10th edn (London, Macmillan, 1959).

EKB Tan, 'Law and Values in Governance: The Singapore Way' (2000) 30 *Hong Kong Law Journal* 91.

Thio Li-ann, '*Lex Rex or Rex Lex*? Competing Conceptions of the Rule of Law in Singapore' (2002–03) 20 *UCLA Pacific Basin Law Journal* 1–76.

——, 'Rule of Law Within a Non-Liberal "Communitarian" Democracy: The Singapore Experience' in R Peerenboom (ed), *Asian Discourse on the Rule of Law: Theories and Implementation of the Rule of Law* (London, Routledge, 2004) 183–224.

——, *A Treatise on Singapore Constitutional Law* (Singapore, Academy Publishing, 2012), at 104–20 and 164–96.

——, 'Between Apology and Apogee, Autochthony: The "Rule of Law" and Beyond the Rules of Law in Singapore' [2012] *Singapore Journal of Legal Studies* 269–97.

WEBSITES

www.mlaw.gov.sg/news/speeches/keynote-address-by-dpm-prof-s-
jayakumar-at-the-iba-rule-of-law-symposium.html (S Jayakumar, 'The
Meaning and Importance of the Rule of Law', keynote address at the
International Bar Association Rule of Law Symposium)
www.mlaw.gov.sg/news/speeches/speech-by-minister-for-law-k-
shanmugam-at-the-new-york-state-bar-association-rule-of-law-
plenary.html (K Shanmugam, Speech at the New York State Bar
Association Rule of Law Plenary Session, 28 Oct 2009)

3

Parliament and Representation

━━━━◆◆◆━━━━

A Brief Historical Outline – Parliament and the Problem
of Representation – The Revival of Local Government? –
Qualification of Members – Duties of Members – Parliamentary
Privilege – Principal Officers of Parliament – Parliament's
Committees – The Conduct of Elections – Concluding Thoughts

I. A BRIEF HISTORICAL OUTLINE

THE HISTORY OF representative government in Singapore
is a relatively short one. There was no elected representative
municipal government in the Straits Settlements until 1867
when control over the three settlements was transferred from the
India Office to the Colonial Office in London. By becoming a Crown
Colony, the Straits Settlements was granted a colonial constitution that
constituted its own Legislative Council or Legco. The Governor of the
Straits Settlements was expected to govern with the help of the Legco,
and later on, in 1877, with the help of his Executive Council (Exco)
as well. The Governor was empowered to convene and prorogue the
Councils, initiate legislation and to assent to, veto or reserve bills 'for
the Royal pleasure'.

While the Legco had law-making powers, it was by no means a
'representative body'. In 1867, it consisted of the Governor, the Chief
Justice, the Officer Commanding the Troops, the Lieutenant-Governor
of Penang, the Colonial Secretary, the Attorney-General, the Colonial
Engineer and four non-official European members nominated by the
Governor. By 1871, the Lieutenant-Governor of Malacca, the Judge of
Penang, the Treasurer, the Auditor-General and two more non-official
members were added to the Council.

The Exco, which was a sort of cabinet, was not responsible to the Legco and official members were bound to support the Governor. The non-official members were not bound as such and could speak their minds and vote according to the dictates of their conscience on all matters. The Governor's executive supremacy was maintained and remained intact until the start of the Second World War. Although many changes were proposed and championed, the system remained fixed and the Legislative Council remained primarily an advisory body to air the views of the various communities.

Following the turmoil of the Second World War, a colonial-style Singapore constitution was introduced. From 1946 to 1948 Singapore was ruled by the Governor with the help of an advisory executive council consisting entirely of officials and nominated non-officials. There were 10 members in the Executive Council (6 officials and 4 nominated members) and the non-officials were in the minority in the Legislative Council. By 1947, the movement towards self-government was already in motion and, as a first step, a new constitution to be implemented in 1948 created an Executive Council with an official majority and a Legislative Council with 9 officials and 13 non-officials, of whom four would be nominated by the Governor, three chosen by the chambers of commerce and the remaining six elected by adult British subjects who had been resident in Singapore for one year prior to the election. This, however, excluded the bulk of the migrant population who were not granted citizenship status.

In 1953 Sir George Rendel headed a commission to review the Constitution and the Commission recommended keeping local government separate and proposed, for the central government, a single-chamber legislative assembly of 32 members (25 elected councillors, 3 ex-officio ministers, and 4 nominated non-officials). It also recommended the replacement of the executive council by a council of nine ministers: three appointed by the Governor, and the remaining six recommended by the leader of the strongest party in the Legislative Assembly who would also enjoy many of the functions of a Prime Minister. With the implementation of the Rendel Constitution in 1955, Singapore saw, for the first time, a meaningful form of representative government although essential matters such as external affairs, internal security and defence remained in the hands of the British.

These arrangements did not last long. The Constitutional Talks of 1956 and 1957 resulted in the granting of a new constitution in 1958 which provided for internal self-government and which created a Legislative Assembly of 51 members elected on the basis of adult suffrage. The Colony of Singapore became the State of Singapore with the British retaining control over foreign affairs and external defence but with power to suspend the Constitution in an emergency only. When Singapore became a constituent state of the Federation of Malaysia in 1963, Singapore gave up control over foreign affairs, defence and security to central government but retained wide-ranging powers over finance, labour and education. Singapore was accorded 15 seats in the 159-member federal legislature but retained her own executive government, her Assembly and her own head of state: the Yang di-Pertuan Negara. Independence and separation from Malaysia in 1965 necessitated changes in Singapore's Constitution. However, the only change in the structure of Singapore's legislature was the disappearance of its 15 seats in the federal legislature.

II. PARLIAMENT AND THE PROBLEM OF REPRESENTATION

Today, Singapore's Parliament is one of the most unique in the world. Outwardly, it looks just like any other legislature derived from the British Westminster model, but as we saw in the previous chapter, a number of changes were made to the legislative structure between 1981 and 1990 that transformed the nature of the chamber dramatically. These changes can be attributed to two factors: (a) the need to ensure minority representation in Parliament; and (b) the People's Action Party's (PAP's) attempt to secure continued dominance of Parliament.

A. Ethnic Representation

Singapore's Parliament is unicameral. This is not altogether remarkable, considering Singapore's small size. However, a two-chamber house had previously been proposed and rejected by both the Rendel Commission in 1954 as well as the Wee Chong Jin Constitutional Commission in 1966. Several members of the Rendel Commission—looking at constitutional developments in Ceylon and British Guyana—were impressed by arguments in favour of a second chamber as they felt that in a 'politically inexperienced' territory like Singapore, a second chamber would 'provide a valuable check against possibly hasty or partisan legislation by the new Legislative Assembly'.[1] Proponents of the two-chamber house were attracted by the idea that an upper house, comprising nominated members would act as an effective check against 'the danger of Party tyranny'.[2] This proposal was rejected on the grounds that: (a) Singapore was too small for a bicameral system, which would add an unnecessary layer to government; (b) such a body would end being 'little more than the mouthpiece of a minority Party, or of vested interests, or even of the Governor himself';[3] (c) the second chamber would be strongly criticised if it were allowed to thwart the will of the majority as expressed through their elected representatives; and (d) it would be difficult 'to find enough suitable candidates to fill all the seats' in the various new institutions.[4] The Rendel Commission thus rejected the proposal in favour of having four nominated unofficial members on the 25-member Legislative Assembly to safeguard various minority and commercial interests.

Twelve years later, the Wee Chong Jin Constitutional Commission had occasion to consider the matter once more. Concerned with how best to provide adequate safeguards of ethnic, religious and linguistic minorities in Singapore, the Commission considered the possibility of an upper house in which members would be nominated or elected to 'represent the racial, linguistic and religious minorities in Singapore'.[5] This proposal was raised in conjunction with two others. The first was to have a Committee of Representatives from the various minority groups which would be entitled to elect three persons from amongst its members to represent the minorities in the elected chamber in Parliament (thus maintaining its unicameral structure); and the second was the change the system of election to one based on proportional representation.

The 'nominated minorities' proposal was rejected outright as the Commission felt that the elected chamber 'should not be diluted by the presence of any member who has not been elected on a general

---

[1] *Report of the Constitutional Commission, Singapore* (Singapore, Government Printer, 1954), at para 77.

[2] ibid, at para 78.

[3] ibid, at para 87.

[4] ibid, at para 90.

[5] *Report of the Constitutional Commission* (Singapore, Government Printer, 1966), at para 46.

franchise'.[6] Participation by non-elected representatives was considered not only 'inappropriate' but also 'retrograde'. The proportional representation proposal was also rejected for several reasons, all of which relate to the intensification of inherent racial or communal divisions:

> The Commission rejects this proposal for the following reasons: First it is convinced that the effect of such a system in Singapore would be the intensification of party politics along racial lines. Secondly, it would result in the formation of more political parties on communal lines. Thirdly, it would encourage politicians to exhort the elector to vote for the party which represents his race in order to ensure racial representation in Parliament. Finally, it must provide a strong incentive to political parties, whether communal or otherwise to base their appeal to the electorate on purely communal lines. The ultimate result would be, in the Commission's view, to perpetuate and accentuate racial differences thereby making increasingly difficult if not impossible the achievement of a single homogeneous community out of the many races that form the population of the Republic.[7]

To best protect minority rights, the Wee Chong Jin Commission recommended first, that the equality clause be entrenched in the Constitution, and second, that an advisory body called the 'Council of State' be created with

> a small membership chosen irrespective of race, colour or creed, from amongst able, mature and respected citizens who shall have either rendered distinguished public service or have attained eminence in their respective walks of life but who should not be member of any political party at the time of their appointments.[8]

The rationale for recommending the Council of State was the Commission's belief that

> it would be one of the most effective means of ensuring against legislation discriminatory of racial, linguistic or religious minorities and … that the members of this body should be chosen from citizens of the highest calibre irrespective of race, colour or creed is motivated by the belief that such a body would help to achieve the objective of building a united people and by the need to avoid any measure which will tend to perpetuate or accentuate racial, religious or linguistic distinctions in public affairs.[9]

---

[6] ibid, at para 47.
[7] ibid, at para 48.
[8] ibid, at para 51.
[9] ibid.

This Council would be tasked with considering all proposed legislation except for supply bills or bills presented on a Certificate of Urgency, and state in its report to Parliament if the bill contained a discriminatory measure or unfairly prejudiced any racial, linguistic or religious minority. This recommendation was accepted by Parliament and in 1969, the Constitution was amended to create the Presidential Council, the composition and functions of which are set out in Part VII of the Constitution. This body was renamed the Presidential Council for Minority Rights in 1973. While acknowledging that this body 'has many of the attributes commonly associated with an Upper House of Parliament' the Wee Commission was anxious that it should remain an advisory body and not form part of the legislature. Minority rights were thus to be protected through a tightly entrenched equality clause and non-discriminatory legislation, rather than through symbolic representation in the legislature.

This view of ethnic representation was radically revised in 1988 with the creation of Group Representation Constituencies. The motivation for the creation of this institution lay in the government's concern that there was 'a voting trend which showed young voters preferring candidates who were best suited to their own needs without sufficiently aware of the need to return a racially-balanced party slate of candidates'.[10] It should be explained that up until this time, Singapore's Parliament had a racially balanced mix of members because the ruling PAP made it its policy to ensure that members of ethnic minorities were fielded at every general election.

There was nothing in the Constitution guaranteeing ethnic minority representation but this was achieved solely because of the PAP's commitment to multi-racialism, and between 1968 and 1981, the PAP won every seat in Parliament, enabling the party to effectively manifest its multi-ethnic policies. However, two small electoral defeats in 1981 and 1984 caused the party's leadership to reconsider how minority ethnic representation could be entrenched. In 1981, the PAP lost one seat in the Anson constituency by-election; in the 1984 General Election, it lost the Anson seat as well as a seat in Potong Pasir. Neither Anson nor the Potong Pasir constituency were sufficiently ethnically distinct

---

[10] See speech of then First Deputy Prime Minister Goh Chok Tong in moving the Second Reading of the Parliamentary Elections (Amendment) Bill *Singapore Parliamentary Debates Official Reports* 11 Jan 1988, vol 50, col 178.

to have affected the vote. Nonetheless, the PAP reasoned that given the success in the public housing programme in breaking up the old ethnic enclaves and redistributing their former residents throughout Singapore, every constituency in Singapore would be predominantly Chinese in composition. Thus, if Singaporeans decided to vote on racial lines, they could well wake up one morning and find no ethnic minorities in Parliament and this would be deleterious to racial harmony.

B. The Group Representation Constituency and Town Councils

To stem the tide and entrench minority ethnic representation in Parliament, the government formulated the Group Representation Constituency (GRC) scheme. Article 39 of the Constitution was amended to provide that Parliament may make provision for 'any constituency to be declared by the President ... as a group representation constituency to enable any election in that constituency to be held on the basis of a group of 3 candidates'.[11] Furthermore, 'at least one of the three candidates in every group shall be a person belonging to the Malay' or 'Indian or other minority communities'. Having eschewed the bicameral solution to minority representation back in 1966, the PAP now sought to entrench minority representation by ensuring that minority candidates would be included in every single election, and regardless of which political party won power, there would always be ethnic minorities in the House. In this way, the minority representatives would be elected, rather than appointed and thus carry the mandate of his constituency's support. On its own, the GRC scheme looked like a good idea, even though criticisms could be made of the 'coat-tails' effect of having relatively unknown candidates (be they minorities or otherwise), being elected into Parliament on the strength of prominent 'team leaders'.

However, the GRC system was introduced in tandem with the Town Council proposal, which was designed to give residents in the public housing estates developed by the Housing and Development Board a say in the running of their estates. The stated objectives of the councils

---

[11] Constitution of the Republic of Singapore, Art 39A(1)(b).

were to: (a) transfer the management of housing estates from the Housing and Development Board (HDB) to a local council thus allowing participation by residents; (b) allow residents to become involved in decision-making on local matters; (c) allow the elected MPs to decide what should be done for the electorate in the new town; and (d) raise the level of social discipline and responsibility among residents.[12]

Under the original proposal, each town council would take charge of three adjoining but hitherto single-member constituencies which were grouped by proximity to the 'town'. The chairman of each council was to be a Member of Parliament, and he or she was empowered to appoint any person to help in the management of the estate. The chairman was given great flexibility in appointing town councillors who were usually residents and grassroots leaders. The clustering of three constituencies into a single town or GRC was thus based on the necessity of including an ethnic minority member in the ward, and the economies of scale and cost savings that came with a larger constituency insofar as the provision of goods and services was concerned. By having all members of the town council come from the same political party, any political bickering that might jettison the efficient running of the town would be obviated.[13]

III. THE REVIVAL OF LOCAL GOVERNMENT?

A. Town Councils as Local Government

The creation of town councils as an added layer to governance has caused some to wonder if this was leading to the revival of local government. When Singapore was part of the Straits Settlements, it had its own municipal government, which was responsible for maintaining the police force and for taking care of public roads, buildings and water

---

[12] See Agnes Wee, Mathew Yap, Irene Ngoo, 'Estates will evolve their own identities' *The Straits Times* 23 Aug 1986, at 12.

[13] On town councils, see generally, Ooi Giok Ling, 'Accountability and Quality Services in Singapore: A Case Study of Town Councils' (1997) 18 *Regional Development Dialogue* 139; and KYL Tan, 'Comment on Ooi Giol Ling's "Accountability and Quality Services in Singapore: A Case Study of Town Councils"' (1997) 18 *Regional Development Dialogue* 150.

supply. The Singapore Municipal Committee was established in 1848 by law, and was augmented over the years by legislative amendment, the most important of which was the Municipal Act of 1856.[14] Under this Act, the old Municipal Committee was transformed into the Municipal Commission. The powers of the Commissioners were enlarged by the Municipal Ordinance of 1887.

The establishment of local government was perfectly logical considering the fact that Singapore was but one of the three territories that made up the Straits Settlements and Singapore's Commissioners would naturally be more concerned with and responsive to its local needs and particularities. While its members were mainly appointed, a number of Municipal Commissioners were initially elected. Prominent local businessmen and community leaders saw membership of the Commission as a prelude to appointment to the more prestigious Legislative Council. As its name suggests, the Municipal Commission took charge of the town or municipal area. The areas beyond the town limits were placed in the hands of a Rural Board in 1908.

Local government was restored in 1946 after the interregnum of the Japanese Occupation. By this time, the Straits Settlements had been disbanded and the territories of Penang and Malacca were absorbed into the new Malayan Union—a federal aggregation of Malay states that were formerly part of the Federated Malay States, the Unfederated Malay States and the Straits Settlements. Singapore was turned into a Crown Colony. In 1951, when Singapore was accorded 'city' status, the Municipal Commission was renamed the City Council. The PAP, who came to power in 1959, had been elected on a platform of efficiency and accountability and vowed to 'bring about smoother and more efficient public service to serve the people' and to raise efficiency, getting rid of duplication of functions.[15] In tandem with the transformation of the Legislative Assembly into a wholly-elected body, the City Council was eventually dissolved by the passage of the Legal Government Integration Ordinance in 1963, which divided up all the functions of

---

[14] Act No 14 of 1856 (India).
[15] Speech of Dr Goh Keng Swee, Second Reading of the Local Government Integration Bill *Singapore Legislative Assembly Reports* 15 Jun 1963, vol 20, col 1385.

the City Council and Rural Board and distributed them among the various government ministries.[16]

The first GRCs were created in time for the 1988 General Elections and represented the theoretical conflation of two fundamentally different objectives: that of ensuring minority representation in Parliament and that of efficiently managing Singapore's public housing estates. This conflation is problematic since it is unclear which object has priority. Since 1988, the GRC scheme has been expanded twice, in 1991, just prior to the general elections,[17] and again in late 1996, again in time for the general elections.[18] In both instances, the number of GRCs in Singapore was increased, and more significantly, the number of members within each GRC team was also increased.

In 1991, the number was increased from three to four on the grounds that population growth required town councils to expand and these expanded bodies needed more MPs or town councillors. The same logic was used in 1996 when the number was once again increased from four to up to six members. Over the years, the number of GRCs oscillated between 13 and 15 while the number of seats encompassed by the GRCs expanded. For example, in the 1988 General Elections, there were 13 GRCs with a total of 39 seats up for grabs at the elections. In the elections in 1991, there were 15 GRCs with 60 seats; in 1997, a total of 74 seats were contested. In the most recent election of 2011, there were 15 GRCs with a total of 75 seats.

Despite the increase in the number of GRC seats, the single-member constituencies (SMCs) were not obliterated altogether. After hitting an all-time low of nine SMC seats in several elections, the government increased the number of SMCs to 12 for the 2011 elections. At the same time, the *minimum* number of minority members in Parliament appears to be capped at 15 since the number of GRCs has not expanded accordingly. The government's rationale that the 'economies of scale' improve as GRCs get bigger is problematic at two levels. First, SMCs

[16] Local Government Integration Ordinance, No 18 of 1963. See the interpretation of its effect in *Yat Yuen Hong Co Ltd v Turquand, Youngs & Co* [1965–1967] SLR(R) 725; [1967] SGFC 19 (Federal Court, Singapore).

[17] On the impact of the expansion of the GRC concept on the general elections, see KYL Tan, 'Constitutional Implications of the 1991 Singapore General Elections' (1992) 13 *Singapore Law Review* 26, at 40–54.

[18] See KYL Tan, 'Is Singapore's Electoral System in Need of Reform?' (1997) 14 *Commentary* 109.

will naturally be discriminated against and do not enjoy these economies of scale unless they become part of an enlarged or amalgamated town council; and second, if this logic were to be taken to its logical conclusion, then the best economies of scale will be enjoyed by the very biggest GRCs. What then is there to stop the Constitution from being amended to transform the whole of Singapore into say, four GRCs or even one mega-GRC?[19]

B. The Community Development Councils (CDCs)

Linked to the town councils are the Community Development Councils (CDCs). In his 1996 National Day Rally speech, then Prime Minister Goh Chok Tong stated that to promote greater social cohesion and harmony in the community, CDCs would be introduced to help take care of the less fortunate members of any community. More significantly, this new body would be linked to town councils. When the scheme was first announced, Goh gave a long list of schemes which would be managed by the CDCs, including improvement projects like Housing and Development Board (HDB) upgrading, more bursaries and scholarships for students who make above average improvements, better kindergartens and better-trained teachers, before and after-school care service centres and programmes to take care of the elderly. However, when the CDCs were eventually set up, three main government schemes in the areas of public welfare and assistance and medical welfare were assigned to them.

The CDC is not a constitutional creature but was created under the People's Association Act,[20] an Act that had been passed in 1960 to promote 'community recreation in Singapore and for matters incidental thereto'. The People's Association (PA) consists of the Prime Minister as chairman, a minister appointed by the Prime Minister to serve as deputy chairman, eight members appointed by the chairman and one member to be appointed by the chairman in consultation with its affiliates.[21] In 1997, the government enacted the People's Association (Community Development Councils) Rules which, among other things,

---

[19] ibid, at 114.
[20] Ordinance 35 of 1960.
[21] ibid, s 4(1).

empowered the Board to 'designate any area in Singapore to be a District' and to 'appoint for that District a committee to be known as a Community Development Council'.[22] Each District would comprise one or more constituencies and the Board 'may designate the Chairman of the Council for a District to be the Mayor of that District'.[23]

The final structure of the CDC scheme was unveiled in August 1997 by Home Affairs Minister Wong Kan Seng. In all, nine CDCs would cover the whole of Singapore, with the two smallest CDCs covering the two then-opposition wards of Potong Pasir and Hougang. The opposition denounced the CDC scheme as nothing more than a ploy to entrench the ruling party. Originally, there were no plans to establish CDCs in the opposition wards. Eventually, the government decided to involve the opposition wards in the CDCs and because the government expected 'residents and other volunteers, community leaders and other leaders working in various other organizations to come forward to support and serve in the CDCs'. More importantly, the chairmen of the two opposition ward CDCs in 1997 were two PAP candidates who lost their electoral bids: the twice-defeated Andy Gan (in Potong Pasir) and Heng Chee How (in Hougang).

Aljunied GRC, which was won by the opposition Workers' Party in 2011, remains within the North East District which is under the charge of Sam Tan, a PAP mayor. Indeed, every mayor is a PAP MP and their appointment is made possible because the PAP controls the government and the Prime Minister, by virtue of his position as chairman of the PAP, is empowered to appoint mayors.

C. GRCs as 'Fixed Deposit' Seats

By clustering several single-member constituencies together, the GRC system made it necessary for contending political parties to form teams that include an ethnic minority. This proved difficult for the opposition political parties for many years. Owing to the PAP's overwhelming dominance of Singapore's political landscape and the non-ideological nature of Singaporean politics, the opposition parties found it difficult to attract members and erstwhile candidates. Most of Singapore's

---

[22] People's Association (Community Development Councils) Rules 1997, s 3.
[23] ibid, s 6.

political parties have, from the late-1940s, been established along multi-ethnic lines. All political parties sought to appeal broadly to the entire electorate rather than any particular sector. As such, personalities and programme have traditionally played a far more important role in the harnessing of votes than ideological positions.

The difficulty experienced by opposition parties was compounded by the need to include ethnic minorities and the expansion of GRCs from three members to up to six members each. The opposition's difficulties were exacerbated by the constant redrawing of electoral boundaries prior to each general election. At the same time, most opposition parties lacked immediately recognisable personalities to helm their GRC teams, unlike the PAP, who strategically placed well-known former cabinet ministers as leaders of their GRC teams.[24]

Between 1988 and 1996, amendments to the Constitution were necessary to increase the number of team members in each GRC. All these amendments were made shortly before the general elections. The very short lead-time between the constitutional changes and nomination day is a cause for some concern. While there is nothing in the Singapore Constitution requiring Parliament to treat all political parties with fairness, principles of natural justice require that sufficient notice of major changes be given to all parties contesting general elections.

This timing problem is compounded by the fact that before any general election is held, the Electoral Boundaries Review Committee must first issue its report setting out the constituencies to be contested. Boundaries of electoral divisions change from time to time because of shifting populations and expansion of wards. They are also changed in accordance with changes made to the Constitution. This means that aspiring political candidates who have been 'working the ground' may sometimes find their 'ground' being swept up from under them. Constituency boundaries are redrawn just months before elections, and a candidate's 'ground' may either be cut up into several parts and merged with other constituencies, or transformed into a GRC. Let us take the example of Sin Kek Tong, the Singapore People's Party's (SPP's) candidate in the 1997 General Election. Sin announced very early on that he was contesting the Braddell Heights seat which was a single-member constituency (SMC). When the Committee's report was

---

[24] ibid; see also Tan, 'Constitutional Implications of the 1991 Singapore General Elections' (n 17).

released on 6 November 1996, he was shocked to find that his intended ward had been merged with Marine Parade GRC.

The problems are thus obvious. How can a political aspirant work the ground with confidence, cultivating the grassroots and seeking the people's mandate if he cannot be sure that the 'ground' on which he may spend years campaigning would remain intact after the Committee's report. Worse still, what if it becomes a six-member GRC? Where is he going to get five other GRC members at such short notice?

The function of law is to give certainty and stability to social, economic and political life. No one can plan ahead if laws are constantly changed at the last moment.[25] Teams can hardly be expected to compete fairly if the rules of the game are constantly being changed. It would be much fairer and more sensible if any change to the electoral system should take effect only in the following election and not the impending one. This will guarantee sufficient lead-time for all parties in the contest and would go a long way in allaying people's fears that the incumbent party will abuse its constitutional powers just to fix the opposition through gerrymandering. Because of the difficulties faced by opposition parties, GRCs have, since their creation in 1988, been seen as safe or 'fixed deposit' seats for the PAP.

This situation changed dramatically at the 2011 General Elections,[26] when the opposition Workers' Party defeated the PAP's team in the Aljunied GRC. The defeat was particularly significant since the PAP's Aljunied team was considered to be a strong one, helmed by Foreign Minister George Yeo, and two other ministers, Lim Hwee Hua and Zainal Abidin Rasheed. More importantly, the Workers' Party succeeded in debunking the myth of PAP invincibility in the GRCs and is now able to demonstrate its competence in running a town council. While town councils are, strictly speaking, not local government in that no separate elections are held for councillors, they effectively function as such. This will invariably create a tension in the minds of the electorate who must decide, at each succeeding general election, whether to vote for politicians who are most able to satisfy their localised needs, or for politicians who are capable of forming a cabinet to govern

---

[25] See discussion on the rule of law in ch 2.

[26] For a study of the ground-breaking shifts in Singapore's electoral politics in the 2011 General Election, see KYL Tan & T Lee (eds), *Voting in Change: Politics of Singapore's 2011 General Election* (Singapore, Ethos Books, 2011).

the country. As was seen in the Aljunied GRC case, having Cabinet ministers as town councillors was considered a handicap since these ministers seldom have time to meet the constituents in their weekly meet-the-people sessions. This political development may well lead to future constitutional changes with respect to the GRC system especially since it will be difficult for the PAP to regain the Aljunied GRC unless the Workers' Party team shows itself incompetent to run the town.[27]

IV. QUALIFICATIONS OF MEMBERS

Under the Constitution, there are three categories of MPs: (a) elected members (from both Group Representation Constituencies (GRCs) and Single-Member Constituencies (SMCs); (b) 'non-constituency Members' (NCMPs) who are not directly elected but obtained the highest number of votes from among the defeated candidates; and (c) Nominated Members of Parliament (NMPs), non-partisan members who are not elected, but appointed.

The qualifications of candidates wishing to stand for election are set out under Article 44 of the Constitution. They are not onerous since candidates need only be Singapore citizens above the age of 21, resident in Singapore and demonstrate an ability to partake in parliamentary proceedings. Grounds for disqualification are few, being of: unsound mind; or undischarged bankrupt; or having been convicted of an offence carrying a prison term of one year or more or a fine exceeding S$2000.

An MP's seat becomes vacant when Parliament is dissolved. A vacancy can also occur if a member: (a) ceases to be a citizen of Singapore; (b) ceases to be a member or is expelled from his political party; (c) resigns his or her seat or is absent for 'two consecutive months in each of which sittings of Parliament ... are held' without the Speaker's permission. Following the 2011 General Election, Parliament consists of 99 members. Of these 87 were popularly elected, 3 are Non-constituency MPs and 9 are Nominated MPs.

---

[27] KYL Tan & T Lee, 'Political Shift' in Tan & Lee (eds), *Voting In Change: Politics of Singapore's 2011 General Election* (n 26) 9–25.

V. DUTIES OF MEMBERS

Elected Members of Parliament (MPs) must represent their constituents by bringing their problems and difficulties to Parliament's attention. Members are also expected to hold the executive accountable for its actions. This duty is not an unfettered licence to criticise the government. The Westminster system assumes a Parliament dominated by two main parties with the opposition's shadow cabinet holding the government accountable for its actions. Opposition MPs also help test the government's legislative initiatives by questioning them with well-prepared speeches in debate.

However, this ideal has no bearing on reality in Singapore. The PAP's total monopoly of Parliament from 1968–81 and its continued dominance of it, does not allow for such forms of control. Indeed, the PAP was so dominant that from 1965 to 1981, backbenchers often took on the role of ersatz 'opposition members'. This form of control was both restricted and unrealistic and amounted to little more than shadow boxing. Under the Westminster model, strict party discipline is taken very seriously and no matter how critical PAP members may be of government policy, they must vote according to the party line. At best, members who disagree vehemently with the government's position abstain from voting. This occurred in 1990 when several PAP MPs objected to the introduction of the Nominated MP scheme. After a fierce debate on the floor and seeing how the Whip had not been lifted, the MPs who opposed the scheme simply abstained. Parliament's ability to constrain the executive and it hold is accountable is thus seriously undermined.

This institutional problem is further compounded by PAP MPs' traditional reluctance to criticise government policies. The backbencher is only able to comment on the details of the legislation before Parliament but cannot criticise the principles of policy. In recent years, this appears to be changing. While PAP MPs are still constrained by the Whip, a number of MPs have been more vocal in criticising government policy. One notable example of this was PAP MP Inderjit Singh, who was scathing in the debate on the *Population* White Paper 2013, where he rebuked his parliamentary colleagues for policy misjudgements in respect of population growth. Singh then absented himself from the final vote, being among only eight PAP MPs who did not vote on the Paper.

VI. PARLIAMENTARY PRIVILEGE

For MPs to perform their duties without harassment or undue influence from the public or the government, they are given a special status carrying with it certain powers, privileges and immunities. These are contained in the Parliament (Privileges, Immunities and Powers) Act[28] and are 'the same as those of the Commons House of Parliament of the United Kingdom and of its Speaker, members or Committees at the establishment of the Republic of Singapore'.[29]

These privileges and immunities enable MPs to speak and debate freely. They protect members from repressive measures or legal actions by the government and others. Parliament has power to summon witnesses, experts and other persons, call for records or papers to assist them in their Committee work. These powers also enable Parliament to punish recalcitrant members of the House or members of the public who abuse their parliamentary privileges.

The main privileges and immunities pertain to the freedom of speech and to immunity from arrest in certain cases. Speeches made in the course of debate or in parliamentary proceedings are not 'liable to be impeached or questioned in any court, commission of inquiry, tribunal or any other place whatsoever out of Parliament'.[30] Furthermore, a member shall not be liable to legal proceedings whatsoever only by reason of any matter or thing brought up before Parliament or committee. Neither may he be arrested or detained in respect of any civil proceedings if he is either attending, sitting or returning from any parliamentary proceedings.

Offences for which members may be punished include failure to comply with rules, orders or summons of Parliament; the use of violence or force on the Speaker or fellow members; publishing false reports or creating a disturbance within the precincts of the House. Parliament regulates its own affairs and the Privileges Committee may, among other things, imprison an errant MP or fine him or her up to S$50,000.

---

[28] Ordinance 11 of 1962.
[29] ibid, s 3.
[30] ibid, s 5.

A. Life of Parliament and Vacancies

Under Article 64(1) of the Constitution, there must be a session of Parliament 'once at least in every year' and Parliament must sit for a new session within six months of the last sitting of the previous session. The lifespan of Parliament is five years[31] although the President can dissolve Parliament at any time 'if he is advised by the Prime Minister to do so' and if the Prime Minister commands the confidence of the majority of the Members of Parliament. A general election must be held within three months of Parliament's dissolution.[32]

Under Article 46(1) of the Constitution, every Member of Parliament shall cease to be a member when Parliament is dissolved. A member's seat also becomes vacant if he or she: (a) ceases to be a citizen of Singapore; (b) ceases to be a member of, or is expelled or resigns from, the political party for which he or she stood in the election; (c) resigns his or her seat; (d) absents him- or herself from sittings of Parliament for two consecutive months without the Speaker's permission; (e) is disqualified under one of the provisions of Article 45; or (f) is expelled from Parliament.[33] In the case of Nominated MPs, his or her seat becomes vacant when the term of office expires, or if he or she stands as a candidate for any political party or as an independent. A Non-Constituency MP must also vacate his or her seat if he or she is elected as a Member of Parliament for any constituency. If a member of a GRC dies or vacates his or her seat in Parliament, no writ of election shall be issued. Indeed, section 24(2A) of the Parliamentary Elections Act[34] stipulates that 'no writ shall be issued ... for an election to fill any vacancy unless all Members for that constituency have vacated their seats in Parliament'. Theoretically, five members of a six-member GRC can resign their seats and leave the remaining member as the sole representative for his or her constituency. In the 2011 elections, there were two six-member GRCs: Ang Mo Kio GRC and Pasir Ris-Punggol GRC, each with about 170,000 electors. The average single-member constituency in Singapore has 25,000 electors.

---

[31] Constitution of the Republic of Singapore, Art 65(4).
[32] ibid, Art 66.
[33] ibid, Art 46(2).
[34] Ordinance 26 fo 1954.

One of the biggest constitutional debates in recent years has been whether the vacation of a seat in Parliament automatically triggers a by-election. In February 2012, Yaw Shin Leong, the Workers' Party MP for the Hougang constituency (single-member ward) was expelled from his party and his seat fell vacant. Yaw's seat was declared vacant by the Speaker on 28 February 2012 and by-elections were anticipated. However, Prime Minister Lee Hsien Loong stated that there was no time period in which he was required to call an election and even intimated that he had ultimate discretion in deciding if a by-election needed to be called. On 2 March 2012, a Hougang constituency resident, Mdm Vellama d/o Marie Muthu filed an application for a declaration that: (a) the Prime Minister does not have unfettered discretion in deciding whether to announce by-elections in the Hougang constituency; and (b) the Prime Minister does not have unfettered discretion to decide when to announce a by-election in the Hougang constituency, and must do so within three months or within such reasonable time as the Court deems fit. In the High Court, Justice Philip Pillai, who delivered his judgment on 1 August 2012, held that the words 'shall be filled by election' in Article 49(1) of the Constitution referred to a process rather than an event. In other words, all vacancies shall be filled by election, as opposed to nomination, and do not require a writ of election to be issued within a specified time.[35] In the meantime, President Tony Tan issued a writ of election on 9 May 2012 and by-elections were held on 26 May 2012. It was won by the Workers' Party's Png Eng Huat. Vellama appealed Justice Pillai's decision and the Court of Appeal overturned the High Court's interpretation of Article 49 of the Constitution, holding that the Prime Minister did not have an unfettered discretion to decide whether or not to hold a by-election when a seat becomes vacant. Furthermore, such a by-election must be 'within a reasonable time',[36] taking all circumstances into consideration:

> The sum total of all this in the context of the present appeal is that while the Prime Minister retains a substantial measure of discretion as to the timing of an election to fill a casual vacancy, his discretion is not unconditional. Thus, it will not be in order for him to declare that he will not be calling an

---

[35] *Vellama d/o Marie Muthu v Attorney-General* [2012] SGHC 155; [2012] 4 SLR 698 (High Court).
[36] *Vellama d/o Marie Muthu v Attorney-General* [2013] SGCA 39 (Court of Appeal), at para 92.

election to fill such a vacancy unless at that point in time, he intends, in the near future, to advise the President to dissolve Parliament. In any event, even if at a particular point in time he feels that it would not be appropriate to call for an election to fill a vacancy, he must still review the circumstances from time to time and call for election to fill the vacancy if and when the circumstances have changed.[37]

VII. PRINCIPAL OFFICERS OF PARLIAMENT

A. The Speaker

The Speaker presides over Parliament. The rules of procedure are found in the Standing Orders of Parliament. Following a general election, Parliament must elect a Speaker. The Speaker need not be a member of the House although someone who does not qualify to stand as an MP cannot be elected. Traditionally, the Speaker is also a Member of Parliament but this has not always been the case. Singapore's first Speaker, Sir George Oehlers (1908–68) was not a member of the House when he was elected Speaker.

Generally, the Speaker's job is to preside over Parliament and to regulate the conduct of debate. The Speaker also tries to ensure that the voice of the minority is heard and rules on matters of procedure and order from which there are no appeals. The Speaker is the guardian of Parliament's prestige and honour and is thus empowered to mete out punishments to errant members. The Deputy Speaker performs all the duties of the Speaker in the Speaker's absence. The Deputy Speaker is elected in the same manner as the Speaker except that the presiding officer in this instance is the Speaker himself.

B. The Clerk of Parliament

The Clerk of Parliament is the House's chief permanent officer. He or she is appointed by the President upon consultation with the Speaker and the Public Service Commission and may only be removed by a two-thirds vote in Parliament. In such an instance, only the President

---

[37] ibid, at para 87.

on consultation with the Speaker can remove him.[38] The Clerk and Assistant Clerks form part of the Secretariat of Parliament. The office of the Clerk of the House is a very specialised one and demands great expertise in legislative procedure and parliamentary administration. He has custody of all votes and proceedings, records, bills and other documents presented to or laid before Parliament and advises the Speaker and members on matters of procedure. The Clerk also administers oaths, presides over the election of the Speaker, and is responsible for the printing and circulation of all bills and motions. When Parliament is in session, the Clerk sits at the Table in front of and below the Speaker's Chair wearing his traditional black gown.

C. The Whip

The word 'whip' is an abbreviation of an eighteenth-century English fox-hunting term 'whipper-in'. The whipper-in kept the hounds from straying from the pack and this is analogous to what government and opposition Whips do in Parliament. They are party disciplinarians tasked with rounding up party support during voting and ensuring that members are present during other occasions. This is essential in the parliamentary system of government, which depends heavily on strong party discipline.

In Singapore, there is only the government Whip as there is insufficient opposition to require an opposition Whip. There are also two deputy government Whips. The Whip ensures the efficient and smooth running of the parliamentary machinery. He lists the speakers for each item of business and estimates the time likely to be required for each item and thereby assists the House to complete its business on time. He also ensures efficient communication within his party; and ensures that backbenchers vote in line with the party's stand. Party MPs may vote according to their conscience only after he has lifted the whip.

The Whip is directly responsible to the Leader of the House and to the Prime Minister. His other duties include advising the government on parliamentary business and procedure and maintaining a close liaison with ministers in regard to parliamentary business which affects

---

[38] Constitution of the Republic of Singapore, Art 51.

their departments. In carrying out his duties, the Whip must work closely with the Leader of the House.

D. Leader of the House

Back when English Prime Ministers were also peers of the realm, they often had to be present in the House of Lords and thus were absent from the House of Commons. To represent them, they appointed a leading minister as the Leader of the House. According to Sir William Gladstone (1809–98), four-time Prime Minister of Britain, the Leader of the House

> suggests, and in a great degree fixes, the course of all principal matters of business, supervises and keeps in harmony the actions of his colleagues, takes the initiative on matters of ceremonial procedure, and advises the House in every difficulty as it arises.[39]

Under Parliament's Standing Orders, the Leader is responsible for making representations to the Speaker on urgent matters of public interest that may require sittings. He also advises the Speaker on the sitting arrangements within the House. In the Prime Minister's absence, the Leader expresses the sense of the House on formal occasions, such as in moving motions of thanks or congratulation. The Leader of the House is also responsible for arranging government business and the legislative programme in the House (in consultation with the government Whip), advising the House on any difficulty which may arise and moving procedural motions relating to the business of the House on formal occasions.

VIII. PARLIAMENT'S COMMITTEES

There are two types of parliamentary committees: (a) those established under the Standing Orders of Parliament; and (b) those established by the People's Action Party and as Government Parliamentary Committees (GPCs). Parliamentary committees provide a closer and more in-depth study of government business and also act as a minor check on the executive. In the case of select committees, they also provide an opportunity for the public to present their views directly to Parliament.

---

[39] WE Gladstone, 'Kin Beyond Sea' (1878) 127 *North American Review* 179, at 207.

A. Committee of the Whole House

A Committee of the whole House comprises all members of the House. In fact, it is the whole House in a less formal capacity and a chairman (rather than the Speaker) presides. Whenever the House goes into Committee, the Speaker leaves the Chair and the Mace is removed from the Table by the Serjeant-at-Arms and placed in the lower brackets. The Speaker then assumes the chairmanship of the Committee but does not sit at the Speaker's Chair. Instead, he assumes his seat at the Table and he enjoys all the powers as the Speaker except that he cannot inflict serious forms of punishment on members. The House may resolve itself into a Committee of the Whole House to consider any matter although it must do this when Parliament considers bills. Usually, the Committee of the Whole House will deliberate bills that are uncomplicated, are of a regulatory measure or are minor amendments. Major or controversial bills or amendments like those amending the Constitution or in which personal or religious sensitivities are involved are usually committed to select committee for more detailed consideration.

B. Select Committees

Select committees are small committees appointed by Parliament for a specific purpose. Usually, it is to scrutinise a particular piece of legislation, for example the Copyright Bill 1986 and the Constitution (Amendment) Bill 1991. Select committees are appointed for this purpose only if the bill is complex, controversial or has wide-ranging impact. They have the power to send for persons, papers and records in the fulfilling of their function and are accountable to the whole House by way of a report in which they express their findings.

C. Sessional Committees

Under the Standing Orders, standing select committees may be established. Each sessional committee consists of a chairman (usually the Speaker) and seven members. Membership in these committees should, as far as possible, reflect 'the balance between the government benches and the opposition benches in Parliament'. There are currently seven standing committees: (a) Committee of Selection; (b) Public Accounts Committee; (c) Estimates Committee; (d) Standing Orders Committee; (e) House Committee; (f) Public Petitions Committee; and (g) Committee of Privileges.

The Committee of Selection is responsible for informing Parliament whenever any member has been appointed to any of the Committees. The job of the Public Accounts Committee is to 'examine accounts showing the appropriation of sums granted by Parliament to meet public expenditure and such accounts laid before Parliament'. The Estimates Committee is charged with the duty to 'examine any of the Estimates, to report what economies consistent with the policy implied in the Estimates might be effected and ... suggest the form in which the Estimates might be presented'. These Estimates form the subject matter of the Finance Minister's Annual Budget, which contains estimates of revenue and expenditure for the fiscal year. They also show the assets and liabilities of the country.

The Standing Orders Committee's duties are to consider from time to time matters pertaining to the Standing Orders of Parliament and to make recommendations for any necessary amendments. The House Committee's duty is to 'consider and advise the Speaker upon all matters connected with the comfort and convenience of Members of Parliament' whilst the Public Petitions Committee considers all petitions referred to it. Finally, the Committee of Privileges is charged with the handling of 'any complaint of breach of privilege or any matter which appears to affect the powers and privileges of Parliament' and to report on them to Parliament.

D. Government Parliamentary Committees (GPCs)

Early in 1987, then First Deputy Prime Minister Goh Chok Tong proposed forming GPCs, each focusing on a specific area affecting the future of Singapore. These GPCs are not like parliamentary committees since they are organs of the PAP. They have no constitutional status but are instead an initiative of the PAP Government. Goh cited three main reasons for setting up GPCs:

> Firstly, unless the PAP suddenly becomes incompetent, it will continue to dominate Parliament. This creates a special problem for the Government

back-benchers. The public sees them with little or no influence over policy formulation, and with little or no independence of mind. That this does grave injustice to our MPs is immaterial. It is how the public sees them that matters.

Secondly, we have better qualified MPs. Most of them have successful careers. They will not find the humdrum demands of constituency work challenging enough. They will want to seek greater satisfaction by having an influence on government policies. They will want their opinions heard and considered, if not followed. If we want better Members of Parliament we have to listen to them, and give weight to their political inputs.

Thirdly, and this is the most compelling reason, we have to look for a new political formula to take us into the next century. Our political culture is one of Government dominance. Government, or specifically, the Cabinet, is the power house that drives Singapore. It is this dominance that holds Singapore together as a nation. Without this dominance, Singapore would have disintegrated long ago.[40]

These GPCs are limited to MPs from the governing party and they closely monitor the policies of particular ministries with the help of Resource Panels, comprising experts and interested laypersons. They provide a wider range of views in Parliament and help Cabinet ministers refine policies. They also serve as sounding boards and provide valuable feedback and suggestions to the relevant ministries on issues of public interest. Each government ministry will have a corresponding GPC each of which consists of five backbenchers, and is chaired by one senior member. Each GPC is backed by a 12-member resource panel and their task is to concentrate on a particular area affecting the government of the country, examining all intended bills in that area and in some instances, they will be consulted even before the bill is drafted.

The creation of GPCs was considered a positive step given the state of oppositional representation in Parliament. Its use as simulated critics of government legislation will definitely be far more effective than expecting backbenchers to take on the role of opposition members. Furthermore, the level of debate and discussion on each policy has, in my opinion, reached a greater level owing to the specialised nature of the GPCs and the utilisation of experts outside of Parliament. This has

[40] Speech by Deputy Prime Minister Goh Chok Tong to the Alpha Society *Singapore Government Press Release* 10 Feb 1987, Release No 17/FEB 05-1/87/02/10.

led community leaders and professionals to participate more actively in the affairs of state, albeit behind the scenes.

IX. THE CONDUCT OF ELECTIONS

Before general elections can be called, the President must dissolve Parliament and issue a writ of election to the Returning Officer. This writ will specify when the nomination of candidates will take place. Once the President issues the writ of election, the Returning Officer will issue a notice of election.

A. Nomination Day

On nomination day, candidates must present their nomination papers, statutory declarations and certificate personally at the nomination centre. At the close of the nomination period, if there is only one candidate (in the case of an SMC), or one group of candidates (in the case of a GRC) for the ward, the Assistant Returning Officer will declare at the nomination centre that the candidate or the group of candidates have been returned as MP(s). However, where there is more than one candidate (SMC) or more than one group of candidates (GRC) nominated, the Returning Officer will adjourn to a date when a poll will be taken, ie polling day.

The Returning Officer will then issue the notice of contested elections giving:

a. the date of the poll (not less than nine days nor more than eight weeks after publication of notice);
b. the names of candidates, their symbols, proposers and seconders; and
c. the names and locations of all polling stations.

B. Campaigning

Candidates can only start their election campaigns after nominations close. Electioneering can carry on right up to the eve of polling day. During that period, they can make house-to-house calls, distribute pamphlets, put up posters and banners and hold election rallies. Political parties will also be given air-time by the Singapore Broadcasting Authority. The length of air-time depends on the number of candidates each party is fielding.

To prevent 'money-politics' and expensive election campaigns, the Parliamentary Elections Act specifies that the maximum amount any candidate or his election agent can pay or incur is: (a) in the case of a GRC, an amount equal to S$3.50 for each elector divided by the number of candidates in the group; or (b) in the case of an SMC, an amount equal to S$3.50 for each elector.

C. Polling Day

Every voter will receive a poll card informing him of polling day and where he may cast his vote in person. Polling takes place from 8.00 am to 8.00 pm. At the end of the day, the ballot boxes are sealed and witnessed by the candidates and/or their agents. The ballot boxes are then delivered to their respective counting centres where they will be opened in front of the candidates and/or their counting agents. The ballot papers are then sorted and counted.

After the count, the Assistant Returning Officer will inform the Group Assistant Returning Officer of the results of counting at the principal counting place. The Assistant Returning Officer will then collate the results and notify the representatives of the candidates (principal election agents, election agents or the candidates) of the results before transmitting them to the Returning Officer who will make his announcement at the Announcement Centre for public consumption. The results will be officially published in the *Government Gazette*.

D. Political Donations

The Political Donations Act and its Regulations came into operation on 15 February 2001. The Act seeks to prevent foreigners from interfering in Singapore's domestic politics by funding candidates and political associations or parties. Political associations and candidates may only accept donations from 'permissible donors' and may not accept more than S$5000 of anonymous donations per annual reporting period.

X. CONCLUDING THOUGHTS

If the numerous changes and innovations to Singapore's Parliament seem bewildering, one ought to only remember that the ruling PAP Government has—like British parliamentarians—all along seen the legislature as the ultimate source of power. Its legitimacy to rule flows directly from the votes cast in an election. However, the structure and logic of the Westminster parliamentary system is premised on binary outcomes—either you are in Parliament or you are not. Put another way, the electorate is forced to speak unequivocally for or against the government, and this lack of nuances has led the PAP Government to 'perfect' Parliament through its various legislative schemes. As then Prime Minister Lee Kuan Yew explained in the aftermath of the 1984 General Election:

> The results of the election show a highly sophisticated electorate. They want a PAP government, they were sure they had one, they wanted to put the pressure on the PAP.

> They wanted some people in Parliament to get us to either go slower—if they don't like to go as fast—or to be more generous in our policies, less austere and so on.

> In no case did they take chance. The result showed an unexpectedly subtle understanding of how to use one vote to maximum effect. We lost two seats, so just one non-constituency candidate. The signal has been sent.[41]

The puzzle for the PAP Government has been this: How to remain in power and yet accommodate alternative and dissident views? The first of these innovations was the NCMP scheme in 1984 which allowed up to three of the 'best losers' in the general election to be appointed to the House. The hope was that these NCMPs would offer an alternative voice, keep the government on its toes and quell all desire to elect an alternative party into power. The scheme failed for two reasons. First, all opposition parties initially rejected offers to have their members appointed NCMPs as they felt that NCMPs lacked legitimacy, having to get into Parliament 'by the back door'. Second, the numbers allocated for NCMP—just three initially, and then later, six—was simply too small to make a difference. It smacked of tokenism, and the public was not convinced.

The GRC scheme was an attempt to entrench multi-racialism in Singapore's Parliament without making the ethnic minorities feel

---

[41] 'PM: What the results mean' *Straits Times* 23 Dec 1984, at 1.

that they owed their places in the House to the colour of their skins. Requiring minorities to be members of GRC teams meant that they were voted into Parliament and thus carry the mandate of their electorate. Having rejected the bicameral legislature proposal on two occasions, this was the party's best effort at ensuring that Singapore's Parliament would always reflect the demographic mix of Singaporean society. If the traditional Westminster-style electoral system was allowed to function unaltered, there was a clear possibility that Singapore's Parliament might one day be filled with only Chinese members. This modification ensured that this would not happen.

Of course, as we saw above, the GRC scheme also provided the PAP Government with a massive advantage in the conduct of electoral politics and succeeded in reducing the opposition parties to contesting seriously only in the small number of single-member wards available. It worked well for over two decades, but by the 2011 General Election, had begun to backfire on the PAP.

The NMP scheme was yet another effort to ameliorate the polarisation of legislative debate practically demanded by the Westminster system. Since the parliamentary form of government is premised on a two-party system, with each party taking turns to form the government, debates are highly partisan. The tendency was thus for opposition parties to object to everything the government proposed because they were expected to do so, even if the proposal was worthy of support. The NMP scheme sought to break this trend and improve the quality of parliamentary debate by bringing alternative voices to Parliament—without creating an upper house—to argue and reason on a non-partisan basis. Good ideas should thus be supported because they were good, and not because they emanated from a particular party. Initially, the NMP scheme was meant to be a temporary measure, especially since many PAP members objected to the scheme. From 1990 onwards, each new Parliament had to vote to retain the NMP provisions. It was, however, made permanent in 2011.

All the changes to the structure of Parliament were premised on certain assumptions—that the PAP would always remain dominant and in power; that opposition voices should be heard as a nod to plurality, but should never derail the common wisdom of the majority; that opposition parties continue to find it difficult to recruit new (and poor quality) members; and that the voting public would continue to choose their government pragmatically by opting for the tried and trusted PAP. All this changed in the 2011 General Election. Although actual gains by the opposition were small, the transformation of the voting milieu had been dramatic.[42] Old assumptions no longer held and Singapore ushered in a new era of electoral politics.

FURTHER READING

Ooi Giok Ling, *Town Councils in Singapore: Determination for Public Housing Estates* (Singapore, Times Academic Press, 1990).

KYL Tan, 'Constitutional Implications of the 1991 Singapore General Elections' (1992) 13 *Singapore Law Review* 26.

———, 'Is Singapore's Electoral System in Need of Reform?' (1997) 14 *Commentary* 109.

———, 'Parliament and the Making of Law in Singapore' in KYL Tan (ed), *The Singapore Legal System* (Singapore, Singapore University Press, 1999) 123–59.

———, 'Singapore: A Statist Legal Laboratory' in A Black & G Bell (eds), *Law and Legal Systems of Asia* (Melbourne, Cambridge University Press, 2011) 330–71.

——— & T Lee, *Voting In Change: Politics of Singapore's 2011 General Election* (Singapore, Ethos Books, 2011).

Li-ann Thio, 'Neither Fish Nor Fowl: Councils, Community Development Councils and the Cultivation of Local Government/Governance in Singapore' in H Kudo, G Laud & L Pegoraro (eds), *Municipi d'Oriente: Il Governo Locale in Europa Orientale, Asia e Australia* (Bologna, Centre for Constitutional Studies and Democratic Development, 2009) 373–411 (in Italian).

WEBSITE

www.parliament.gov.sg (official website of Singapore's Parliament)

---

[42] Tan & Lee (eds), *Voting In Change: Politics of Singapore's 2011 General Election* (n 26).

4

Law-making

———◆———

Introduction – Rule Formulation – Introduction of Bills in
Parliament – The Legislative Process – The Presidential
Council for Minority Rights and Presidential Assent – Executive
Law-making – Legislative Powers in an Emergency

I. INTRODUCTION

P ARLIAMENT HAS SEVERAL functions, the most important
of which is law-making. Passing legislation is the quintessential
legislative act. After all, Parliament's elected representatives carry
the mandate of 'the People', and the corresponding legitimacy to make
laws on their behalf. Indeed, it was the lack of legislative response in
the 1840s and 1850s that caused Singapore's merchants to agitate relent-
lessly for the Straits Settlements to have its own legislature. This eventually came to pass in 1867 when the Straits Settlements was transferred
to the control of the Colonial Office in London and the Settlements
was given its own Legislative Council.

Under Article 58 of the Constitution, 'the power of the Legislature
to make laws shall be exercised by Bills passed by Parliament and
assented to by the President'. Ideally, Members of Parliament (MPs)
should introduce measures and laws that reflect the aims and aspirations of society. However, this is seldom the case in Westminster-style
parliaments as legislative initiative often comes from the government
rather than from individual MPs.

In Singapore, this problem is compounded by the fact that at both
formulation and actual law-making stages, MPs assume a muted and
passive role, abdicating their once exclusive domain in favour of the
executive. Professor Chan Heng Chee pointed out, as far back as in
1976, that MPs lack legislative initiative and that almost all legislation

comes from the Cabinet acting on its own initiative or on the advice of senior civil servants.[1] During the passage of bills in Parliament, MPs are again reluctant to speak out against bills and policies. The government is thus able to set its goals and values for society through laws passed in Parliament. Nonetheless, Parliament performs the crucial symbolic role of legitimising both the government's rule and the laws it passes through established and accepted procedures.

II. RULE FORMULATION

The majority of bills that are introduced in Parliament are initiated by the Executive. These are known as government bills. Non-government bills are known as private members' bills and they are a rarity in Singapore. Government bills begin life as executive policies that may be forged from within the public service or through public feedback on existing law. This is usually the case when the new laws amend existing statutes. Next, the Permanent Secretary of the ministry initiating the legislation will prepare a draft of the bill or a detailed statement of its proposed contents and refer it to the Cabinet for 'in-principle' approval of the policy and then onto the Attorney-General's Chambers (AGC) for advice and drafting. Drafting is the responsibility of the Legislation and Law Reform Division of the AGC. Once the bill has been printed and vetted by the AGC, a copy of the Memorandum to the Cabinet is sent to the Permanent Secretary for the Ministry of Law for approval before submission to the Cabinet. Only after the Cabinet approves the bill will it be read in Parliament.

Private members' bills are extremely rare. The last time such a bill was successfully introduced was when Nominated MP Walter Woon proposed the Maintenance of Parents Bill in 1994. It was passed into law in 1995. A key reason why such bills are rare is the strict party discipline enforced by the political parties in Singapore. As the ruling People's Action Party (PAP) has been continuously in power since 1959, there has been no real opportunity for its backbenchers to introduce legislation of their own since the party is already in government. MPs belonging

---

[1]   Chan Heng Chee, 'The Role of Parliamentary Politicians in Singapore' (1976) 1(3) *Legislative Studies Quarterly* 423–41.

to opposition parties—and there have only been at most eight such MPs in any Parliament—will not propose bills that will certainly be defeated by the ruling party.

III. INTRODUCTION OF BILLS IN PARLIAMENT

A. Government Bills

Any member may introduce a bill into Parliament provided sufficient notice is given to the House. The period of notice is two clear days for government bills, and four clear days for private members' bills. Bills that either directly or indirectly provide for tax collection, state expenditure involving the Consolidated Fund or matters relating to the financial obligations of the government, may not be introduced or moved unless it is recommended by the President and signed by a Minister.

On the actual day of the bill's introduction, the member introducing the bill will read aloud the long title of the bill and then present the bill to the Clerk at the Table. The Clerk will then read aloud the short title of the bill. The bill will then have been introduced into Parliament with no questions put and this is known as the First Reading of the bill. After this, a date will be fixed for the Second Reading of the bill.

B. Private Members' Bills

Since Singapore became independent in 1965, only four private members' bills have been introduced. The first was in fact a government bill but was raised by a backbencher because of the religious nature of the bill. The others were true private members' bills. The first of these was the Roman Catholic Archbishop of Singapore Bill. In August 1974, Padma Selvadurai, a backbench member of the PAP, introduced a bill to incorporate the Titular Roman Catholic Archbishop of Singapore. The bill was read for the first time on 28 August 1974. The object of the bill was 'to incorporate the title of the Roman Catholic Archbishop of Singapore as a body corporate with perpetual succession and a corporate seal'. This change in the law was necessitated by the split in the Archdiocese of Malacca-Singapore into the Diocese of Malacca-Johor and the Archdiocese of Singapore. At the Second Reading on

23 October 1974, only Selvadurai spoke and there was no debate before the bill was committed to select committee. There were no public representations on the bill and it was returned to Parliament in November the following year with minor textual amendments by the committee. It was accordingly read a third time and passed on 11 November 1975.

It would be close to two decades before the next private members' bill was tabled. In May 1994, Nominated MP Walter Woon sought leave to introduce the first real private members' bill—the Maintenance of Parents Bill. The bill was controversial as it was seen by several quarters as a pro-Confucian law to legislate filial piety as it allowed financially dependent or indigent parents to take out maintenance orders against their children if the latter failed to support them in their old age. The original version of the bill as drafted by Woon had a fairly weak enforcement mechanism as Woon, being a Nominated Member of Parliament, was in no position to commit the government to additional expenditure to enforce the law. However, as the bill received strong support from the government through the Ministry of Community Development, the final bill had much greater bite than the original. The bill was read for the first time on 23 May 1994. It proceeded to a Second Reading on 25 July 1994 and after almost three days of impassioned debate by some 30 MPs, a division was called to decide if the bill has been read a second time. Of the 63 MPs present, 50 voted in favour, 11 against and 2 abstained.[2]

At the close of the debate at the Second Reading, Woon proposed that it be committed to a select committee comprising the Speaker (as chairman) and seven other MPs. Wong Kan Seng, Leader of the House, then proposed that 'as the bill has provoked so much debate in this House and interest in the public', three more members would be added to the select committee.[3] The committee reported back to Parliament in October 1995 after receiving over a thousand representations from the public and questioning scores of representors.[4] The bill was

---

[2] See Debate on Maintenance of Parents Bill *Singapore Parliamentary Debates* 27 Jul 1994, vol 63, cols 318–62.

[3] Wong Kan Seng, Speech *Singapore Parliamentary Debates* 26 Aug 1994, vol 63, col 587.

[4] Singapore Parliament, *Report of the Select Committee on the Maintenance of Parents Bill (Bill No 13 of 1994)*, Parl 2 of 1995.

then read a third time on 2 November 1995 and passed without further debate. It was signed into law and became operational on 1 June 1996.

During the time that the Maintenance of Parents Bill was being deliberated in select committee, another Nominated MP, Kanwaljit Soin, proposed another private members' bill, the Family Violence Bill. Soin explained that she and members of the Society Against Family Violence and a number of other voluntary welfare organisations had worked on the bill since mid-1994 as they felt that existing laws were insufficient to deal with the rising tide of family violence. While Soin received support from other NMPs, the PAP MPs, and in particular, the government front bench did not support the bill. Abdullah Tarmugi, the Acting Minister for Community Development said:

> Sir, I oppose the passage of the Bill, not for what it seeks to achieve, ie, to enhance the protection of victims or potential victims of family violence, but for its approach and tone and for the fact that there is already existing legislation in the Women's Charter to address the same problem and which can be amended to enhance its effectiveness.[5]

After two days of debate, the bill was defeated at the Second Reading and proceeded no further. Without the support of the government of the day and of the majority of the House, a private members' bill is destined for failure, even if it succeeds in provoking much discussion and debate. At the same time, the Whip is not imposed for private members' bills, thus allowing MPs to speak more freely and in good conscience. The latest attempt by a private member to introduce a bill is PAP MP Christopher De Souza, who made plain his intention to introduce a Prevention of Human Trafficking Bill. De Souza obtained permission from the Ministry of Home Affairs to introduce the bill and the ministry further directed the Singapore Inter-Agency Taskforce on Trafficking on Persons to work with him in hammering out the specifics of the bill. At press time, the bill has yet to be introduced but with the full support of the government and after four public consultations, this bill will almost be certain to pass into law.

---

[5] A Tarmugi (acting Minister for Community Development), Speech *Singapore Parliamentary Debates* 2 Nov 1995, vol 65, col 184.

IV. THE LEGISLATIVE PROCESS

A. The First Reading

During the First Reading, the long title of the bill is read to serve notice to everyone that a fresh bill is before the House. Thereafter, a date would be set for the bill's Second Reading. This is usually at the next available scheduled parliamentary sitting. On rare occasions, a bill may be rushed through to Second Reading on the same day under a Certificate of Urgency. Section 86 of the Standing Orders of Parliament provides that 'when a certificate of urgency signed by the President' accompanies a bill, that bill may 'be proceeded with throughout all its stages until such Bill has been read the third time'. Urgent bills usually relate to public order or security matters, or tax or fiscal bills. Since independence in 1965, only 27 bills have been passed under a Certificate of Urgency, and of these 23 were passed before 1976.

B. The Second Reading

After the bill's first reading, the Clerk will: (a) publish the bill in the *Gazette*; (b) print the bill; and (c) circulate it to Members. All this must be done at least seven clear days before the Second Reading. If an amendment is to be made to the bill after the First Reading, two clear days' notice of amendment, signed by a Cabinet Minister, must be given to the Clerk. This does not, however, include urgent bills which may be read three times and passed within the day.

During the Second Reading, the Minister moving the bill usually delivers a speech outlining the objectives of the bill. Members will then debate the bill. At the end of the debate a motion is put 'That the Bill be now read a Second Time'. At this point, a vote is taken on the bill. Voting is generally by voice vote and there is seldom an official division. Under the Standing Order of Parliament, a division—a more formalised form of vote counting—may be called so long as at least five MPs support the division. Once a division is called, the division bells are rung, after which the Serjeant-at-Arms locks the door of the Chamber and voting begins. Because of the PAP's overwhelming dominance of Parliament, no division was called for many years. It was only when Nominated MPs entered the House that this procedure was revived.

Once the bill passes its Second Reading, it moves on to the Committee Stage.

C. The Committee Stage

After the Second Reading, the bill will be committed either to a select committee or to the Committee of the Whole House. If the bill goes to select committee, a chairman and his committee is appointed and given powers to call persons, records and other documents. The committee must list its findings and recommendations in a select committee report. If the bill is not being committed to select committee, the House resolves itself into the Committee of the Whole House and deliberates the bill in great detail, going through each clause. The Committee may only discuss the details of the bills and not its underlying principles.

At the Committee Stage, amendments to the bill may be made but the bill cannot be rejected outright since that power is reserved for the House. After the bill has been dealt with in Committee, a report must be made to the House. This is known as the Report Stage. The chairman of the select committee or of the Committee of the Whole House (whichever the case may be) will report the findings of the committee to Parliament. If amendments are made, the amendments are put to the House and they may either be accepted or rejected although the latter alternative is rarely the case. Once the House accepts the amended bill, a motion may be moved that 'The Bill be read a Third Time'.

D. The Third Reading

The Third Reading is similar to the Second Reading although the debate is usually far more limited. Amendments to correct errors or oversights may be made with the Speaker's permission but no amendments of a material character may be made. The Minister moving the Third Reading may again make a speech outlining the changes made and perhaps explain what repercussions the legislation would have. At the end of the debate, the bill is put to a vote and, once accepted, will have been passed by Parliament. However, further steps are needed before the bill becomes law.

V. THE PRESIDENTIAL COUNCIL FOR MINORITY
RIGHTS AND PRESIDENTIAL ASSENT

After the final reading and before the bill is presented to the President
for his assent, the Speaker will send an authenticated copy to the
Presidential Council for Minority Rights for its consideration. The
Council must consider the bill and make a report to the Speaker
within 30 days. This 30-day limit may be extended if the bill is particularly complex or difficult. If the Council presents no report within
the time limit, it is presumed that no provision of the bill contains a
'differentiating measure'.

The Presidential Council for Minority Rights is established under
Part VII of the Constitution. It comprises a chairman (appointed for
3 years), not more than 10 members appointed for life and not more
than 10 members appointed for 3 years appointed by the President on
the Cabinet's advice. To qualify for membership, a person must be a
Singapore citizen, resident in Singapore and at least 35 years old. He
must not be of unsound mind, an undischarged bankrupt or have been
convicted of an offence carrying a term of imprisonment lasting one
year or more or a fine of 2000 dollars or more.

It is the particular function of the Council 'to draw attention to any
Bill or to any subsidiary legislation if that Bill or subsidiary legislation
is, in the opinion of the Council, a differentiating measure'. Article 68
of the Constitution defines a 'differentiating measure' as

> any measure which is, or is likely in its practical application to be, disadvan-
> tageous to persons of any racial or religious community and not equally
> disadvantageous to persons of other such communities, either directly by
> prejudicing persons of that community or indirectly by giving advantage to
> persons of another community.

However, three types of bills are exempted from the Council's scrutiny:
'money bills', bills on a Certificate of Urgency and bills which affect
the defence, security, public safety, peace or good order of Singapore.

A. Role of the Elected President

If the Council issues an adverse report, Parliament can either amend
the bill and re-submit it to the Council or proceed to present the bill
for the presidential assent in spite of the adverse report. The latter

course of action is only feasible if Parliament passes the motion for presentation by 'an affirmative vote of not less than two-thirds of the total membership of Parliament'. If the report presented to Parliament is not adverse, then it goes to the President for his assent without further delay. Once the President assents to the bill, it becomes an Act of Parliament, ie law. Of course, the President may, in areas where his personal discretion is invoked under the Constitution—such as budgets or the raising of loans or giving of guarantees by the government—refuse to assent to a bill duly passed by Parliament.

An Act comes into force only at the date of its publication in the *Gazette*. The publication date of a law and its commencement date are two different things. An Act may be published in the *Gazette* but may not be in force because of a clause providing for the date of commencement to be decided by the Minister. Often the date of commencement depends on the drafting of necessary subsidiary legislation.

VI. EXECUTIVE LAW-MAKING

A. Subsidiary Legislation

Owing to time constraints and other practical considerations, Parliament delegates legislative powers to the executive. Many Acts contain provisions empowering the Minister in charge to promulgate necessary subsidiary legislation. To prevent abuse by the executive, all subsidiary legislation is made pursuant to its parent Act. Under the ultra vires doctrine, the Minister cannot promulgate legislation that is not substantively or procedurally provided for in the parent Act. Procedures for promulgating subsidiary legislation vary from Act to Act. Generally, subsidiary legislation is drafted by legal officers acting on behalf of the Attorney-General based on a draft prepared by the responsible Permanent Secretary.

All subsidiary legislation is also subject to scrutiny by the Presidential Council for Minority Rights' scrutiny. The Minister in charge must, within 14 days of the legislation's publication, submit an authenticated copy to the Council. The Council has 30 days to consider it and report to the Speaker and the appropriate Minister whether the subsidiary legislation contains any differentiating measure. If, in the opinion of the Council, there appears to be a differentiating measure, then the offending provision can either be revoked or amended within six months. Alternatively, Parliament can pass a resolution confirming the provision in question. If the Council does not report within the 30-day period, it is presumed that the Council is of the opinion that the subsidiary legislation contains no provision that is a 'differentiating measure'.[6]

Under Article 58 of the Constitution, legislative power is exercised by Parliament through the laws it passes. Parliament may also confer executive functions on any persons under Article 23(2). Section 36 of the Interpretation Act provides that the Minister may sub-delegate his powers to another official 'with the approval of the President and by notification in the Gazette' provided there is no written law to the contrary. However, the Minister must personally exercise the power to make delegated legislation; he cannot delegate it.

Section 23(1) of the Interpretation Act requires that all subsidiary legislation be published in the *Gazette*. Failure to do so will render the legislation void. This exact issue arose in the case of *Cheong Seok Leng v Public Prosecutor*,[7] where the appellant had been charged for being unlawfully absent from duty from his post in the Vigilante Corps. One argument raised was that the Minister's assignment of Cheong to the Vigilante Corps was ultra vires the Vigilante Corps Act. The High Court held that the Minister's assignment was subsidiary legislation as it had legislative effect, and since it had not been published in the *Gazette*, it was invalid.

In an administrative state like Singapore, many more rules are in fact to be found in subsidiary legislation than in primary legislation. Beyond the usual test of constitutionality, all subsidiary legislation must be made well within the powers of the primary enabling statute. Typically, principal statutes contain enabling provisions giving the Minister in charge of the ministry responsible for enforcing the law wide discretionary powers to make rules for the proper administration of the Act. Take the Accountants Act[8]—alphabetically the first Act listed in the Singapore Statutes—for example. Section 64(1) of the Act provides that the Accounting and Corporate Regulatory Authority 'may, with the approval of the Minister, make rules to give effect to his Act'. Similarly,

---

[6] See ibid.
[7] [1988] 1 SLR(R) 530 (High Court, Singapore).
[8] Act 4 of 2004.

under the Animals and Birds Act,[9] section 80 provides that the 'Minister may make rules for the carrying out of the purposes of this Act and for any matter which is required under this Act to be prescribed'. In almost every Act, provisions such as these enable the executive to promulgate subsidiary legislation having the force of law. The requirement that they be published in the *Gazette* thus becomes important in ensuring that the state's laws are clear and made known to the public at large. Naturally, all such subsidiary legislation is also subject to judicial review by the courts.

B. Other Forms of Executive Rule-making

Besides subsidiary legislation, rules may also be promulgated by way of administrative guidelines. While administrative guidelines do not have the force of law, they may be relied on and enforced by the promulgating agency under certain circumstances. This was made clear in the High Court decision in *Lines International Holding (S) Pte Ltd v Singapore Tourist Promotion Board*.[10] In this case, the plaintiff cruise operator sought judicial review of a set of guidelines issued by the Port of Singapore Authority (PSA).

These guidelines had been issued in an effort to limit the numbers of 'cruises to nowhere' which were really gambling cruises. Under the guidelines, all cruise operators were limited to the total number of 'cruises to nowhere' they could offer. The plaintiff failed to comply with these limits and, as a consequence, was denied berthing rights. The question before the court was whether the guidelines issued by the PSA were legally enforceable. Justice Judith Prakash held that a body exercising an administrative discretion was entitled to adopt a general policy provided that the policy was not unreasonable in the *Wednesbury* sense, the policy was made known to all persons affected, and the authorities did not fetter their discretion and were prepared to hear out individual cases or deal with exceptions.[11]

---

[9] Ordinance 3 of 1965.
[10] [1997] 1 SLR(R) 52.
[11] ibid, at 79.

VII. LEGISLATIVE POWERS IN AN EMERGENCY

Parliament's legislative powers are extensively amplified in an emergency. Notwithstanding anything in the Constitution, Parliament 'make laws with respect to any matter, if it appears to Parliament that the law is required by reason of the emergency'.[12] Parliament may also bypass the President's assent (Article 150(4)). Such laws are valid even if they are inconsistent with any provision of the Constitution (Article 150(5)(a)), except for: (a) provisions of Article 5(2A), relating to the President's discretion in disallowing amendments to certain parts of the Constitution; (b) the provisions specified in Article 5(2A) relating to areas where the President can act in his personal discretion; and (c) the provisions relating to religion, citizenship or language (art 150(5)(b)).

Article 150 is a special provision because it confers wide legislative powers on the executive. Under Article 150(2), the President may legislate only when the emergency is declared and Parliament is not sitting. Thereafter, the President is required to summon Parliament as soon as is practicable. He has powers to promulgate ordinances until Parliament is sitting. Under Article 150(3), a Proclamation of Emergency may be revoked, or may be annulled by a resolution of Parliament. A lot of delegated legislation is often passed during an emergency. While ordinary legislation inconsistent with the Constitution may be validated by Article 150(5)(a), this provision does not appear to protect delegated legislation.

FURTHER READING

KYL Tan, 'Parliament and the Making of Law in Singapore' in KYL Tan (ed), *The Singapore Legal System* (Singapore, Singapore University Press, 1999) 123–59.

WEBSITE

www.parliament.gov.sg (official website of the Singapore Parliament)

---

[12] Constitution of the Republic of Singapore, Art 150(4).

5

The Executive

Introduction – Singapore's Prime Minister – The Cabinet and its Ministers – Unique Features of Singapore's Cabinet – Ministerial Salaries – Code of Conduct for Ministers – Policy Formulation, Decision-making and Collective Responsibility – The Attorney-General – The Executive: An Elected Dictatorship?

I. INTRODUCTION

IT IS IRONIC that in the Westminster *parliamentary* system of government, the most powerful branch of the government is the *executive*. In Singapore, the executive branch of government consists of the President, the Prime Minister and the Cabinet.

The Cabinet is a body of high-ranking members of government. In some countries, they may be referred to as the Council of Ministers. Under the parliamentary system of government, the Cabinet wields tremendous power and determines and directs state policy. In some other countries, such as the United States, the Cabinet functions largely as an advisory council to the President or head of state. Interestingly, the functions and powers of the Cabinet in the present-day United States are far more similar to the traditional role of Cabinets.

Historically, Cabinets emerged in England during the reigns of Kings George I (1714–27) and George II (1727–60). Both monarchs came from Hanover in Germany and spoke very little English. As such, they relied heavily on a small group of advisors to help them decide state policy. The most important of these advisors was Sir Robert Walpole (1676–1745) who became, over a period of 21 years, England's first Prime Minister. The modern Cabinet system developed further and acquired greater and greater powers in nineteenth century England under the prime ministerships of Lord Henry Palmerston (1784–1865),

Benjamin Disraeli (1804–81) and William Gladstone (1809–98). The title of Prime Minister was unofficial and unrecognised under British law until the passing of the Crown Act 1937.

In Singapore, the modern Cabinet emerged from the old Executive Councils established under the British. The first Executive Council, or Exco for short, was established in 1877 to advise the Governor of the Straits Settlements. The Governor was expected to consult the Exco on all affairs of importance even though the Governor had tremendous veto powers over both the Exco and the Legislative Council. Singapore's first modern Cabinet emerged from the Rendel Constitution of 1954, and following the 1955 General Elections, David Saul Marshall of the Labour Front became Singapore's first elected Chief Minister and led the first Cabinet or Council of Ministers comprising six elected members and three ex-officio official members appointed by the Governor.

The office of Chief Minister within the rubric of a colonial admin-istration was not the same as that of a Prime Minister in an independ-ent state. The Chief Minister was still outranked by the Governor, the Colonial Secretary, the Financial Secretary and the Attorney-General. When Singapore became a self-governing colony in 1959, the post of Governor was abolished and replaced by that of the High Commissioner and the post of Chief Minister was transformed into that of the Prime Minister. Thus, when the People's Action Party won the 1959 General Election, its leader, Lee Kuan Yew became Singapore's first Prime Minister.

II. SINGAPORE'S PRIME MINISTER

Under Article 25(1) of the Constitution, the President must appoint as Prime Minister, the person who 'in his judgment is likely to com-mand the confidence of the majority of the Members of Parliament'. Singapore has only seen two Chief Ministers and three Prime Ministers since 1955. David Saul Marshall (1908–95) and Lim Yew Hock (1914–84) were both leaders of the Labour Front while Lee Kuan Yew (b 1923), Goh Chok Tong (b 1941) and Lee Hsien Loong (b 1952) were all leaders of the People's Action Party (PAP).

Since 1959, the PAP has dominated Parliament and, consequently, Singapore politics and transitions between the Prime Ministers have been carefully stage-managed affairs. The PAP's leader, just like that of most other political parties in Singapore, is the party's secretary-general and not its chairman. This does not mean that the secretary-general automatically becomes the Prime Minister. When Lee Kuan Yew stepped down as Prime Minister in 1990, he continued as the PAP's secretary-general till 1992. Lee Hsien Loong succeeded Goh Chok Tong as Prime Minister on 12 August 2004 but Goh remained secretary-general of the party until December 2004.

The Prime Minister is the most powerful member of the Cabinet. This is not only because of his appointment but because of his control over his party which commands the majority of Parliament's seats. In Singapore, political parties observe very strict *party discipline*. This means that members of a particular political party will loyally vote according to that party's dictates. No member of a political party will vote against his own party's policies, legislation or proposals. If he does so, he will be taken to task by the party's disciplinarian, the *Whip*. He might even lose his party membership, and thus lose his seat in Parliament. Occasionally, the Whip will be lifted and all parliamentarians be allowed to vote according to conscience rather than along party lines. The Whip can be lifted at the special request of party members or where the bill is particularly controversial. There is no Whip in the case of private members' bills.

III. THE CABINET AND ITS MINISTERS

Article 24(1) of the Constitution provides that there shall be 'a Cabinet which shall consist of the Prime Minister and such other Ministers as may be appointed in accordance with Article 25.' Nothing is said about the size of the Cabinet or how many ministries there can be. It is up to the government of the day to decide. In 2014, Singapore's Cabinet comprises 18 elected Members of Parliament, each heading a government department or 'ministry'. Each Cabinet member is known as a 'minister' rather than the more traditional British title of 'secretary of state'. The Cabinet is responsible for state policies and the day-to-day administration of the country. Constitutionally, the Cabinet is collectively responsible to Parliament.

Other than the key ministers who form the Cabinet, there are also junior ministers or Ministers of State who, though not members of the

Cabinet, assist in running the various government ministries. Ministers are drawn from the ranks of elected parliamentarians. In Singapore's case, all the ministers have been drawn from the ranks of PAP MPs since 1963. This is because the PAP has such an overwhelming majority in Parliament that it has not been necessary for the party to accommodate any opposition members in the Cabinet line-up.

In some countries, where the majority of the leading party is much less clear or where the ruling party does not command a majority of seats in the legislature, opposition members may be included in a coalition government and in the Cabinet as well. The only time in which Singapore had a coalition government was in the aftermath of the 1955 General Election. Although David Marshall's Labour Front won the most number of seats overall, it only secured 10 of the 25 seats in the Legislative Assembly. As no political party secured an overall majority, the Governor invited Marshall to form a coalition government which he did by forming an alliance with the UMNO-MCA Alliance[1] which won three seats. With a total of 13 seats, the Labour Front and UMNO-MCA Alliance was able to form a majority government. As part of the electoral bargain, Marshall had to appoint Abdul Hamid bin Haji Jumat, leader of UMNO, as his Minister for Communications and Works.

While the Prime Minister is appointed by the President, acting in his discretion, he must appoint the other ministers 'acting in accordance with the advice of the Prime Minister'.[2] The Prime Minister may choose any Member of Parliament to be a member of his Cabinet. Nominated MPs as well as Non-Constituency MPs are eligible for appointment although this has never happened. However, in moving the Constitution (Amendment) Bill in 1990, then Deputy Prime Minister Goh Chok Tong opined:

> The Government does not intend to appoint NMPs as Ministers or other office holders. But when I looked into the future, I wondered whether it was necessary or desirable to expressly prevent a future government from appointing an NMP as Minister. ...

---

[1] This was an alliance formed between two leading ethnically based parties from the Federation of Malaya: the United Malays Nationalist Organisation (UMNO) and the Malayan Chinese Association (MCA).

[2] Constitution of the Republic of Singapore, Art 25(1).

In coming to this decision, my guiding principle is what is in the national interests. For a country to be well run and the people to enjoy growth and prosperity, it must have effective government. This means having suitable people to do the specialised complex jobs like Finance, Trade and Industry and Law. If there is no elected MP who can do such jobs adequately, it is in the people's interest that a competent person is appointed to do so from the non-elected MPs.[3]

The swearing-in of ministers will take place at an official ceremony where the minister-to-be will take an oath of allegiance before the President and is handed his letter of appointment. The appointment will then be published in the *Government Gazette*.

The Prime Minister is responsible for selecting and emplacing his ministers. Under Article 30 of the Constitution, the Prime Minister is empowered to 'charge any Minister with responsibility for any department or subject' as well as to 'revoke or vary any directions given'. The Prime Minister may also 'retain in his charge any department or subject'. This means that the Prime Minister can hold additional posts, such as Finance Minister or Defence Minister. For example, when Lee Hsien Loong took over as Prime Minister in 2004, he retained his post as Finance Minister.

The Cabinet line-up also includes junior ministers, called Ministers of State, but none of these offices are specifically provided for in the Constitution. The Constitution does, however, provide specifically for the appointment of Parliamentary Secretaries and Permanent Secretaries. Under Article 31(1), the President, acting on the Prime Minister's advice, may appoint 'Parliamentary Secretaries from among the Members of Parliament to assist Ministers in the discharge of their duties and functions'.

Article 34(1) mandates that there shall be one or more Permanent Secretaries for each ministry. These Permanent Secretaries are senior civil servants whose job is to 'exercise supervision over the department or departments to which he is allocated' under the minister's general direction and control. Like all other key appointments, Permanent Secretaries are appointed by the President acting on the Prime Minister's advice. However, the choice of candidates is limited to a list of names submitted by the Public Service Commission. Unlike junior ministers

---

[3] Goh Chok Tong, Speech on Second Reading of Constitution (Amendment) Bill *Singapore Parliamentary Reports* 29 Mar 1990, vol 55, col 1016.

and Parliamentary Secretaries, the Permanent Secretary is not a political appointee. This senior official remains in office regardless of the change in his political masters; hence the term 'permanent'. However, the Prime Minister is vested with the power to determine where each Permanent Secretary is allocated.

IV. UNIQUE FEATURES OF SINGAPORE'S CABINET

Although the structure of Singapore's Cabinet follows closely that of the United Kingdom, it has some unique features. Since 1980, the Cabinet has included a *Minister Without Portfolio* who was also secretary-general of the National Trades Union Congress (NTUC). The history of how this unique post came about goes back to 1951 when, with the backing of the British authorities, a federation of trade unions known as the Singapore Trades Union Congress (STUC) was established. The STUC comprised unions of all political stripes and in 1961, it split into the NTUC, which supported the PAP, and the Singapore Association of Trade Unions (SATU), which supported the opposition Barisan Sosialis. SATU collapsed and was deregistered two years later after most of the Barisan leaders were preventively detained under the Internal Security Act in Operation Coldstore, leaving the NTUC as the sole federation of trade unions in Singapore.

The NTUC's support for the PAP was made possible by the close personal alliance between the PAP's Lee Kuan Yew and CV Devan Nair, the NTUC's powerful secretary-general. In 1968, after the PAP won every single seat in the general election, Parliament amended the Industrial Relations Act to severely restrict workers' rights to strike. The following year, after being warned by Finance Minister Goh Keng Swee to change its attitude towards employers, the NTUC adopted a cooperative approach towards employers. In 1980, after the PAP once again won all the seats in the 1980 General Election, Prime Minister Lee Kuan Yew expressed concern that the personal alliance he had forged with Devan Nair might not flow naturally to the new generation of leaders of both the PAP and the NTUC. He then proposed formalising ties between the party and the Congress. In June 1980, a special PAP-NTUC Liaison Committee was established and NTUC secretary-general Lim Chee Onn—who was also MP for Bukit Merah— was appointed Minister without Portfolio in the Cabinet. Lim left the cabinet abruptly in 1983 and was succeeded by Ong Teng Cheong who later became Deputy Prime Minister and then President.

Another oddity in the Cabinet since 1988 has been the post of *Senior Minister in the Prime Minister's Office*. This post was first occupied by the former Foreign Minister, S Rajaratnam (1915–2005) from 1988 to 1991. It then went to two successive prime ministers: Lee Kuan Yew from 1991 to 2004; and Goh Chok Tong from 2004 to 2011. When Goh stepped down from this position, he was given the post of Emeritus Senior Minister. It is an honorary title carrying neither ministerial power nor responsibility.

When he became Singapore's third Prime Minister, Lee Hsien Loong created yet another new Cabinet post, that of *Minister Mentor* for Lee Kuan Yew, who occupied this post from 2004 to 2011. Unlike the Emeritus Senior Minister, the Minister Mentor—whose main responsibility was to mentor the Cabinet and use his considerable status to help solve issues—was a ranking minister of the Cabinet, and drew a full ministerial salary.

V. MINISTERIAL SALARIES

The salaries of government ministers is not constitutionally guaranteed but provided for by annual supply bills. Singapore's ministers are the highest paid politicians in the world; the computation of their salaries and bonuses has, since 1994, been the subject of intense and divisive debate. In October 1994, the government issued a White Paper entitled *Competitive Salaries for Competent and Honest Government: Benchmarks for Ministers & Senior Public Officers*.[4]

The paper proposed pegging the salaries of ministers and civil servants at two-thirds of the average earned income of the top four earners in six professions (accounting, banking, engineering, law, local manufacturing and multi-national corporations). These professions were identified as those in which its top earners had the kind of general management skills ministers would also possess. At the same time, by pegging it to only two-thirds of the average, the one-third 'discount' symbolised the 'sacrifice' involved in a person becoming a minister.

[4] Cmd 13, 1994.

Controversial though this proposal was, it was approved by Parliament in November 1994. Over the next two decades, ministerial salaries became one of the most hotly debated topics in Parliament and in the coffeshops. Ministerial salaries rose steadily over the years, peaking in 2007 when the Prime Minister earned S$3.1 million per annum. In years when economic performance was poor, ministerial salaries dipped accordingly. For example, during the economic crisis of 2008–09, ministerial salaries dropped an average of 22 per cent.

High ministerial salaries became a major election issue in the 2011 General Election. Having successfully commoditised the public service and government, the executive bore the brunt of the public's displeasure when essential services were found wanting. Forced to accept these high salaries, the electorate raised their expectations of their ministers and expected top performance for top dollar. And when they thought things went wrong, the government got all the blame and paid for it in votes. Following the 2011 General Election, the Prime Minister appointed the Committee to Review Ministerial Salaries, which recommended an overall lowering of salaries by as much as 31 per cent.

VI. CODE OF CONDUCT FOR MINISTERS

Cabinet ministers are not allowed to hold any 'office of profit'[5] or be actively engaged in any commercial enterprise. One of the planks upon which the PAP was initially elected was its incorruptibility. The party adopted an all-white party uniform to visually demonstrate their commitment to clean government. Indeed, one of the first pieces of legislation passed by the PAP Government after winning power in 1959 was a major amendment to the Prevention of Corruption Ordinance of 1937. In moving the bill, Home Affairs Minister Ong Pang Boon explained the rationale:

This Government has, during the first eight months of its period of office, given ample proof of its dedication of purpose, its honesty of action and

---

[5] Under Art 2 of the Constitution, 'office of profit' is 'any whole time office in the public service' except for the offices of President, Prime Minister, Chief Justice, Speaker, Deputy Speaker, Minister, Parliamentary Secretary, Political Secretary, Member of Parliament, Ambassador and High Commissioner.

its abhorrence of corruption. Its civil service is on the whole a well-trained, efficient and honest one and compares favourably in these respects with those of other countries in this part of the world. But it would be dishonest to deny that corruption does not exist and that there is no problem of corruption in the public services. Although it may not be so rife as to create public alarm and despondency, yet it nevertheless calls for unceasing vigilance and all possible remedial measures.

Corruption on the part, of some must not be allowed to smirch the good name of the present Government and the large majority of its civil servants. Therefore, this Government is determined to take all possible steps to see that all necessary legislative and administrative measures are taken to reduce the opportunities of corruption, to make its detection easier and to deter and punish severely those who are susceptible to it and engage in it shamelessly.[6]

The Prevention of Corruption Act 1960 gave wide-ranging powers to the Corrupt Practices Investigation Bureau (CPIB), a department of the Attorney-General's Chambers that had been established in 1952.[7] Significantly, all offences under the Act were made seizable offences, thus enabling the CPIB to 'deal with offenders more speedily and effectively', including the investigation of 'any bank account, share account or purchase account' of any suspect.[8] Most significantly, the CPIB was placed directly under the control of the Prime Minister's Office so that even Cabinet ministers could be investigated for corruption. And if the Prime Minister himself is to be investigated, the Director of CPIB may do so with the concurrence of the President.

This tough legislation further buttressed a *Code of Conduct for Ministers* which had been in place since 1954. This Code, which was based on British practice, was introduced in the run-up to the 1955 General Election in which the first elected government of Singapore would assume power. This Code was revised in 1979 and then again in 2005. It provides rules governing the participation of ministers in business and other professional capacities and requires ministers to make full disclosure of their private interests, directorships, partnerships and other

---

[6] Ong Pang Boon, Second Reading, Prevention of Corruption Bill *Singapore Legislative Assembly Debates* 13 Feb 1960, vol 12, cols 376–77.
[7] On the fight against corruption, see JST Quah, *Combating Corruption Singapore-Style: Lessons for Other Asian Countries*, Maryland Series in Contemporary Asia No 2, 189 (Baltimore, University of Maryland School of Law, 2007).
[8] Ong Pang Boon (n 6) at col 379.

appointments to the President. At the same time, ministers are enjoined to exercise great care to avoid conflict of interests in the conduct of their financial affairs; not to use their influence on civil servants; and to avoid accepting gifts that would place them in a position of obligation to the giver. In May 2011, shortly after the general election, Prime Minister Lee Hsien Loong reiterated the importance of rectitude and prudence in the conduct of public affairs in an open letter to all PAP MPs. None of this is legally binding but does establish benchmarks of political behaviour that are regarded as practically binding in the same way as a convention in the United Kingdom. It was even suggested by one academic that the Code be made law.[9]

VII. POLICY FORMULATION, DECISION-MAKING AND COLLECTIVE RESPONSIBILITY

Cabinets make decisions affecting all aspects of the political life of the country. So long as the ruling party maintains its majority in Parliament, the Cabinet can practically do anything it wants—declare war, make treaties, raise taxes, make laws and so on. As Walter Bagehot noted in his classic book *The English Constitution*, the efficiency of British government lay in the 'close union and nearly complete fusion of the executive and legislative powers' and this is certainly the case in Singapore.

Under Article 28(1), the Cabinet can only be summoned by the Prime Minister, and the Prime Minister must, as far as possible, 'attend and preside at meetings of the Cabinet'. If the Prime Minister is indisposed or is overseas, he may appoint another minister to preside in his place. Under Article 29, all proceedings of the Cabinet are confidential and are valid even if some unauthorised person took part in its proceedings or voted at the meeting.

Before decisions are taken at Cabinet level, a process of policy formulation is set in motion. Typically, key decision-makers identify issues and problems, analyse their causes and formulate solutions for an effective response. In Singapore, most public policies are formulated by the Cabinet. Article 24 of the Constitution provides that 'Cabinet shall have the general direction and control of the Government'. This means that

---

[9] See G Koh, 'Made codes of conduct law' *The Straits Times* 15 Jul 2005, at 31.

each minister has control over and direction of the civil servants and staff in his ministry. Oftentimes, the ministry staff initiate the policy-making process by highlighting issues and problems to the minister in charge. These issues and problems are then discussed and ironed out at Cabinet meetings.

Outside the Cabinet, policies may also be formulated by civil servants, but this is rare. Cabinet ministers typically meet weekly. Prior to their full Cabinet meetings, they attend pre-Cabinet meetings which are informal lunchtime sessions preceding full Cabinet meetings. It appears that it is at the pre-Cabinet meetings that some kind of consensus building takes place among the inner circle and key decision-makers. Recently, it was publicly acknowledged that when Goh Chok Tong was Prime Minister, he kept Lee Kuan Yew out of the pre-Cabinet meetings.

Whatever decisions are taken at Cabinet, all ministers are collectively responsible to Parliament.[10] This means that once the Cabinet makes a decision, every member of that Cabinet is bound by it and held personally responsible for it. He or she must also support and defend it in public even if he or she disagrees personally with it. Thus, if a policy proves unsuccessful or highly unpopular with Parliament, the entire Cabinet must resign. While this principle of collective responsibility is mandated under the Constitution, there has never been an occasion of it being put to test. This is possibly due to two reasons. The first is the fact that a single party—in this case, the PAP—controls almost all seats in Parliament. Since the Cabinet is made up of the most senior and important members of the party, the MPs are not likely to want to have them removed. Second, the strict party discipline imposed by the party Whip ensures that no one votes against the government line anyway.

VIII. THE ATTORNEY-GENERAL

The office of the Attorney-General[11] is typically considered part of the executive arm of government. The office originated in England in medieval times and the term came into use in 1461. By the mid-1500s, the Attorney-General was chief legal advisor to the Crown. Singapore's

---

[10] Constitution of the Republic of Singapore, Art 24(2).
[11] See Tan Boon Teik, 'The Attorney-General' (1988) 2 *Malayan Law Journal* lviii.

first Attorney-General was appointed in 1867 after the Straits Settlements was transferred to the control of the Colonial Office in London. Sir Thomas Braddell, a practising lawyer was appointed Attorney-General of the Straits Settlements and served until 1883. Throughout this period, Braddell was allowed to continue legal practice while serving as Attorney-General. This privilege was abolished in 1893. Unlike his British counterpart, the Attorney-General in Singapore is not a political appointee. The Attorney-General's office is established under Article 35(1) of the Constitution, and he or she is appointed by the President acting in his discretion provided he concurs with the advice of the Prime Minister. Except in the event of the death of the incumbent Attorney-General, the Prime Minister is duty-bound to consult the outgoing Attorney-General, the Chief Justice and the Chairman of the Public Service Commission.[12]

The Attorney-General does not enjoy the same security of tenure as the judges of the Supreme Court as he may be appointed for a specified period.[13] Since 2006, appointments of the Attorneys-General in Singapore have been for brief two-year periods. However, the Attorney-General may only be removed from office by the President provided that the President, acting in his discretion, concurs with the Prime Minister's advice. The Prime Minister may not tender such advice except when the Attorney-General is, by reason of infirmity of body or mind or any other cause, unable to discharge the functions of his office; or for misbehaviour. And even in respect of such occasions, the Prime Minister must seek the concurrence of a special tribunal comprising the Chief Justice and two judges of the Supreme Court convened by the Chief Justice for this specific purpose.[14]

The Attorney-General, like his ancient counterpart, acts as the government's principal legal advisor. Article 38(7) makes it the Attorney-General's duty 'to advise the Government on such legal matters and to perform such other duties of a legal character, as may from time to time be referred or assigned to him by the President or the Cabinet'. However, the Attorney-General is also the Public Prosecutor and is responsible for instituting, conducting and discontinuing any proceedings for any offence.[15] His remuneration is not constitutionally protected from diminution though he is paid out of the Consolidated

---

[12] Constitution of the Republic of Singapore, Art 35(2).
[13] ibid, Art 35(4).
[14] ibid, Art 35(6)(a).
[15] ibid, Art 35(8).

Fund.[16] In the exercise of his prosecutorial function, the Attorney-General is independent and is not subject to control by the government. Even so, the Attorney-General's prosecutorial discretion is subject to review by the courts. In *Ramalingam Ravinthran v Attorney General*,[17] the Court of Appeal considered the limits of the Attorney-General's prosecutorial discretion and held:

> Although the courts are entitled to presume that the prosecutorial power has been properly exercised in a particular case, its exercise is nevertheless subject to legal limits. As a requirement of the rule of law, all legal powers are subject to limits ... An inherent limitation on the prosecutorial power is that it may not be exercised arbitrarily, and may only be used for the purpose for which it was granted and not for any extraneous purpose.
>
> ...
>
> The Attorney-General is the custodian of the prosecutorial power. He uses it to enforce the criminal law not for its own sake, but for the greater good of society, ie, to maintain law and order as well as to uphold the rule of law. Offences are committed by all kinds of people in all kinds of circumstances. It is not the policy of the law under our legal system that all offenders must be prosecuted, regardless of the circumstances in which they have committed offences. Furthermore, not all offences are provable in a court of law. It is not necessarily in the public interest that every offender must be prosecuted, or that an offender must be prosecuted for the most serious possible offence available in the statute book. Conversely, while the public interest does not require the Attorney-General to prosecute any and all persons who may be guilty of a crime, he cannot decide at his own whim and fancy who should or should not be prosecuted, and what offence or offences a particular offender should be prosecuted for. The Attorney-General's final decision will be constrained by what the public interest requires.[18]

IX. THE EXECUTIVE: AN ELECTED DICTATORSHIP?

With so much power centred on the Prime Minister and Cabinet, what is there to prevent them from abusing it? The theory of the separation of powers which we discussed earlier requires that as far as possible,

---

[16] ibid, Art 35(10).
[17] [2012] 2 SLR 49.
[18] ibid, at 74–75.

legislative and executive power should repose in two different and distinct bodies. In the Westminster parliamentary system of government, the distinction between the legislative and executive branches of government is blurred by the combination of two factors: (a) Prime Minister and Cabinet being drawn from members of Parliament; and (b) strict party discipline which requires members of the same political party to vote according to party lines.

This situation is exacerbated by the fact that since 1968, there has never been any real opposition in the Singapore Parliament. From 1968 to 1981, the PAP held every single seat in Parliament. Since 1981, there has, at most, been only seven elected opposition politicians at any one time. In a Parliament of 87 members, this makes hardly a dent on the ruling party's majority in the House. As such, the idea that the Prime Minister and Cabinet are answerable to Parliament is tenuous at best since Parliament has little real power to shape or change a decision already made by the Cabinet.

In other countries, where there is a substantial opposition, it will be much more difficult for the Cabinet to secure the majority it needs in Parliament to push its political agenda forward. Outside these constitutionally prescribed control mechanisms, Cabinets in other countries, such as Great Britain are subject to checks and balances through the actions of pressure or special interest groups as well as a critical press. These external checks are practically absent in Singapore and there is really little to check the executive's power on a daily basis. The only way the Cabinet and government can be controlled is through the ballot box, but even that is illusory if there is little chance of displacing the incumbent party.

FURTHER READING

PN Pillai & KYL Tan, 'Settling Into the Foundations: Development of Singapore's Constitutional System 1965-1985' in KS Sandhu & P Wheatley (eds), *Management of Success: The Moulding of Modern Singapore* (Singapore, Institute of Southeast Asian Studies, 1989) 647–68.

KYL Tan, 'Singapore: A Statist Legal Laboratory' in A Black & G Bell (eds), *Law and Legal Systems of Asia* (Melbourne, Cambridge University Press, 2011) 330–71.

WEBSITES

www.pmo.gov.sg/content/pmosite/home.html (official website of the Prime Minister's Office)

www.cabinet.gov.sg/content/cabinet/index.html (official website of the Singapore Cabinet)

https://app.agc.gov.sg/ (official website of the Attorney-General's Chambers)

6

The Elected President

————◆◆◆————

Introduction – Singapore's Presidential Executive: A Short
History – The President's Traditional Discretionary Powers
– The Elected President – The Elected President Scheme in
1991 – Post-1991 Changes – 'Loans' under Article 144(1) – The
President Exercises his Discretion – Some Unique Aspects of
the Presidency

I. INTRODUCTION

UNTIL 1991 SINGAPORE had a head of state with nominal
powers. Much like the Queen in England—who reigns but
does not rule—the President had few real discretionary powers. All powers were to be exercised in the name of the President, on
behalf of the state, on the advice of the Prime Minister and his Cabinet.
Real power lay in in the hands of Prime Minister and his Cabinet. The
office was thus largely titular and ceremonial. This quirk was an accident
of history since the English monarch did in fact have much real power
before the Glorious Revolution of 1688. Indeed, many of these former
British colonies soon abandoned the Westminster model in favour of a
limited presidential executive where the head of government and head
of state reposed in a single office, and where the President, as head of
government, wielded more effective power.

Among post-colonial states, Singapore was unique in refusing to follow this trend. From independence in 1965 to 1991, Singapore's non-
executive President had very limited powers, similar to that of other
ceremonial heads of state. This changed in 1991, when a major constitutional amendment was effected to transform the post of President
into an elected one. The sweeping changes to the presidency were the
last in the line of constitutional changes that the PAP Government put

in place following the loss of the Anson constituency to the Workers' Party in 1981. All the changes—mainly to the legislature, and then to the presidency—were designed to forestall a 'freak election result' that would displace the PAP as Singapore's government.

II. SINGAPORE'S PRESIDENTIAL EXECUTIVE: A SHORT HISTORY[1]

During the colonial era, Singapore's chief executive was the Governor. He was appointed by the Crown and acted on its behalf. In 1959, when Singapore was granted self-governing status, the office of the Governor was transformed into that of the Yang di-Pertuan Negara (Malay for 'Head of State'). Like the Governor, the Yang di-Pertuan Negara was appointed by the Queen, but only after consultation with the government.

During the transition from colony to self-governing state, Singapore's last British Governor, Sir William Goode (1907–87), became the first Yang di-Pertuan Negara, and held this office for six months before becoming the first United Kingdom High Commissioner. To complete the transition, Goode resigned his office as Yang di-Pertuan Negara and Yusof bin Ishak (1910–70), a former journalist, succeeded him to the post. He thus became the first and only Malayan-born Yang di-Pertuan Negara of Singapore. When Singapore joined the Federation of Malaysia in 1963, Yusof remained as Yang di-Pertuan Negara and upon Singapore's independence in 1965, the post of Yang di-Pertuan Negara was abolished and replaced by the office of President.

Yusof was Singapore's first President. He died in office in 1970 and was succeeded by world-renowned Eurasian gynaecologist Benjamin Henry Sheares (1907–81) who also died in office in 1981. Singapore's third President was former trade unionist CV Devan Nair (1923–2005), who resigned in 1985 under a cloud and was replaced by former journalist Wee Kim Wee (1915–2005) who was President from 1986 to 1993. Wee was Singapore's last non-executive president and Singapore's first 'elected' president. In 1993, the first ever presidential election

---

[1] On the evolution of the office of the President, see Huang Jianli, 'The Head of State in Singapore: A Historical Perspective' in KYL Tan & Lam Peng Er (eds), *Managing Political Change: The Elected Presidency* (London, Routledge, 1997) 9–51.

was held and former unionist and Deputy Prime Minister Ong Teng Cheong (1936–2002) won the election. When Ong stepped down at the end of his six-year term in 1999, former senior civil servant SR Nathan (b 1924) 'won' the election as the sole candidate in the election. Nathan served two terms as President and stepped down in 2011 when former Cabinet Minister, Tony Tan Keng Yam (b 1940) narrowly won a hotly contested election. We will consider the landmark 2011 elections in greater detail below.

III. THE PRESIDENT'S TRADITIONAL DISCRETIONARY POWERS

The President's 'traditional' discretionary powers are those that existed prior to the 1991 amendments, ie discretion in: (a) the appointment and dismissal of the Prime Minister; (b) dissolution of Parliament; and (c) during a national emergency.

A. Appointment and Dismissal of the Prime Minister

Article 25(1) provides that the President

> shall appoint as Prime Minister a Member of Parliament who in his judg-ment is likely to command the confidence of the majority of the Members of Parliament, and shall, acting in accordance with the advice of the Prime Minister, appoint other Ministers from among the Members of Parliament.

The key words here—*in his judgment*—indicate the exercise of a personal discretion. However, does this mean that the President can act in any way he likes, or must he arrive at his decision in some kind of logical fashion? In this context, how should the President determine whether or not a particular Member of Parliament 'is likely to commend the confidence' of the House.

There is no local case law on this matter, but there is a very interesting Sabah High Court case, *Tun Datu Haji Mustapha bin Datu Harun v Tun Datuk Haji Mohamed Adnan Robert, Yang di-Pertua Negeri Sabah & Datuk Joseph Pairin Kitingan (No 2)*,[2] which may prove instructive. The issue

---

[2] [1986] 2 MLJ 420.

before the court was the legality of the Governor's (Yang di-Pertuan Negeri's) appointment of one Tun Mustapha as Chief Minister of the state after the conclusion of general elections. Justice Tan Chiaw Thong held that the head of state could not:

> [C]onstitutionally exercise or make his judgment on the appointment of a Chief Minister without taking into account the number of elected seats secured by each and every political party and, for that matter, by the independent candidates, in the election. It is clear that, if he omits to take into account the number of seats obtained by any particular political party which participated in the election, it cannot be said that he had exercised or made his judgment under art 6(3) for, if he did so, he would be acting unlawfully and unconstitutionally by ignoring or not complying with the requirement, in particular of art 6(3). In such circumstances, it is equally clear, in my view, that he has made no judgment under art 6(3). In this connection, I see no difference between this situation and the case where the Head of State appoints as Chief Minister a person who is not a member of the Legislative Assembly, contrary to the express requirement of art 6(3).

Juxtaposing the Sabah situation with Singapore's context, it is clear that the President cannot act on his whim in determining who he should appoint as Prime Minister. The appointee must be someone who clearly commands the confidence of the House, and this is determined by taking into account the electoral majorities of the various parties following the general election.

Likewise, under Article 26(1)(b), the President may declare the office of the Prime Minister vacant if he is *satisfied* that the Prime Minister has ceased to command the confidence of Parliament. What does it mean for the head of state to be 'satisfied'?

Again there are no local authorities on the matter, but two different approaches have been adopted by other Commonwealth courts. In the Privy Council decision of *Adegbenro v Akintola*[3] from Nigeria, the Judicial Committee held that 'support' for the Premier could be ascertained by means other than a formal vote on the floor of the legislature. Closer to home, the Sarawak High Court held, in the case of *Stephen Kalong Ningkan v Tun Abang Haji Openg and Tawi Sli*,[4] that support could only be ascertained by a formal vote in the legislature. Interestingly, the

---

[3] [1963] 3 *Weekly Law Reports* 63.
[4] [1966] 2 MLJ 187.

Federal Court—Malaysia's highest court—favoured the Privy Council's interpretation when it considered the Sultan of Perak's exercise of discretion in the appointment of a Chief Minister in the case of *Dato' Seri Ir Hj Mohammad Nizar bin Jamaluddin v Dato' Seri Dr Zambry bin Abdul Kadir (Attorney General, intervener).*[5]

B. Proroguing and Dissolving Parliament

Article 65(1) of the Constitution provides that the President may prorogue Parliament by proclamation in the *Gazette*. It further provides that if at any time the office of Prime Minister is vacant, the President shall dissolve Parliament

> as soon as he is satisfied, acting in his discretion, that a reasonable period has elapsed since that office was last vacated and that there is no Member of Parliament likely to command the confidence of a majority of the Members

The wording of Article 65 makes it clear that the President has a personal discretion in determining whether or not the office of Prime Minister has been vacated and whether any Member of Parliament is likely to command the confidence of the majority in the legislature. Once he makes this determination, he must dissolve Parliament to pave the way for general elections.

Under Article 65(3), the President may also dissolve Parliament if the Prime Minister advises him to do so, but he must first be 'satisfied that, in tendering that advice, the Prime Minister commands the confidence of a majority of the Members of Parliament'. However, the President cannot exercise a discretion to dissolve Parliament after he has notice of a motion proposing an inquiry into his own conduct under Article 22L(3). This is to prevent the President from dissolving Parliament to pre-empt any inquiry into his capabilities or any offences he may have committed in his capacity as President. Naturally, if Parliament passes a resolution requesting the President to dissolve Parliament, he must do so.

---

[5] [2010] 2 MLJ 285. See A Harding, *The Constitution of Malaysia: A Contextual Analysis* (Oxford, Hart Publishing, 2012) ch 4.

C. Discretion during an Emergency

Part XII of the Constitution, entitled 'Special Powers Against Subversion and Emergency Powers', contains provisions to deal with situations warranting the declaration of a national emergency. Under Article 150 of the Constitution, a state of grave emergency exists if 'the security or economic life of Singapore is threatened'. This section further provides that if the President is 'satisfied' that such an emergency exists, he may issue a Proclamation of Emergency. This can happen whether Parliament is sitting or not. If Parliament is not sitting (ie prorogued), the President is duty-bound to summon Parliament 'as soon as practicable' and 'may, until Parliament is sitting, promulgate ordinances having the force of law, if satisfied that immediate action is required' (Article 150(2)). The key issues here concern the nature of the President's discretion, its application, and whether the court may judicially review the exercise of this discretion.

D. Justiciability of the President's Discretion

The President's exercise of discretion may be legally challenged in court. In the case of *Yong Vui Kong v AG*,[6] the Court of Appeal had occasion to consider the nature of the President's discretion with respect to the granting of pardons to death-row prisoners. The Court made several important observations. First, it rejected the appellant's argument that the President could act in his *personal discretion* under the Article 22P pardoning powers; and second, it held that the President's discretionary power was justiciable. With respect to the justiciability point, the Court considered authorities from the United Kingdom, Caribbean, Canada, Australia, New Zealand, India, Hong Kong and Malaysia and concluded that:

> Given that the clemency power is a constitutional power vested exclusively in the Executive, it is not justiciable on the merits, firstly, on the basis of the doctrine of separation of powers ... and, secondly, on the basis of established administrative law principles ... In our local context, this entails that, assuming the clemency power is exercised in accordance with law, the merits

---

[6] [2011] 2 SLR 1189; [2011] SGCA 9.

of the clemency decision made will fall outside the purview of our courts. Our courts cannot look into whether a clemency decision is wise or foolish, harsh or kind; neither can they substitute their own decision for the clemency decision made by the President simply because they disagree with the President's view on the matter. ...

However, this conclusion—viz, that the merits of a clemency decision are not reviewable by our courts—does not, in my view, entail that the clemency power in our constitutional context is therefore an 'extra-legal' power in the sense of being a power beyond any legal constraints or restraints. ...

... In *Chng Suan Tze*, this court formulated the *Chng Suan Tze* principle as follows:

> In our view, the notion of a subjective or unfettered discretion is contrary to the rule of law. All power has legal limits and the rule of law demands that the courts should be able to examine the exercise of discretionary power.

More accurately stated, the principle is that 'all legal powers ... have legal limits[;] [t]he notion of a subjective or unfettered discretion is contrary to the rule of law'[7]

However, there are several instances in which the President's discretion cannot be challenged. In other words, it is non-justiciable. In *Lee Mau Seng v Minister for Home Affairs*,[8] the High Court was asked to consider the President's exercise of discretion under section 8(1) of the Internal Security Act. This section provides that the President may order a person to be detained without trial if he is 'satisfied' it is necessary to prevent that person 'from acting in any manner prejudicial to the security of Singapore or any part thereof or to the maintenance of public order or essential services therein'. Chief Justice Wee Chong Jin held that the words in section 8(1) were not intended to give the President a personal discretion but that the President should act according to the Cabinet's advice. This was because the power to preventively detain someone without trial is a legislative power and it was inconceivable that Parliament intended to confer an arbitrary power on a constitutional head of state.

Under section 8B(2) of the Internal Security Act, there can be no judicial review 'of any act done or decision made by the President or

---

[7] [2011] 2 SLR 1189, at 1232–33.
[8] [1970–1971] SLR(R) 135; [1971] 2 MLJ 137.

the Minister' under the Act except on questions 'relating to compliance with any procedural requirement of this Act governing such act or decision'. Furthermore section 8B(1) froze the courts' interpretation of the President's 'satisfaction' to that which applied on 13 July 1971—the date of the decision in *Lee Mau Seng's* case—and estopped the courts from referring to the decisions of any other Commonwealth country in respect of the principles of judicial review. It should be noted that the High Court in *Lee Mau Seng's* case further held that the court could not examine the grounds and allegations of fact supplied to the detainee to determine 'whether or not some or all of them are so vague, unintelligible or indefinite as to be insufficient' to enable the detainee to make an effective representation against the order of detention.

IV. THE ELECTED PRESIDENT

In 1984, then-Prime Minister Lee Kuan Yew mooted the idea of converting the office of President into an elected one.[9] Having lost a single seat in the Anson constituency by-election, Lee worried incessantly about what would happen to Singapore if, in a 'freak election', an opposition party displaced the ruling PAP as its government. Reflecting on this constitutional change in 2011, Lee said:

> I'm running a system where I'm hoping if the PAP loses, not everything will be lost for Singapore. And if you change all the permanent secretaries, military chiefs, commissioner of police, heads of statutory boards, then you'll ruin the system. For five years, the President can prevent that. And our past reserves cannot be raided. But if you're clever enough and you can win a second term with a two-thirds majority, you can change the constitution and unscramble the double-key safeguard. … So with these safeguards, it may be possible to salvage the situation for Singapore if it goes wrong in one or two elections. If we don't have this safety net, the country can go down after one freak election. It is a risk Singapore cannot afford to take.[10]

---

[9] See KYL Tan, 'The Presidency in Singapore: Constitutional Developments' in KYL Tan & Lam Peng Er (eds), *Managing Political Change: The Elected Presidency* (London, Routledge, 1997) 51–87.

[10] Han Fook Kwang et al, *Lee Kuan Yew: Hard Truths to Keep Singapore Going* (Singapore, Straits Times Press, 2011), at 73.

In July 1988, just two months before the general election, Deputy Prime Minister Goh Chok Tong released the first White Paper on the elected presidency. In August 1990, a second White Paper outlining the specific proposals was issued with an accompanying Constitution Amendment Bill. Following lengthy debates in Parliament, a select committee was appointed. Several amendments were made to the original bill and it was finally passed into law in January 1991.

A. The Rationale and the Initial Proposals

The proposal offered several reasons why an elected presidency was necessary. The first was the fear of popular vote-buying that would potentially bankrupt the state. This should not happen to Singapore which had the fortune of having a responsible government that had accumulated over US$30 billion in national reserves. If a future irresponsible government were elected into office, the temptation to raid Singapore's coffers would be great and if succumbed to, would lead to financial ruin. The White Paper also identified Singapore's public service as a cornerstone of its success and highlighted the importance of preserving the civil service's integrity and competence. If the wrong people were appointed through nepotism and corruption, Singapore would also suffer. As nothing in the Constitution prevented any government from squandering all of Singapore's reserves nor the irresponsible appointment of key civil servants, a new institution had to be created to act as a check and as a second key to the nation's coffers.

In designing a constitutional safeguard, the White Paper also found several considerations vital. First, it determined that the parliamentary system of government should be preserved and the Prime Minister and his Cabinet should retain governmental initiative. Second, the safeguard mechanism should be able to act quickly to avert a potentially disastrous situation. Third, the person exercising this power had to have strong moral authority gained through an election and must be a person with previous ministerial, high executive or administrative experience to 'balance the demands of political expediency and the public interest'; and finally the Constitution should require presidential candidates to have such experience and qualities.

The government considered several options, such as

creating an upper legislative body, reposing the power of the veto in the Presidential Council for Minority Rights or some other body analogous to the Federal Reserve Board, or requiring decisions on financial assets to be subject to the approval of the electorate in a referendum

but found them unsuitable. It was thus decided to transform the office of President into an elected one with the President holding the 'second key' to the nation's financial reserves. His powers were to be confined to two specific areas—government spending and the appointment of key posts in the public service.

B. The Second White Paper

In the Second White Paper issued in 1991, several additional considerations were brought into play. First, the President would be required to check against possible executive abuse of power in preventive detention cases under the Internal Security Act. Second, the President's discretion was extended to the making of prohibition orders under the Maintenance of Religious Harmony Act; and third, in the interests of upholding the integrity of the Cabinet, the Director of the Corrupt Practices Investigation Bureau was to report directly to the President.

A fourth change related to the President's advisory panel. The original 'Presidential Committee for the Protection of Reserves' was renamed Council for Presidential Advisors (CPA) and would comprise six members instead of the original five. The President, the Chairman of the Public Service Commission and the Prime Minister would nominate two members each. In addition, the role of Council of Presidential Advisors was defined as giving the President advice on all matters in which he had discretionary powers, although the President was legally obliged to consult the Council only on questions involving the budgets of the government, statutory boards and key government companies. Finally, a new provision allowed Parliament to override the presidential veto. In addition to these changes, other provisions relating to the qualification and disqualification of candidates, terms of office, specific government statutory boards and companies to be included under the President's purview were specifically spelled out.

Parliament debated the bill vociferously during the Second Reading before committing it to select committee. The select committee's report was presented to Parliament on 18 December 1990. A month later, the bill and its amendments were passed into law.

V. THE ELECTED PRESIDENT SCHEME IN 1991

The creation of an elected presidency in Singapore entailed a major amendment to the Constitution. The original length of the Constitution grew by a third and the provisions relating to the presidency are extremely convoluted and complex. The final scheme that emerged in 1991 placed tremendous emphasis on the qualifications of candidates. Beyond being a Singapore citizen, the presidential candidate had to be at least 45 years old, not a member of a political party on the date of nomination, resident in Singapore for at least 10 years and satisfy the Presidential Elections Committee (PEC) that 'he is a person of integrity, good character and reputation', and has for a period of not less than three years, held office in one of numerous capacities laid down under Article 19(2)(g).

Specifically, these offices are: Minister; Chief Justice; Speaker; Attorney-General; Chairman of the Public Service Commission; Auditor-General; Permanent Secretary; chairman or chief executive officer of one of the statutory boards referred to in Article 22A read with Schedule 5 (viz Board of Commissioners of Currency, Singapore, Central Provident Fund Board, Housing and Development Board, Jurong Town Corporation, Monetary Authority of Singapore, and the Post Office Savings Bank of Singapore); chairman of the board of directors or chief executive officer of a company incorporated or registered under the Companies Act with a paid-up capital of at least S$100 million or its equivalent in foreign currency; or in any other similar or comparable position of seniority and responsibility in any other organisation or department of equivalent size or complexity in the public or private sector which, in the opinion of the PEC, has given him such experience and ability in administering and managing financial affairs as to enable him to carry out effectively the functions and duties of the office of the President.

A. Presidential Elections

Article 17(2) of the Constitution provides that the President 'shall be elected by the citizens of Singapore in accordance with any law made by the Legislature'; in this case, the Presidential Elections Act 1991. Under the Act, elections will be held within six months after the office of the President becomes vacant, but not more than three months before the expiration of the incumbent's term. After the notice of election and at least two clear days before nomination day, each candidate must apply to the PEC for a certificate stating that the PEC is satisfied that he is a qualified candidate under Article 19 of the Constitution. If there is only one candidate in a presidential election, that candidate will be declared elected as President (Presidential Elections Act, section 15).

In the first presidential election in 1993, Ong Teng Cheong defeated Chua Kim Yeow for the post. However, in the 1993 and 1999 elections, there was only one candidate—SR Nathan—who was duly declared elected as President on both occasions.

The 2011 presidential election was the most hard-fought and competitive election in the institution's history. For the first time, four candidates were qualified to stand in the election. Two of them—both former PAP stalwarts—were well known to the public. Dr Tony Tan Keng Yam, a former Deputy Prime Minister and chairman of the powerful Singapore Press Holdings group, was the government's preferred candidate. His former PAP colleague, Dr Tan Cheng Bock was a popular veteran politician well known for his vocal and critical views. The third candidate was Tan Jee Say, a former senior civil servant and hedge fund manager who had just contested the general election as a candidate of the Singapore Democratic Party. The fourth candidate, Tan Kin Lian, was a well-known figure in corporate circles, having been the long-time chief of NTUC Income, one of Singapore's largest insurance companies.

Coming hot on the heels of the 2011 General Election—which was keenly fought and which saw the PAP suffer its biggest loss since 1963—campaigning for the presidential election was highly politicised. And unlike past elections, which were generally sedate, dignified affairs, the candidates campaigned vigorously, using all media platforms to push their messages through. Various civic groups and opposition political parties nailed their colours to the mast. At least two of the candidates urged voters to elect them as alternatives to Parliament, and claimed extra-constitutional powers. This prompted the Law Minister to explain and clarify the constitutional powers of the President. At the end of nine-day campaign, Tony Tan Keng Yam defeated Tan Cheng Bock by just over 7000 votes. Tony Tan obtained 35.2 per cent of the vote, compared to Tan Cheng Bock's 34.85 per cent. Coming in third in the election was Tan Jee Say, and Tan Kin Lian, who scored just 4.91 per cent of the vote, lost his election deposit.

Tony Tan's narrow win and the fact that he secured only 35.2 per cent of the popular vote led many to question his legitimacy to check Parliament. The original idea behind having the President elected was to ensure that he had moral authority to refuse concurrence with the legislature which had the general mandate of the voting public.

B. Term of Office, Powers and Immunities

The President's term of office is six years. Under Article 21 of the Constitution, he must exercise his functions on the advice of the Cabinet or of a minister acting under the authority of the Cabinet. The President retained his old discretionary powers in the appointment of the Prime Minister, and withholding consent to a request for the dissolution of Parliament. In addition to these traditional powers, the President may act in his personal discretion in withholding his concurrence to: (a) bills that circumvent or curtail his powers; (b) guarantees given or loans raised by the government; (c) borrowings that would lead to a drawing down of Singapore's reserves; (d) appointments of key civil servants; (e) budgets of various statutory boards; (f) the detention or further detention of any person under the Internal Security Act; and (g) the issue of prohibition orders under the Maintenance of Religious Harmony Act.[11]

In addition, the President may consent to investigations undertaken by the Corrupt Practices Investigations Bureau (CPIB) even if the Prime Minister refuses his consent.12 When exercising his discretion, the President is, in some cases, bound to consult the CPA, and in others, he may refer these matters to it for advice. The President is

---

[11] Constitution of the Republic of Singapore, Art 21(2).
[12] ibid, Art 22G.

immune from any court proceedings for anything he does or omits while acting in his official capacity.[13]

C. Removal of the President

Under Article 22L, the President may be removed from office if he 'is permanently incapable of discharging his functions of his office by reason or physical infirmity' or has been found guilty of intentionally violating the Constitution; treason; misconduct or corruption involving the abuse of the powers of his office; or any offence involving fraud, dishonesty or moral turpitude.

To determine whether the President is guilty, a Tribunal appointed by the Chief Justice and consisting of no fewer than five judges of the Supreme Court would be constituted.

Before the President can be removed under Article 22L, 'Prime Minister or not less than one-quarter of the total number of the Members of Parliament' must 'give notice of a motion alleging his unsuitability under the terms of this article'. If the motion has been adopted 'by not less than half of the total number of the Members of Parliament, the Chief Justice must appoint a tribunal to inquire into the allegations against the President. If the Tribunal reports to the Speaker that in its opinion the President is either permanently incapable of discharging his functions or has been guilty of one of the allegations, Parliament 'may by a resolution passed by not less than three-quarters of the total number of the Members of Parliament remove the President from office'. This has never happened. All of Singapore's Presidents, save one, served out their terms of office without incident. Only Singapore's third President, CV Devan Nair, resigned before the end of his first term in office, ostensibly to seek treatment for his alcoholism.

D. Entrenchment of Office

The office of the President is now more tightly entrenched than most other provisions under the Constitution, including Singapore's

---

[13] ibid, Art 22K.

parliamentary system of government, judiciary and fundamental liberties. Article 5(2A) now requires that any bill to amend Articles 17 to 22, and 22A to 22O of the Constitution[14] cannot be passed by Parliament unless it has been supported at a national referendum by not less than two-thirds of the total number of votes cast. As such, provisions relating to the presidency cannot be amended unless a referendum is carried out. Interestingly, the government never brought the new Article 5(2A) into force and it has been held in abeyance since 1991. Some scholars have questioned the way in which these new provisions were introduced, as well as the need to entrench these provisions so tightly in the Constitution.

E. *Constitutional Reference No 1 of 1995*

In early 1995 a problem arose with respect to the interpretation of Article 22H, one of the 'protected provisions' under Article 5(2A). Specifically, Article 22H (as it then read) provided that the President 'may, acting in his discretion' withhold his assent 'to any Bill passed by Parliament (other than a Bill to which Article 5(2A) applies) if the bill provides, directly or indirectly, for the circumvention or curtailment' of his discretionary powers. This problem arose mainly because Article 5(2A) was (and continues to be) held in abeyance and Article 22H (which is operational) refers directly to Article 5(2A). As a result, some provisions relating to the presidency are protected by Article 5(2A) while others are not. However, since Article 5(2A) is not yet operational, the question before the Tribunal was whether the President could exercise his discretion to refuse assent to a bill to amend Article 22H if it circumvented or curtailed his discretionary powers.

In early 1995, President Ong Teng Cheong referred this constitutional question to the Special Tribunal under Article 100. The Special Tribunal ruled that even though Article 5(2A) was not in force, the suspended provision represented Parliament's will and intention that it had become part of the law. As such, the President could not enlarge his personal discretion on account of the fact that Article 5(2A) was not

---

[14] Arts 17 to 22 establish the elected presidency scheme while Arts 22A to 22O set out the President's powers.

yet in force since Article 22H, when enacted, did not confer on the President such a wide discretion.[15]

VI. POST-1991 CHANGES

Since 1991, provisions relating to the elected President have been amended several times. Most of these changes reflect an about-turn in the government's thinking about the President's powers. The first major amendment came in September 1994. Some of more important changes and their implications are dealt with in this section.

A. President to State Reasons for Spending Reserves

The first important amendment, Article 148H, provides that if the President consents to the government drawing down the reserves, he must publish his reasons in the *Gazette*. He must thus publish the rationale for his actions, whether he exercised his presidential veto or not.

B. Transfer of Surpluses

In the 1994 amendment, transfers of surpluses from statutory boards or government companies were deemed not to be a draw on their reserves. In 2004, these provisions were again amended, this time allowing statutory boards and government companies to transfer their surpluses either to the government or to each other without the President's scrutiny. Under the new Article 148I, the government is now permitted to transfer its past reserves to any statutory board or a Schedule 5 government company (at present, only Jurong Town Corporation, the Monetary Authority of Singapore, the Housing and Development Board and the Central Provident Fund Board) without the President's consent.

---

[15] *Constitutional Reference No 1 of 1995* [1995] 1 SLR(R) 803. See Thio Li-ann, 'Working out the Presidency: The Rites of Passage' [1995] *Singapore Journal of Legal Studies* 509; and Chan Sek Keong, 'Working out the Presidency: No Passage of Rights' [1996] *Singapore Journal of Legal Studies* 1.

C. Advisory Capacity of the Supreme Court

A new Article 100 was added in 1994 to establish a Special Tribunal consisting of no fewer than three judges of the Supreme Court. The President may refer to this Tribunal 'for its opinion any question as to the effect of any provision' of the Constitution. The Tribunal is under a duty 'consider and answer the question so referred as soon as may be and in any case not more than 60 days after the date of such reference'. Any dissenting opinions of any judge must accordingly be reflected in the opinion rendered to the President although the majority decision shall be considered the opinion of the Tribunal and shall be pronounced in open court. The opinion is not subject to challenge in any court.

This amendment was significant since an important question had arisen with respect to the interpretation of the President's powers under Article 22H. This was dealt with in *Constitutional Reference No 1 of 1995*. Lee, in moving the amendment, pointed out that unlike in Malaysia, the 'Singapore Constitution does not have any provisions for referring questions of interpretation of the Constitution to the Courts for an advisory ruling'.

D. Reduction of Veto Powers

In 1994, a new Article 151A was inserted. With this change, the President no longer has a veto on 'any defence and security measure'. This is defined as

> any liability or proposed transaction which the Prime Minister and the Minister responsible for defence, on the recommendations of the Permanent Secretary to the Ministry of Defence and the Chief of Defence Force, certify to be necessary for the defence and security of Singapore.

This certificate cannot be challenged in court and is 'conclusive evidence of the matters specified therein'.

This amendment created an uproar in Parliament. Some MPs pointed out that the new provision could be abused by unscrupulous politicians. Nominated MP Walter Woon argued that it would be all too easy to circumvent the safeguards in the Constitution since 'national security' was 'such a wide thing that it would be possible to fit any sort of handouts within the rubric'. However, the government's position was that since the Prime Minister and the Cabinet are responsible for deciding whether the country goes to war, they must have the power to execute the decision, and the country cannot risk a tussle between the Prime Minister and the President over whether spending is necessary for defence and security.

In 1996, a 'deeming provision' was inserted under a new Article 5A(6). This provides that the President will be *deemed* to have assented to a bill 30 days after the bill is presented to him for his assent, if he does nothing. New articles were added to Article 22, 22A and 22C—concerning the President's power to veto appointment of public officers, members of statutory boards and directors of government companies. This change provides that where the President acts contrary to the CPA's recommendation by refusing to make an appointment or refuses to revoke an appointment, Parliament may override the President's decision by passing a resolution of not less than two-thirds majority.

VII. 'LOANS' UNDER ARTICLE 144(1)

In November 1997, a constitutional controversy broke out when it was announced that Singapore was to grant a US$5 billion loan to crisis-hit Indonesia. According to newspaper reports, the decision was made by Prime Minister Goh Chok Tong in consultation with Senior Minister Lee Kuan Yew. The Workers' Party issued a two-page statement alleging that this move ran counter to the Constitution as it violated Article 144(2). The Finance Minister responded by saying that Workers' Party chief, JB Jeyaretnam had 'misread the Constitution'. Attorney General Chan Sek Keong gave a written opinion on the matter and concluded that there was no need to secure the President's assent for such a loan.

The Attorney-General argued that Article 144(1) of the Constitution—which provides that '[n]o guarantee or loan shall be given or raised by the Government' except where the Parliament has so resolved, *and* where the President has concurred—must be read '*reddendo singula singulis,* that is, to render each to each, applying each verb to its appropriate subject'. Thus, the words in Article 144(1) should be read as 'No guarantee shall be given' or 'No loan shall be raised'. Jeyaretnam then offered to refer the matter to the High Court if the state would bear the costs. When his offer was rejected by the government, the matter was dropped and was not pursued in the courts.

Interestingly, the same issue was raised once again by JB Jeyaretnam's son, Kenneth (who took over the leadership of the Reform Party from his late father), in 2012, but in relation to a completely different situation. On 20 April 2012, the Monetary Authority of Singapore (MAS) announced that Singapore had offered a contingent loan of US$4 billion to the International Monetary Fund (IMF) as part of an international effort involving more than 30 countries to ensure that the IMF had enough resources to deal with the global financial crisis. The loan was to the IMF and not to countries borrowing from the IMF. Jeyaretnam argued that this contingent loan contravened the provisions of Article 144(1) of the Constitution and had to be approved by Parliament and the President, and sought prerogative orders and a declaration against the government. In the High Court, Justice Tan Lee Meng adopted the *reddendo singular singulis* interpretation of the Attorney-General from 1997.[16] Jeyaretnam appealed to the Court of Appeal and judgment is pending at the time of writing.

VIII. THE PRESIDENT EXERCISES HIS DISCRETION

The financial crisis that broke out in the United States in 2007 spread like a wild fire throughout the world and by 2008 and because of its open economy and its heavy reliance on exports to the United States and Europe, Singapore was immediately affected by the contagion. In the fourth quarter of 2008, Singapore's economy shrank by 12.5 per cent while it declined 5.4 per cent in the July-September quarter. It was the third consecutive quarterly decline in gross domestic product. Growth in the economy was only 1.5 per cent for 2008, compared with 7.7 per cent for 2007. By the end of 2008, the government was predicting that Singapore's economy would contract by 2 per cent in 2009.

The economy was bleeding so badly that the government announced that it was bringing forward the budget debate from March to 22 January. Rumour was rife about the government needing to draw down on its past reserves to meet the crisis. On 17 February 2009, President

---

[16] *Jeyaretnam Kenneth Andrew v AG* [2013] 1 SLR 619.

SR Nathan announced that he agreed to the first-ever draw on Singapore's past reserves. Nathan's announcement, while not wholly unexpected, nonetheless attracted much interest from the public who were keen to understand the process under which the President exercised his discretion.

Under Article 148A(1) of the Constitution, the President may,

> acting in his discretion, withhold his assent to any Supply Bill, Supplementary Supply Bill or Final Supply Bill for any financial year if, in his opinion, the estimates of revenue and expenditure for that year … are likely to lead to a drawing down on the reserves which were not accumulated by the Government during its current term of office, except that if the President assents to any such Bill notwithstanding his opinion that the estimates, supplementary estimates or statement of excess are likely to lead to a drawing on those reserves, the President shall state his opinion in writing addressed to the Speaker and shall cause his opinion to be published in the Gazette.

If the President withheld his assent to the supply bill, Parliament could vote to overrule the President within 30 days by passing such a resolution with a two-thirds majority. If such an overruling action was not feasible, Parliament could authorise the use of expenditure from the Consolidated Fund in an amount not exceeding the previous year's budget. This means that if President Nathan had not given his assent, Parliament—which is overwhelming controlled by the ruling PAP—would have had no problem overruling his decision.

In any case, that did not happen. Indeed, Nathan took great pains to explain to the public how the decision was made to support the government's two new schemes to alleviate the economic hardship of Singaporeans—the Jobs Credit Scheme and the Special Risk Sharing Initiative—especially since a number of observers were concerned that he was able to come to his decision within 11 short days. He explained that throughout 2008, he and his CPA members received regular briefings by officials from the Ministry of Trade and Industry and the Monetary Authority of Singapore and were kept apprised of the state of the global and Singapore economies.

On 18 January, he was approached by Prime Minister Lee Hsien Loong, who explained the dire state of the economy to him and told him that extraordinary measures were needed to give confidence to the people and to address the impact of the economic crisis on the people, especially those in the low-income bracket. In this connection, the

Prime Minister underscored the severity of the situation and requested the President's assent to use the past reserves. What happened next was revealed in President Nathan's interview:

> The CPA and I were already aware of the circumstances that were prevailing and how they were impacting on us. So I agreed at that stage to give every consideration to the proposal when it was submitted to me.
>
> After that, the Minister for Finance came to see me and he formally made a request the next day for the specifics of the scheme and sought a meeting to discuss this in greater detail.
>
> So a meeting was convened with the CPA and myself and it was addressed by the Minister for Trade and Industry, Minister for Finance and it was attended by people from the Attorney-General's Chambers (and the) Accountant-General.
>
> The Minister for Finance and the relevant officials went through the Resilience Package of $20.5 billion with (its) focus on saving jobs, keeping companies afloat and the long-term infrastructure and capability development that have to be embarked upon.
>
> When the CPA was convened on my direction, two briefings were provided—first by the Minister for Trade and Industry and his officials and the Monetary Authority of Singapore, and the second by the Ministry of Finance.

After the briefing, President Nathan left the meeting to allow the CPA to deliberate the proposals. The CPA reviewed the details of the proposal, sought legal advice on the constitutional implications of the request, and agreed to a formal proposal being tabled by Minister of Finance Tharman Shanmugaratnam on 19 January. In all, the process of obtaining the President's assent took 11 days 'from the time the matter was first broached'.

IX. SOME UNIQUE ASPECTS OF THE PRESIDENCY

Singapore's elected President scheme is unique in a number of ways. First, unlike the American or French Presidents, Singapore's President has substantially limited powers. Indeed, these powers are of a reactive rather than a proactive nature. As such, even though the President's power to say 'No' is an extremely potent one, he is in no position to formulate or promote particular policies or platforms. The nature of the elected President's powers became a hot topic of discussion during the presidential elections of 2011. Several candidates urged voters to choose them by promising to be 'active' while in office. Tan Kin Lian, for example, told voters that if elected, he would establish a personal Presidential Council to manage interactions with the public and secure their feedback; Tan Jee Say went further to propose the dismantling of government companies and to act as a proxy for citizens who did not vote for the present government; while Tan Cheng Bock proposed moving the Prime Minister's office out of the Istana grounds, and adding six advisors who were experts in finance and constitutional law to his Council of Presidential Advisors. These extravagant claims to powers met with rebuttals from Law Minister K Shanmugam and former Law Minister S Jayakumar both of whom clarified the constitutional position with respect to the President's powers.

Second, the President is political but non-partisan. Unlike the American President who can hail either from the Democratic or Republican parties, the Singaporean President cannot be a member of any political party. If he is, he must resign from the party before nomination day. A great deal of debate was generated on this point during the select committee hearings as many feared that if any member of a political party should become the President, he might be biased towards his party and would therefore not be effective as a check against a deviant or unscrupulous government.

Third, the office of the President is now a competitive one. This represents a marked departure from the established Westminster model of government. In the past, the head of state has often been seen as a unifying component in the Westminster constitutional set-up. The role of the ceremonial head of state, no matter how trivial and formal, is an important one. Loyalty is owed to the state as epitomised by the President, and it is he who provides the rallying point for all nationalist sentiment. This function is especially important in multi-racial, multi-religious Singapore.

Previously, the President represented Singapore's multi-racial and multi-religious make-up. Even though Singapore's population is predominantly Chinese, the other minority races—Malays, Indians, Eurasians and other minorities—are given due recognition by having members of their communities elected as President. Singapore's first President, Yusof bin Ishak, was a Malay. He was succeeded by

Dr Benjamin Henry Sheares, an Eurasian, and when Sheares died, CV Devan Nair, an Indian, succeeded to the post of President. The first Chinese President was Wee Kim Wee, a Peranakan or a Straits-born Chinese. Now, this key function is obliterated. Race can no longer be used to unite the nation through the symbol of the President. Indeed, as the 2011 presidential election demonstrated, electoral competition creates fractures and enhances existing fissures. This led PAP Member of Parliament, Denise Phua to call for the elected presidency scheme to be scrapped and a return to the time when the presidency was largely ceremonial:

> I long for the day of a senior statesman who can represent our country as a head of state in the likes of ex-Presidents Yusof bin Ishak and Dr Benjamin Sheares; statesmen who need not be lugged through yet another political campaigning process that divides the country instead of healing and uniting the people of Singapore.[17]

FURTHER READING

Chan Sek Keong, 'Working out the Presidency: No Passage of Rights' [1996] *Singapore Journal of Legal Studies* 1.
KYL Tan & Lam Peng Er (eds), *Managing Political Change: The Elected Presidency* (London, Routledge, 1997).
Thio Li-ann, 'Working out the Presidency: The Rites of Passage' [1995] *Singapore Journal of Legal Studies* 509.

WEBSITE

www.istana.gov.sg/content/istana/index.html (Official website of the President's Office)

[17] Denise Phua, debate on President's Address *Singapore Parliament Reports* 27 May 2014, vol 92.

7

The Judiciary

———••———

Introduction – Judicial Power: Meaning, Nature, Content and Scope – Constitution of Singapore's Judiciary – Judicial Independence – Jurisdiction of the Courts – Establishing Jurisdiction and *Locus Standi* – Judicial Control of Administrative Action – Limits on Judicial Review – Public Law Remedies – Doctrine of Prospective Overruling – Conclusion

I. INTRODUCTION

O F THE THREE branches of government, Singapore's judiciary has changed the least since its inception. The courts were the first local institutions established by the colonial government. Starting with the Court of Judicature of Prince of Wales Island, Malacca and Singapore in 1827—the year the Second Charter of Justice 1826 arrived—the judicial branch of government developed slowly during the colonial period (1826–1942). During this period, growth was primarily in terms of an expansion of jurisdiction, and in the staffing of the courts.

While one Recorder travelling on circuit sufficed in the 1820s and 1830s, two judges were deemed necessary by 1855, when a Third Charter of Justice was issued, and by the time the Straits Settlements Supreme Court was established in 1867, it had a Chief Justice, a Senior Puisne Judge, a Junior Puisne Judge, and a Judge of Penang. The main structural and jurisdictional changes were brought about first, by Singapore becoming a Crown Colony in 1946, and when Singapore joined the Federation of Malaysia in 1963.

The changes in 1946 were minimal, given that Singapore was still a colony; the old Straits Settlements Supreme Court became the Supreme Court of Singapore but not much else changed. However, when Singapore joined the Federation of Malaysia, the Supreme Court of Singapore was replaced and subsumed under the federal system of courts. There was a High Court of Singapore, with concurrent jurisdiction with the sister High Courts of Malaya (for mainland Malaya) and the High Court of Borneo (for the territories of Sabah and Sarawak). Each of these High Courts had their own Chief Justices and appeals lay to the Federal Court (sitting in Kuala Lumpur), which stood at the apex of the Malaysian judicial system. Appeals from the Federal Court to the Judicial Committee of the Privy Council were retained. The head of the federal judiciary was, in 1963, the Lord President of Malaysia.

When Singapore seceded from the Federation of Malaysia in 1965, it retained the Federal Court as its intermediate court of appeal, and the Privy Council as its final appellate court. The reason for this, as we noted in chapter one, was the suddenness of Singapore's independence and the need to prioritise other legal changes. At the same time, the government was anxious to assure would-be foreign investors that their legal rights would be protected by an independent judiciary. The situation was only resolved in 1969 with the passage of the Constitution (Amendment) Act and the Supreme Court of Judicature Act.[1] Appeals to the Privy Council were abolished in 1994[2] and the Singapore Court of Appeal became Singapore final appellate court.

While the judiciary is often considered one of the three branches of government, it defines itself and its powers by its independence from the other branches. The judiciary's role in maintaining law and order according to the Constitution is crucial if the democratic system of government is to function properly. It is the judiciary which is empowered under the Constitution to check on the arbitrary use of power and administrative abuse through the exercise of its judicial power.

II. JUDICIAL POWER: MEANING, NATURE, CONTENT AND SCOPE

Any study of the judiciary and its powers must begin with an understanding of the meaning, nature, content and scope of 'judicial power',

---

[1] Act 24 of 1969.
[2] Judicial Committee (Repeal) Act, No 2 of 1994.

as distinct from 'executive power' or 'legislative power'. Article 93 of
the Constitution provides that the 'judicial power shall be vested in a
Supreme Court and such subordinate courts as may be provided by any
written law for the time being in force'. The significance of this vesting
of judicial power and the ambit of this power was considered in the
High Court case of *Mohammad Faizal bin Sabtu v Public Prosecutor*.[3]

The petitioner in this case (Mohammad Faizal) had been charged
with one count of consuming morphine under the Misuse of Drugs
Act.[4] As he had been admitted to a drug rehabilitation facility on two
previous occasions, the law mandated a minimum mandatory punishment to be meted out on him, as a repeat offender. He argued that this
mandatory provision violated the principle of the separation of powers
since the legislature required the judiciary to impose a mandatory minimum sentence on him.

In the course of deciding the case, Chief Justice Chan Sek Keong
made some important observations about the meaning of Article 93
and 'judicial power'. The Chief Justice started off by considering the
nature of the Westminster model of constitutional government and
noted that under the Singapore Constitution, 'the sovereign power of
Singapore is shared among the same trinity of constitutional organs'
as that of the United Kingdom (UK).[5] 'All constitutions based on the
Westminster model' noted Chan CJ, 'incorporate the principle of separation of powers as part of their constitutional structure in order to
diffuse state power among different organs of state'.[6]

There were, however two fundamental differences between Singapore's
Constitution and that of the UK. The first difference is that in the
UK, Parliament is supreme, whereas in Singapore, the Constitution
is supreme. The second difference is that while the judicial power of
the UK vests in the British courts either at common law or by statute,
the judicial power of Singapore vests in the Supreme Court and other
subordinate courts by virtue of Article 93 of the Constitution. The
constitutional vesting of judicial power in the courts makes the judicial
power 'co-equal in constitutional status with the legislative and executive

[3] [2012] 4 SLR 947; [2012] SGHGC 163.
[4] Act 5 of 1973.
[5] [2012] 4 SLR 947, at 957.
[6] ibid.

power'.[7] Having established the place of the judiciary in the pantheon of powers, Chan CJ went further to hold as Article 93 exclusively vested judicial power in the courts, this must also mean that judicial power cannot vest 'in any entity which is not a "court"'. The exclusivity of the judicial power is thus safeguarded under Part VIII of the Constitution which is 'designed to secure the independence of the judiciary'.[8]

After setting out the nature of judicial power, Chan CJ then proceeded to discuss the ambit of what it constitutes by quoting the classic definition of 'judicial power' in the Australian case of *Huddart Parker Pty Ltd v Moorehead*:[9]

> [T]he words 'judicial power' as used in sec 71 of the Constitution mean the power which every sovereign authority must of necessity have to decide controversies between its subjects or between itself and its subjects, whether the rights relate to life, liberty or property. The exercise of this power does not begin until some tribunal which has power to give a binding and authoritative decision (whether subject to appeal or not) is called upon to take action.

Chan CJ then quoted various other Australian cases, the American Supreme Court decision in *Prentis v Atlantic Coast*,[10] as well as the UK's Donoughmore Committee,[11] and concluded that even if the term 'judicial power' was difficult to define, there was 'a reasonably clear judicial consensus' as to its nature:

> In essence, the judicial function is premised on the existence of a controversy either between a State and one or more of its subjects, or between two or more subjects of a State. The judicial function entails the courts making a finding on the facts as they stand, applying the relevant law to those facts and determining the rights and obligations of the parties concerned for the purposes of governing their relationship for the future.[12]

The Court noted that none of the cases referred to by counsel for both sides 'touch on the question of whether the power to impose punishments on offenders is part of the judicial power'. After reviewing the historical development of the power, various academic opinions and the structural arrangement of Singapore's Constitution, Chan CJ concluded that a reduction of sentencing discretion in itself did not

---

[7] ibid, at 958.
[8] [2012] 4 SLR 947, at 959.
[9] (1908–1909) 8 CLR 330 (High Court, Australia).
[10] 211 US 210 (1908).
[11] *Report of the Committee on Ministers' Powers* (Cmd 4060, 1932).
[12] [2012] 4 SLR 947, at 960.

constitute 'an unconstitutional derogation from the core of the judicial function'.[13] In Singapore, the power to prescribe punishments for offences was part of the legislative power and not the judicial power, and 'it is the duty of the courts to inflict the legislatively-prescribed punishments on offenders'.[14]

One question that has arisen in several jurisdictions has been whether judicial power must be explicitly vested in the courts by the Constitution? The short answer is 'No'. This issue was discussed in great depth by the Privy Council in *Liyanage v The Queen*,[15] in which 11 appellants were convicted for their involvement in an abortive coup. The government was determined to mete out a severe deterrent punishment on the conspirators and passed the Criminal Law (Special Provisions) Act No 1 of 1962. This Act was made retrospective to 1 January 1962 and was directed at the coup conspirators. The Ceylonese Supreme Court held section 9 of this Act unconstitutional and the government then passed the Criminal Law Act No 31 of 1962. On 6 April 1965, 11 of the 26 accused were convicted and sentenced to 10 years' rigorous imprisonment and ordered to forfeit all their properties. They appealed to the Privy Council, challenging the validity of their convictions.

The Privy Council held, inter alia, that even though the Ceylon Constitution did not expressly vest judicial power in the judiciary, judicial power still vested in the judiciary as could be seen from the scheme of the Constitution. This position was similarly adopted in the Singapore High Court in *Mohammad Faizal*'s case where Chan CJ held that the 'principle of separation of powers, whether conceived as a sharing or a division of sovereign power between these three organs of state, is therefore part of the basic structure of the Singapore Constitution'.[16]

III. CONSTITUTION OF SINGAPORE'S JUDICIARY

Singapore's judiciary consists of the Supreme Court and the State Courts. The Supreme Court comprises the Court of Appeal (as Singapore's highest court) and the High Court, while the State Courts

---

[13] ibid, at 967.
[14] ibid, at 970.
[15] [1967] AC 259.
[16] [2012] 4 SLR 947, at 957.

comprises a number of courts, including the Magistrates' Court, District Court and even the Small Claims Tribunal.

A. The Court of Appeal

The Court of Appeal consists of the following judges: (a) the Chief Justice as President of the Court; (b) Vice Presidents of the Court of Appeal; (c) Judges of Appeal (other than Vice-Presidents); and (d) other puisne judges of the High Court who may be appointed from time to time. As its name suggests, the Court of Appeal has only appellate jurisdiction over all civil and criminal matters. It sits as a bench of at least three judges, but may sit as a bench of five or even seven.

Under the Supreme Court of Judicature Act, a Judge of Appeal may also preside in the High Court when he is otherwise unoccupied in the Court of Appeal. This means that the Chief Justice and the Judges of Appeal can sit in the High Court exercising original or appellate jurisdiction.[17] At the same time, if help is needed up in the Court of Appeal, the Chief Justice is empowered to appoint a puisne judge to sit in the Court of Appeal.[18] These provisions enhance the efficiency of the courts. The Court of Appeal's decision is also binding on all other courts in the judicial hierarchy except itself. To qualify for appointment to the Court of Appeal, a person must have the same qualifications required for that of a puisne judge.

B. The High Court

The High Court consists of puisne judges and Judicial Commissioners. To qualify to be a Supreme Court judge, a candidate has to be a 'qualified person' within the meaning of the Legal Professions Act of at least 10 years' standing. The High Court has both original and appellate jurisdictions. In its appellate jurisdiction, the High Court hears appeals from the subordinate courts, especially appeals from the Magistrates' Courts. In its original jurisdiction, it hears cases which are beyond the jurisdiction of the subordinate courts. Certain types of cases, for

---

[17] Supreme Court of Judicature Act, No 24 of 1969, s 10(3).
[18] ibid, s 29(3).

example the offence of murder, can only be tried at the High Court. Likewise, cases where the damages involved amount to more than S$250,000 must be heard in the High Court. In addition to its original and appellate jurisdictions, the High Court also has supervisory and revisionary jurisdictions.

Specialist courts within the Supreme Court, such as the Admiralty Court and Intellectual Property Court (both created in 2002), have been established. These courts function like the High Court in all respects except that the judges who preside over them have specialist knowledge in these areas of law. One 'specialist' court that is constituted on an ad hoc basis is the Constitutional Tribunal, which hears questions referred to it by the President on the effect of constitutional provisions.[19] There is no appeal from decisions of this court.

C. Special Constitutional Tribunal

In September 1994, a new Article 100 was inserted into the Constitution. It established a *Special Tribunal* consisting of not less than three judges of the Supreme Court. The President of Singapore may refer to this tribunal 'for its opinion any question as to the effect of any provision' of the Constitution. The Tribunal is under a duty to 'consider and answer the question so referred as soon as may be and in any case not more than 60 days after the date of such reference'. Any dissenting opinions of any judge must accordingly be reflected in the opinion rendered to the President although the majority decision shall be considered the opinion of the tribunal and shall be pronounced in open court. The Tribunal's opinion is not subject to challenge in any court.

D. The State Courts

The lower courts in Singapore were known as Subordinate Courts right up until January 2014 when they became known as State Courts. The change in nomenclature was to recognise the importance of these courts within Singapore's judicial system. In moving the amendments to the Subordinate Courts Act, Senior Minister of State for Law, Indranee

---

[19] Constitution of the Republic of Singapore, Art 100.

Rajah pointed out that 95 per cent of the judiciary's total caseload was handled by the subordinate courts and that the change in name would 'better reflect the primary position that these courts occupy within our judicial system'.[20]

Under the State Courts Act,[21] the following courts are subordinate courts: (a) District Courts; (b) Magistrates' Courts; (c) Coroner's Court; (d) Juvenile Court; and (e) the Small Claims Tribunal. Previously, the Family Court was also part of the State Courts system, but the Family Justice Act of 2014 established a whole new system of Family Justice Courts which included the Family Division of the High Court and Family Courts and Youth Courts.[22] With the 2014 amendments to the State Courts Act, the office of the Chief District Judge was replaced by that of the Presiding Judge of the State Courts.[23] In addition, the person appointed as Presiding Judge of the State Courts would now be a person with the rank of judge or Judicial Commissioner of the Supreme Court.[24]

E. The Syariah Court

Under the Administration of Muslim Law Act,[25] the Syariah Court has jurisdiction 'to hear and determine all actions and proceedings in which all the parties are Muslims, or where the parties were married under the provisions of the Muslim law' in respect of (a) marriage; (b) divorce; (c) betrothal, nullity of marriage or separation; (d) disposition or disposal of property on divorce; or (e) payment of *mas-kahwin*, maintenance and consolatory gifts or *matta'ah*.[26]

However, the Family Division of the High Court has concurrent jurisdiction with the Syariah Court over civil proceedings relating to maintenance of wife and child, custody and disposition and division

---

[20] *Singapore Parliament Reports* 21 Jan 2014, vol 91.

[21] This Act was originally enacted as the Subordinate Courts Act, Act 19 of 1970. In 2014, it was amended and retitled the State Courts Act.

[22] See Part II, Family Justice Act, Act 27 of 2014.

[23] State Courts Act, s 8A(1).

[24] ibid, s 8A(3).

[25] Act 27 of 1966.

[26] ibid, s 35(2).

of property on divorce in the case of Muslim marriages.[27] The Syariah Court is presided over by a President who is appointed by the President of Singapore. Cases from the Syariah Court are appealable to the Appeal Board or the Majlis Ugama Islam, Singapura or Council of Muslim Religion, Singapore (MUIS). The President of MUIS is also appointed by the President of Singapore and its decision is final. The Syariah Court is, however subject to the supervisory jurisdiction of the High Court.

IV. JUDICIAL INDEPENDENCE

In Singapore, judicial independence is ensured by the traditional method of institutionalising within the Constitution: (a) security of tenure; and (b) security of remuneration.

A. Appointment and Tenure of Judges

In Singapore, all judges (including Magistrates) are appointed by the President. In appointing the Chief Justice, the Judges of Appeal and the Judges of the High Court, the President acts on the Prime Minister's advice. However, the President may, acting on his personal discretion, refuse to concur with the Prime Minister on his recommendations.[28] Before the Prime Minister tenders his advice to the President, he 'shall consult the Chief Justice' in all cases except for the appointment of the Chief Justice himself.[29] In the appointment of State Court judges (ie District Judges and Magistrates), the President acts on the Chief Justice's advice.[30] Article 98(1) provides that 'a judge of the Supreme Court shall hold office until he attains the age of 65 years or such later time, not being later that 6 months after he attains that age, as the President may approve'.

---

[27] See generally, ibid, s 35A.
[28] Constitution of the Republic of Singapore, Art 95(1).
[29] ibid, Art 95(2).
[30] State Courts Act, ss 9(1) and 10(1).

The idea behind safeguarding a judge's tenure is not new. As far back as in 1701, the British Parliament promulgated the Act of Settlement[31] which, among other things, guaranteed judicial tenure. Article III of the Act provided that 'judges commissions be made *quamdiu se bene gesserint*,[32] and their salaries ascertained and established; but upon the address of both Houses of Parliament it may be lawful to remove them'. The significance of this legislation is that it took the appointment and tenure of judges out of the hands of the executive branch (in this case, the king), and placed it in Parliament.[33]

British judges thus enjoyed a degree of judicial independence and security of tenure and remuneration from the eighteenth century onwards. However, this protection was not extended to colonial judges who held office at the Governor's pleasure. Interestingly, this point was established in a case involving Arthur Koberwain á Beckett Terrell (1881–1956), former Acting Chief Justice of the Federated Malay States.[34]

When Singapore became self-governing in 1959, the Constitution provided that judges had security of tenure to age of 62 and could only be removed for inability to discharge the functions of their office or for misbehaviour.[35] This scheme of protection has been preserved until today although the retirement age for judges is now 65 instead of 62. This applies for all judges except for Judicial Commissioners and those on contract.

B. Security of Remuneration

Article 98(6) provides that 'Parliament shall by law provide for the remuneration of the judges of the Supreme Court, and the remuneration

[31] 12 & 13 Will III, c 2.

[32] Literally meaning, 'As long as he shall behave himself well', or in present day language, 'on good behaviour'.

[33] On the development of judicial independence in the UK and common law world, see CH McIlwain, 'The Tenure of English Judges' (1913) 7(2) *American Political Science Review* 217–29; and IR Kaufman, 'The Essence of Judicial Independence' (1980) 80(4) *Columbia Law Review* 671–701.

[34] See *Terrell v Secretary of State for the Colonies* [1953] QB 482. Terrell was informed by the Secretary of State that his office had been abolished just 17 months short of his mandatory retirement age of 62. He claimed that as he held office on good behaviour, his office could not be terminated before his 62nd year. Lord Goddard CJ held that all colonial judges held their office at the pleasure of the Governor.

[35] The Singapore (Constitution) Order-in-Council (SI 1958/293), Art 91.

shall be charged on the Consolidated Fund'. Furthermore, the Supreme Court judges' remuneration and terms of office, including pension rights 'shall not be altered to his disadvantage after his appointment'.[36] This ensures that judges cannot be threatened with diminution of their salaries or abolishment of their offices.

C. Shortage of Judges: Judicial Commissioners and Supernumerary Judges

From the 1950s until the 1990s, Singapore Government had a major problem trying to attract suitable persons to the bench. Even in colonial times, there were not enough judges in the High Court. For example, William Munro, senior partner of the firm of Allen & Gledhill, was asked to act as a temporary High Court Judge in June 1951 until a replacement arrived from England, and this was shortly after Murray Buttrose arrived as new puisne judge in March 1951.[37] Munro was not relieved until the appointment of Justice Whitton as third puisne judge in January 1953. In 1986, *Straits Times* court reporter TF Hwang recalled how acute the shortage of judges was:

> I remember particularly well the 1960s when the shortage of judges was more than acutely felt. Vacancies went a-begging for want of suitable would-be appointees prepared to sacrifice their lucrative practices and modes of life for judiciary posts ... even temporarily with the chance to resume law practice thereafter.

> During the 1960s, there were seven courtrooms in the High Court building for seven judges. But there arose several protracted periods when only three courts were functioning most of the time. And that was more than the norm than the exception.[38]

In 1971, the shortage of High Court judges led to an amendment to Article 94 of the Constitution to permit the appointment of 'supernumerary' or 'contract' judges. This allowed judges of the Supreme Court who were compelled by the Constitution to retire at the age of 65 to stay on as judges on a contractual basis, usually for terms of between

---

[36] Constitution of the Republic of Singapore, Art 98(8).
[37] 'Acting as Judge' *Straits Times* 21 Jun 1951, at 7.
[38] TF Hwang, 'The role of Singapore's Judicial Commissioner' *The Straits Times* 12 Jun 1986, at 15.

one to three years. The first judge to be renewed under this scheme was Justice Tan Ah Tah, the senior puisne judge whose service was retained after his 'retirement' in November 1971.[39] Retaining the services of senior judges did not solve the government's problem as the number of judges willing to be extended and who could carry on as judges was necessarily limited as well.

This led to the government coming up with the Judicial Commissioner scheme in 1979. Judicial Commissioners can be appointed on a temporary basis and this allows practitioners who take up such appointments to return to private practice when their terms are up. The terms of appointments for Judicial Commissioners, like those of supernumerary judges, are for between six months and three years, and are often viewed as a prelude to a full judgeship. The scheme was not popular and the first Judicial Commissioner—Chan Sek Keong, who would later become Chief Justice—was appointed only in 1986. By this time, the government was getting extremely anxious about the shortage of High Court judges and there was talk about appointing foreign judges for Singapore courts.[40] In an article published upon the impending elevation of Yong Pung How to the High Court bench a local journalist stated the problem thus:

> The nub of this shortage problem, which is expected to continue to besiege the higher judiciary in the next few years, lies in the very small pool of private practitioners and senior legal officers worthy of elevation to the Bench.

> For senior lawyers in private practice, notwithstanding the recent salary revision, the income gap between the successful senior partner and a Supreme Court judge is still wide enough to discourage many from taking up a career on the Bench.[41]

One other scheme the government launched to deal with this shortage was the 'Approved Graduate Programme' that was introduced at the Faculty of Law at the National University of Singapore in 1984. Under this programme, top engineers—all scholarship holders working in the civil service—are able to complete a law degree within two

---

[39] 'Farewell, not goodbye Mr Justice Tan' *The Straits Times* 21 Nov 1971, at 4.

[40] TF Hwang, 'No foreign judges for High Court yet …' *The Straits Times* 5 Oct 1981, at 38.

[41] Cheng Shoong Tat, 'Shortage of judges still the main problem facing the judiciary' *The Straits Times* 30 Jun 1989, at 30.

years. These graduates would form a pool from which talents for the High Court Bench could be drawn.[42] This scheme proved controversial because of its elitist premises and assumptions, and was abandoned by the early-1990s. Among the graduands of this scheme, two became High Court judges, one a Senior Counsel and another Solicitor-General. By the 1990s, a more permanent solution was found; the government increased the salaries of judges substantially such that the gap in earnings between judges of the High Court and those of the top legal practitioners was narrowed significantly.

The issue of judges' salaries had long been a regular subject of discussion in Parliament. In 1967, during a debate on the judiciary's budget, Law Minister EW Barker explained the dilemma thus:

> Sir, everyone wants a rise in salary, but one increase leads to another. The Member says, 'Increase the Judges' salaries, because the practitioners outside get more money.' I agree that because of our present scales of salary, it is very difficult for anyone at the Bar to give up his practice to become even the Chief Justice. The amount of income tax any leading lawyer pays exceeds the salary of any of the Judges. But if you up the Judges' salaries, how far do you go? A Minister gets $2,500 a month.[43]

In 1969, the salary of the Chief Justice was revised from S$2570 a month to S$3500 a month and that of puisne judges from S$2100 a month to S$2700 a month.[44] Three years later, calls were made by Members of Parliament to adjust the salaries of Singapore judges to keep them in line with the salaries of judges of the Supreme Court of Malaysia. A slew of changes in judges' remuneration took place between 1973 and 1994 when the salaries of judges became pegged to a formula developed by the government for top civil servants and government ministers. The salaries of judges were raised four times between 1973 and 1989; the Chief Justice's salary from S$7500 in 1973, to S$28,950 in 1989, and that of puisne judges from S$6000 in 1973 to S$19,550 in 1989. In 1994, Parliament decided to peg the salaries of judges, ministers and senior civil servants to the earnings of their counterparts in

---

[42] Oei Sin Giok, '2-Year Law Course for Civil Servants' *The Singapore Monitor* 19 Jul 1984, at 6; and J Tan, 'Engineers taking two-year law course: Move to rectify shortage of top legal brains' *The Straits Times* 20 Jul 1984, at 1.

[43] *Singapore Parliamentary Debates, Official Reports* 15 Dec 1967, vol 26, cols 645–46.

[44] Judges' Remuneration (Amendment) Act 1969 (now repealed).

the public sector.[45] In the case of judges, their salaries were pegged to the top-earning lawyers in town. The current formula for calculating the salaries of judges is: 60 per cent of the median income of the top 1000 Singapore citizen income earners.

Before the major salary revisions in 1994, the government tried one other refinement to the Judicial Commissioner scheme. In 1993, a new Article 94(5) was inserted into the Constitution that 'the President may appoint a person qualified for appointment as a judge of the Supreme Court to be a Judicial Commissioner to hear and determine a specified case only'.[46] In other words, the Prime Minister, with the concurrence of the Chief Justice, can advise the President to nominate a *particular* person to act as a Judicial Commissioner for a single case. The object of this amendment, explained Law Minister S Jayakumar, was to reduce the number of part-heard cases:

> At present, a Judicial Commissioner must be appointed for a specified period. After the amendments take effect, a Judicial Commissioner may, for instance, be appointed to hear a case for which he may have special expertise. Or he may be appointed to hear a case which is originally fixed before a Judge so that that Judge can complete an ongoing case which would otherwise have to be adjourned as part-heard. In this way, the number of part-heard cases can be reduced, thereby improving the administration of justice in the High Court.[47]

Laudable though such a provision might be from an administrative efficiency point of view, it also makes the judiciary vulnerable to executive manipulation and interference. For instance, the government could, if it were minded to, advise the President to appoint a Judicial Commissioner it believes may be likely to convict an accused rather than one who was not so inclined. This possibility is a clear violation of the judiciary's independence and a violation of the judicial power. This article has never actually been implemented nor challenged in court.

---

[45] On the policy to pay civil servants highly competitive salaries, see JST Quah, *Public Administration Singapore-Style* (London, Emerald Group Publishing Ltd, 2010), at ch 6: 'Compensation: Paying for the "Best and Brightest"'.

[46] Constitution of the Republic of Singapore (Amendment) Act 1993, Act No 17 of 1993, s 3(d).

[47] *Singapore Parliamentary Debates Official Reports* 12 Apr 1993, vol 61, col 90.

D. Judicial Independence and the Power to Punish for Contempt

In addition to the institutional and constitutional safeguards discussed above, courts secure their independence through their inherent power to punish for contempt of court. Action is by way of contempt proceedings initiated by the Attorney-General. There are two ways in which contempt of court can be committed. The first is where a court order has been disobeyed, and the second is contempt by 'scandalising the court'. In respect of the latter, the Singapore courts have adopted Lord Russell of Killowen's classic definition in *R v Gray* as to what this means:

> Any act done or writing published calculated to bring a court or a judge of the court into contempt, or to lower his authority, is a contempt of court. That is one class of contempt. Further any act done or writing published calculated to obstruct or interfere with the due course of justice or the lawful process of the courts is a contempt of court. The former class belongs to the category which Lord Hardwicke CJ characterized as 'scandalising a court or a judge'. That description of that class of contempt is to be taken subject to one and an important qualification. Judges and courts are alike open to criticism, and if reasonable argument or expostulation is offered against any judicial act as contrary to law or the public good, no court could or would treat that as contempt of court. The law ought not to be astute in such cases to criticize adversely what under such circumstances and with such an object is published; but it is to be remembered that in this matter the liberty of the press is no greater and no less than the liberty of every subject of the Queen. Now, as I have said, no one has suggested that this is not a contempt of court, and nobody has suggested or could suggest, that it falls within the right of public criticism in the sense I have described. It is not criticism: I repeat that it is a personal scurrilous abuse of a judge as a judge.[48]

From 1974—when the first major contempt by scandalising the court case was heard[49]—to 2010, Singapore's courts took the position that the test for contempt in such cases was the 'inherent tendency' test. In *Attorney-General v Barry Wain*, the High Court held that it was 'sufficient to prove that the words complained of have the inherent tendency to interfere with the administration of justice'.[50] Such a test set the

---

[48] [1900] 2 QB 36.
[49] *Attorney-General v Pang Cheng Lian* [1974–1976] SLR(R) 271.
[50] [1991] 1 SLR(R) 85, at 101.

threshold very low and did not require the Attorney-General to prove anything against the alleged contemnor save that the words uttered were derogatory and called into question the judiciary's independence. Indeed, in *Attorney-General v Hertzberg Daniel & Ors*,[51] Justice Tay Yong Kwang referred to the Australian Law Reform Commission's (ALRC) *Report on Contempt* (1987) and pointed out that the ALRC had concluded that the term 'inherent tendency' means 'calculated'. In other words, an 'inherent tendency' to interfere with the administration of justice means the same thing as 'calculated to interfere with the administration of justice'; the statement 'is simply one that conveys to an average reasonable reader allegations of bias, lack of partiality, impropriety or any wrongdoing concerning the judge in the exercise of his judicial function'.[52] Justice Tay further held that this test had two advantages: first, dispensing with the need to adduce detailed proof on matters that were often unprovable; and, second, the opportunity for the courts to intervene before the damage actually occurs.[53]

The first break away from the 'inherent tendency' test was in the High Court case of *Attorney-General v Shadrake Alan*.[54] In this case, a British author, Alan Shadrake wrote a book entitled *Once a Jolly Hangman: Singapore Justice in the Dock*, which dealt with the cruelty of the death penalty. Shadrake was accused of scandalising the judiciary by alleging or insinuating that: (a) the judiciary succumbed to economic and political pressures whenever it decided whether or not an accused was to be sentenced to death; (b) it was biased against the weak, poor and less educated; and (c) it was a tool of the People's Action Party and was used by the party to muzzle political dissent in Singapore. Justice Quentin Loh held that the High Court was not bound by its previous decisions, rejected the 'inherent tendency' test in favour of a 'real risk' test.

The case went on appeal, thus affording the Court of Appeal an opportunity to pronounce authoritatively on the matter since all decisions on contempt by scandalising the court were hitherto High Court decisions. In *Shadrake Alan v Attorney-General*,[55] the Court of Appeal

---

[51] [2009] 1 SLR 1103.
[52] ibid, at 1125.
[53] ibid.
[54] [2011] 2 SLR 445.
[55] [2011] 2 SLR 506.

upheld Justice Loh's decision and rejected the 'inherent tendency' test in favour of the 'real risk' test:

> [T]he 'real risk' test is an adequate formulation in and of itself and requires no further theoretical elaboration. It is, at bottom, a test that means precisely what it says: is there a real risk that the impugned statement has undermined—or might undermine—public confidence in the administration of justice (here, in Singapore)? In applying this test, the court must avoid either extreme on the legal spectrum, *viz*, of *either* finding that contempt has been established where there is only a remote or fanciful possibility that public confidence in the administration of justice is (or might be) undermined *or* finding that contempt has been established *only* in the *most* serious situations (which is, as we shall see in the next section of this judgment, embodied within the 'clear and present danger' test). In undertaking such an analysis, the court must not substitute its own subjective view for the view of the average reasonable person as it is clear that the inquiry must necessarily be an objective one. Much would depend, in the final analysis, on the precise facts and context in which the impugned statement is made.[56]

The Court further held that 'fair criticism' was not a defence against a charge of contempt although it was a mitigating factor. In determining whether criticism was 'fair', the Court of Appeal adopted the four factors listed by the High Court in another contempt case, *Attorney-General v Tan Liang Joo John*:[57] whether the statement was (a) made in good faith; (b) based on reasoning; (c) made respectfully and expressed in a temperate manner; and (d) directed at the personal character, integrity or impartiality of the judges or the courts.

V. JURISDICTION OF THE COURTS

A. Original and Appellate Jurisdiction

From its earliest days, the jurisdiction of Singapore's courts has been established by statute. The Second Charter of Justice 1826 established a Court of Judicature with 'such Jurisdiction and Authority as Our Court of King's Bench and Our High Court of Chancery and Our Courts of Common Pleas and Exchequer respectively' and 'give

---

[56] ibid, at 795, para 37.
[57] [2009] 2 SLR(R) 1132.

and pass Judgment and Sentence according to Justice and Right'. In criminal matters, the Court was to 'administer criminal Justice in such or the like Manner and Form … as our Courts of Oyer and Terminer and Goal Delivery do'. Today, the jurisdiction of Singapore's courts is circumscribed by the Supreme Court of Judicature Act[58] and the State Courts Act.[59]

Generally speaking, a court's jurisdiction can be divided into: (a) criminal and civil jurisdictions; and (b) original and appellate jurisdictions. The first distinction is not so important in Singapore since most courts possess both criminal and civil jurisdictions. They have power to hear both civil and criminal cases. A few courts, such as the Family Court or the Small Claims Tribunal have only civil jurisdiction.

In most cases, monetary limits (in the case of civil cases) or the power to inflict punishment (in criminal cases) limit a court's jurisdiction. The higher up the court is in the judicial hierarchy, the greater is its jurisdiction. For example, the High Court has an unlimited jurisdiction in that it can hear any type of case, regardless of how trivial or important it may be. This does not mean that the court will hear very small claims. The jurisdictional threshold for the High Court in Singapore for civil actions is S$250,000. Claims less than that are heard in the State Courts. The High Court's jurisdiction is unlimited as to the amount or punishment involved. However, jurisdiction may still be limited by statute.

B. Inherent Jurisdiction

This refers to a superior court's power to hear and determine cases. It is a necessary corollary of the judicial power and it is a jurisdiction asserted and claimed by the highest common law courts. The court's inherent jurisdiction is part of its general jurisdiction as a superior court of record and is unlimited in scope except where explicitly taken away by legislation. As Lord Morris said in the English case of *Connelly v DPP*:

> There can be no doubt that a court which is endowed with a particular jurisdiction has powers which are necessary to enable it to act effectively within such jurisdiction. I would regard them as powers which are inherent

[58] Act 24 of 1969.
[59] Act 19 of 1970, as amended by Act 5 of 2014.

in its jurisdiction. A court must enjoy such powers in order to enforce its rules of practice and to suppress any abuses of its process and to defeat any attempted thwarting of its process.[60]

Historically, the High Court's inherent jurisdiction consisted mainly of the power to punish for contempt of court (discussed above) and to regulate the practice of the court to prevent an abuse of its processes. The English High Court has always assumed such inherent powers. What about Singapore? The combined effect of sections 15 and 16 of the Supreme Court of Judicature Act—which spell out the criminal and civil jurisdiction of the High Court respectively—appear to confer only limited jurisdiction on the Singapore High Court, but are these sections are exhaustive?

Article 93 of the Constitution vests the judicial power 'in a Supreme Court and such subordinate courts as may be provided by any written law for the time being force'. What is vested is the entirety of the judicial power and not only such parts as provided by law. There is no law providing for the judicial review of statutes but a reading of Article 4—which proclaims the Constitution to be the 'supreme law of the Republic of Singapore'—in conjunction with Article 93 affords the High Court the power of constitutional review. Article 4 further provides that 'any law enacted by the Legislature after the commencement of this Constitution which is inconsistent with this Constitution shall, to the extent of the inconsistency, be void'. Read together, it must be surmised that only the courts, duly vested with judicial power, have jurisdiction to authoritatively determine if a law is inconsistent with the Constitution, and if so, to declare it void.

C. Supervisory Jurisdiction

The High Court's *supervisory jurisdiction* refers to its power to control the actions of subordinate courts or tribunals. General supervisory jurisdiction of the High Court is provided under section 27 of the Supreme Court of Judicature Act, which provides that the High Court 'shall have general supervisory and revisionary jurisdiction over all subordinate courts'. The supervisory jurisdiction of the High Court is not to be

---

[60] [1964] AC 1254.

confused with its appellate jurisdiction. In the words of Justice Lai Kew Chai in *Re Mohamed Saleem Ismail* (1987):

> [I]n the exercise of the High Court's supervisory jurisdiction over inferior tribunals including administrative officers exercising judicial or quasi-judicial functions under a statute or subsidiary legislation the High Court is supervising and not reviewing; the High Court in its supervisory capacity cannot substitute its own views for those of the tribunal or officer which or who had been statutorily entrusted to make the decision.[61]

The supervisory jurisdiction of the High Court depends entirely upon the use of its prerogative order such as quashing or mandatory orders. Traditionally, English courts could intervene in certain circumstances by the issue of prerogative writs: quashing orders (formerly known as *certiorari*); mandatory orders (*mandamus*); prohibiting orders (*prohibition*); and review of detention (*habeas corpus*).

D. Revision Jurisdiction

This is the High Court's power to call for the records of a subordinate court for review. The general revisionary power is found in section 27 of the Supreme Court of Judicature Act under which the High Court may 'exercise powers of revision in respect of criminal proceedings and matters in subordinate courts' and to

> call for and examine the record of any civil proceedings before any subordinate court for the purpose of satisfying itself as to the correctness, legality or propriety of any decision recorded or passed, and as to the regularity of any proceedings of any such subordinate court.

The powers of revision cannot be exercised if an appeal lies from the decision of the subordinate court. This power may be invoked when 'it appears desirable in the interests of justice' either of the court's own motion, or at the instance of an interested party.

VI. ESTABLISHING JURISDICTION AND *LOCUS STANDI*

While the courts are vested with extensive powers of judicial review, there are instances where judicial review is not permitted. Generally,

---

[61] [1987] SLR(R) 380, at 384.

courts will only pronounce on or decide real disputes brought by litigants before them. Singapore courts, like other common law courts, do not render advisory opinions. The questions before the court should be real and not theoretical. The leading local authority on the requirement of standing in respect of declaratory relief is the Court of Appeal decision in *Karaha Bodas Co LLC v Pertamina Energy Trading Ltd*,[62] which held that three requirements for *locus standi* are required:

(a) the applicant must have a 'real interest' in bringing the action;
(b) there must be a 'real controversy' between the parties to the action for the court to resolve; and
(c) the declaration must relate to a right which is personal to the applicant and which is enforceable against an adverse party to the litigation.

The need for three requirements to be satisfied in determining *locus standi* was affirmed in two other Court of Appeal decisions: *Tan Eng Hong v Attorney-General*[63] and *Vellama d/o Marie Muthu v Attorney-General*.[64] In *Tan Eng Hong v Attorney-General*, the Court of Appeal held that while constitutional rights 'are personal' to every Singapore citizen, a violation of any constitutional right does not give *any* Singapore citizen *locus standi* to bring an action before the courts. The applicant 'must demonstrate a violation of *his* constitutional rights' before he has *locus standi*.[65]

Under the doctrine of *ripeness*, the court is prohibited from giving advisory opinions. The court does not act as a roving commission to investigate into every single wrongdoing, nor does it institute its own proceedings. Whether a matter is justiciable is up to the court to decide. Although no collusive cases—cases in which the parties conspire to bring a hypothetical case to court—have arisen in the Singapore courts, such cases will almost certainly be denied a hearing.

VII. JUDICIAL CONTROL OF ADMINISTRATIVE ACTION

Judicial review is not concerned with the 'rightness' or substantive merits of a decision, but its legality. If a decision is illegal, the court

---

[62] [2006] 1 SLR(R) 112.
[63] [2012] 4 SLR 476; [2012] SGCA 45.
[64] [2013] SGCA 39.
[65] [2012] 4 SLR 476, at 514–15.

quashes it (ie renders it a nullity) and directs the relevant public authority to decide the issue again. The merits of a case can only be heard on an appeal. In conducting judicial review, courts are more willing to intervene in questions of law rather than questions of fact. Of course, the court will not hesitate to intervene if a tribunal's factual findings are so seriously flawed that there is no evidential support for its conclusion. Similarly, if a tribunal has reached a totally unreasonable conclusion on the basis of certain facts, the court can intervene.

A. Precedent or Jurisdictional Facts

Courts will scrutinise more stringently cases where precedent or juris-dictional facts are involved. A precedent fact is one upon which the exercise of an administrative power depends. The court will determine if the administrative body or tribunal has made a correct or right find-ing. For example, a statute may give a minister discretion to order the temporary detention of anyone 'who is a repeat offender'. The prec-edent fact in this instance would be whether the subject is indeed a 'repeat offender' or not. It would be insufficient if the minister suspects him to be a 'repeat offender'. The question as to whether a precedent fact has been satisfied involves a true/false proposition rather than a reasonable opinion.

Here, the court must ask if the facts justified the decision. Where a non-precedent fact is involved, a less rigorous standard is applied: the issue is whether one can reasonably come to a decision on the evidence. In reviewing this, the court must inquire into the existence of the facts upon which the evaluation was made. In *Re Fong Thin Choo*,[66] Justice Chan Sek Keong cited with approval what Lord Wilberforce said in the House of Lords case of *Secretary of State for Education and Science v Tameside MBC*:

> If a judgment requires, before it can be made, the existence of some facts, … the court must inquire whether those facts exist and have been taken into account, whether the judgment has been made upon a proper self-direction as to those facts, whether the judgment has not been made upon other facts which ought not to have been taken into account. If these requirements

---

[66] [1991] 1 SLR(R) 774.

are not met, then the exercise of judgment, however bona fide it may be, becomes capable of challenge.[67]

B. Errors of Law

Traditionally, a distinction was drawn between jurisdictional errors of law and non-jurisdictional errors of law. A jurisdictional error is said to go *to jurisdiction* (or affect jurisdiction) and is thus ultra vires since it affects the tribunal's power to act. However, when an error is committed *within jurisdiction* the court will decline to interfere unless there is an *error of law on the face of the record*: one which is evident just from an examination of the record.

However, recent decisions from the English courts have eradicated this distinction. The current approach is that adopted in *Page v Hull University Visitor*,[68] which was followed by the Malaysian Court of Appeal in *Syarikat Kenderaan Melayu Kelantan Bhd v Transport Workers' Union*,[69] where Gopal Sri Ram JCA quoted with approval, the following words of Lord Browne-Wilkinson in *Page v Hull*:

> In my judgment, the decision in *Anisminic* ... rendered obsolete the distinction between errors of law on the face of the record and other errors of law by extending the doctrine of ultra vires. Thenceforward it was to be taken that Parliament had only conferred on the decision-making power on the basis that it was to be exercised on the correct legal basis: a misdirection in law in making the decision therefore rendered the decision ultra vires.[70]

C. The Control of Substantive Discretion

Any discretionary power is limited and subject to judicial review. However, not every decision is subject to judicial review. The decision-maker must be empowered by public law to make decisions leading to administrative action. An improper exercise of discretion arises in

---

[67] [1977] AC 1014, at 1047.
[68] [1993] AC 682.
[69] [1995] 2 MLJ 317.
[70] [1993] AC 682, at 701.

several instances. First, the exercise of discretion requires the application of the official's own mind to the matter. If that official is merely acting under someone else's instruction or has simply delegated this discretion to another, the decision may be impugned. At the same time, if the exercise of discretion has been fettered, for example, by too rigid an adherence to a policy or set of guidelines, that would also be invalid.

D. The Grounds of Judicial Review

In a now-classic judgment in the *Council of Civil Service Unions v Minister for the Civil Service* (the '*GCHQ* case'),[71] Lord Diplock categorised the grounds for the judicial review of government action as: (a) illegality; (b) irrationality; (c) procedural impropriety; and (d) possibly proportionality. This categorisation was expressly adopted by the Singapore Court of Appeal in in *Chng Suan Tze v Minister of Home Affairs*.[72] A contravention of any of these grounds will render a decision ultra vires. Let us consider each of these grounds briefly.

i. Illegality

Illegality occurs when a public authority exercises a power it does not possess. The same can be said if it acted in a manner contrary to the policy and objects of the Act in question. Naturally, the wider the object of a law is framed, the wider the powers of the executive authority. In Singapore, the courts have adopted a broad approach to the 'purpose' test in *PP v MM Pillay*,[73] where the High Court held that an administrative measure need not directly relate to the statute's purpose but merely be 'incidental thereto'.

ii. Irrationality

By 'irrationality', Lord Diplock was referring to what can be succinctly called '*Wednesbury* unreasonableness'. In *Associated Picture Houses v*

---

[71] [1985] AC 374.
[72] [1988] 2 SLR(R) 525.
[73] [1977–1978] SLR(R) 45.

Wednesbury Corporation,[74] Lord Greene held that the authority exercising discretion must take into consideration relevant factors set out in the statute, ignore irrelevant collateral matters, have due regard for public policy, and not be 'unreasonable'. The kind of unreasonable decision referred to by Lord Greene is one

> which is so outrageous in its defiance of logic or of accepted moral standards that no sensible person who had applied his mind to the question to be decided could have arrived at it.[75]

In *Ng Hock Guan v Attorney-General* (2004), the plaintiff Ng was a senior investigation officer of the Anti-Vice Branch of the Criminal Investigation Department (CID) of the police Force. He was charged for allegedly slapping three Filipina suspects and disciplinary proceedings were preferred against him. After a 15-day hearing involving 19 witnesses, the Authorised Officer found Ng guilty and dismissed him from the police force. Ng sought judicial review of the Authorised Officer's decision. Justice Lai Kew Chai held that the manner in which the Authorised Officer arrived at his decision, especially his prejudicial attitude towards some key witnesses, was 'irrational and one which no rational and fair-minded arbiter properly directing himself would have made'.

iii. Procedural Impropriety

'Procedural impropriety' refers to instances when executive action fails to comply with: (a) common law principles of natural justice; and (b) statutorily requirements of procedural fairness. Natural justice, in this context, refers to two procedural rules: (a) the rule against bias (*nemo iudex in causa sua*); and (b) the right to a fair hearing (*audi alteram partem*). In *Stansfield Business International Pte Ltd v Minister for Manpower*,[76] Justice Warren Khoo explained the nature of the rules of natural justice:

> Rules of natural justice are not some arcane doctrine of law. They represent what the ordinary man expects and accepts as fair procedure for the resolution of conflicts and disputes by a decision making body that affects his interest. The ordinary man will feel he has not been fairly heard if he has not

---

[74] [1948] 1 KB 223.
[75] [1985] AC 374, at 410.
[76] [1999] 2 SLR(R) 866.

been allowed a reasonable opportunity to present his case. He will equally feel that he has not been fairly heard if he has not been fully informed of what his opponent has to say or if he has not been given an opportunity to answer it or correct it. He will similarly feel aggrieved if a point is taken by the tribunal and he has not been given an opportunity to answer it or correct it. So the rules of natural justice require simply, first, that a party is told of the case he has to meet and of the allegations made against him; secondly, that he is given not only a fair opportunity to put his own case, but also a fair opportunity to correct or contradict the case and the allegations of the other party; thirdly, if a significant point is to be taken against him by the tribunal, he should have a similar opportunity.[77]

The rule against bias requires that a person may not be a judge in a case in which he has a personal or pecuniary interest. In *Chiam See Tong v Singapore Democratic Party*,[78] for example, the court held the members of the Singapore Democratic Party's Central Executive Committee to be biased in view of its members' confrontational and hostile tone.

Two major tests have been developed to determine the extent of bias necessary to disqualify an adjudicator: (a) reasonable suspicion of bias; and (b) real likelihood of bias. The former offers a lower threshold than the latter. Both these tests were considered by the Court of Appeal in *Jeyaretnam Joshua Benjamin v Lee Kuan Yew*,[79] which approved the test as laid down by Ackner LJ in *R v Liverpool City Justices, ex parte Topping*: 'would a reasonable and fair-minded person sitting in court and knowing all the relevant facts have a reasonable suspicion that a fair trial for the applicant was not possible'.[80]

'Fair hearing' requires that an accused be given due notice of the charges made against him and the right to be heard before an unbiased tribunal. An accused must be given adequate notification of the date, time and place of the hearing as well as detailed notification of the case he is to meet. In *Chiam See Tong v Singapore Democratic Party*,[81] Chiam was never told the real nature of the grievance against him and was thus not fully apprised of the case against him.

---

[77] ibid, at 875.
[78] [1993] 3 SLR(R) 774.
[79] [1992] 1 SLR(R) 791.
[80] [1983] 1 All ER 490, at 494.
[81] [1993] 3 SLR(R) 774.

The hearing must also be conducted fairly and properly. In *Tan Boon Chee David v Medical Council of Singapore*,[82] the members of the Medical Council were found to be very slipshod in their attendance at the disciplinary hearings. Some of them did not even stay through the whole proceeding and thus did not hear all the oral evidence and submissions made. The court held that this conduct substantially prejudiced the appellant Tan and constituted a fundamental breach of natural justice.

A right to a fair hearing does not automatically import the right to legal representation. Tribunals have discretion to admit or bar legal counsel, depending on the circumstances, including: (a) the seriousness of the charge and of the potential penalty; (b) whether any points of law were likely to arise; (c) the capacity of a particular accused to present his own case; (d) procedural difficulties faced by the accused in conducting their own defence, for example, lack of access to potential witnesses; (e) the need for reasonable speed in making the adjudication; and (f) the need for fairness as between the accused and between accused and accusers.

Tribunals must also give reasons for their decisions. This will enable an aggrieved individual to know the possible grounds upon which the decision may be challenged. This also helps ensure that decisions are carefully thought through. In *Re Siah Mooi Guat*,[83] the High Court held that there was no common law duty requiring an authority or administrative tribunal to give reasons. The House of Lords held in *R v Secretary of State for the Home Department, ex parte Doody*[84] that while there was no general duty at common law to give reasons for an administrative decision, 'it is equally beyond question that such a duty may in appropriate circumstances be implied'.[85]

iv. Proportionality

In addition to Lord Diplock's 'Three 'I's', the ground of proportionality has been invoked in some local cases. Proportionality is concerned with the balance between the objects of the statute and the means by which the objects are to be achieved. In *PB Chapman v Deputy Registrar of*

---

[82] [1979–1980] SLR(R) 523.
[83] [1988] 2 SLR(R) 165.
[84] [1994] 1 AC 531.
[85] ibid, at 564.

Companies,[86] the court held that the appellant's acts were not dishonest or criminal and as such did not merit the extreme penalty of permanently being disqualified from holding a securities dealer's licence. The doctrine of proportionality was discussed by the Court of Appeal in several cases under the heading of 'irrationality'.[87]

VIII. LIMITS ON JUDICIAL REVIEW

Even after a court has established its jurisdiction to hear a case, it may still decline to hear it for a number of reasons. These may broadly be divided as follows: (a) political questions; (b) legislative prohibition; (c) laches; (d) judgments of superior court; and (e) *res judicata*.

A. Political Questions

Generally, a court will decline jurisdiction in cases where political questions are involved. This is because questions that are political in nature are best resolved through political, rather than judicial means. Any attempt by the judicial branch to decide purely political questions is tantamount to a breach of the separation of powers doctrine and a usurpation of the executive and legislative powers. As Lord Diplock stated in *Gouriet*, the 'only kinds of rights with which courts of justice are concerned are legal rights; and a court of civil jurisdiction is concerned with legal rights only when the aid of the court is invoked by one party claiming a right against another party, to protect or enforce the right or to provide a remedy against that other party for infringement of it, or is invoked by either party to settle a dispute between them as to the existence or nature of the right claimed'.[88] This passage was cited by the Court of Appeal in *Karaha Bodas* with approval.[89]

---

[86] [1977] 2 *Malayan Law Journal* 5.

[87] See *Chan Hiang Leng Colin & Ors v Minister for Information and the Arts* [1996] 1 SLR(R) 294; *Chng Suan Tze v Minister for Home Affairs* [1988] 2 SLR(R) 525; and *Kang Ngah Wei v Commander of Traffic Police* [2002] 1 SLR(R) 14.

[88] *Gouriet v Union of Post Office Workers* [1978] AC 435, at 50.

[89] [2006] 1 SLR(R) 112, at 121.

The political question doctrine has not been argued in the local courts and there are no cases discussing it. Nevertheless, the approach taken in some decided cases suggests that so long as the issues are not wholly political, the jurisdiction of the court will not be ousted. If the issues are partially political or 'smack of political flavour', that alone does not oust the jurisdiction of the courts.

These sentiments were also echoed by Abdul Hamid CJ (Malaya) in *Dato Menteri Othman bin Baginda & Anor v Dato Ombi Syed Alwi bin Syed Idrus* (1981) when delivering the judgment of the Supreme Court of Malaysia in the same case when he said:

> The mere fact that a litigant seeks the protection of a political right does not mean that it presents a political question. Whether a matter raises a political question; whether it has been committed by the Constitution to another branch of government is itself a matter for judicial determination because the Constitution has made the Courts the ultimate interpreter of the Constitution. The Courts accordingly cannot reject a bona fide controversy as to whether some action denominated 'political' exceeds constitutional authority.[90]

B. Legislative Prohibition: Ouster Clauses

In Singapore, as elsewhere, Parliament has attempted to curtail or preclude judicial review through statutory ouster clauses, for example, under the Internal Security Act[91] and the Maintenance of Religious Harmony Act.[92] The clause may stipulate that that any determination by an administrative body is 'final and conclusive' or 'shall not be called into question in a court of law'. Typically, the following devices are used: (a) Finality Clauses; (b) '*Non-Certiorari*' Clauses; (c) 'Shall Not be Questioned' Clauses; and (d) 'As if Enacted' and 'Conclusive Evidence' Clauses.

Typically, finality clauses provide that a minister's decision shall be 'final' or that a tribunal's decision shall be 'final'. The idea behind this tactic is to render the decision unreviewable or unassailable. The courts have not been deterred. In the seminal case of *R v Medical Appeal*

---

[90] [1981] 1 MLJ 29.
[91] Act 18 of 1960 (Malaya).
[92] Act 26 of 1990.

Tribunal, ex parte Gilmore, Denning LJ (as he then was) held that the only effect of the finality clause was to prevent an appeal, and did not preclude judicial review of decisions made ultra vires:

> In stopping this abuse the statutes proved very beneficial, but the court never allowed those statutes to be used as a cover for wrongdoing by tribunals. If tribunals were to be at liberty to exceed their jurisdiction without any check by the courts, the rule of law would be at an end.[93]

Even when the right to *certiorari* has been expressly taken away through *non-certiorari* clauses, the courts will invoke their power of judicial review on the assumption that Parliament could not possibly have intended that a tribunal of limited jurisdiction be permitted to exceed its authority without the possibility of direct correction by a superior court. Again, Denning LJ in *ex parte Gilmore* said:

> [T]he remedy by certiorari is never to be taken away by any statute except by the most clear and explicit words. The word 'final' is not enough. That only means 'without appeal.' It does not mean 'without recourse to certiorari. It makes the decision final on the facts, but not final on the law. Notwithstanding that the decision is by statute 'final', certiorari can still issue for excess of jurisdiction or for error of law on the face of the record.[94]

Another method used by the legislature to exclude the courts is a *shall not be questioned* clause, which was encountered in *Southeast Asia Firebricks Sdn Bhd v Non Metallic Mineral Products Manufacturers Employees Union,*[95] and it may or may not be used in conjunction with a '*non-certiorari*' clause.

Finally, *as if enacted and conclusive evidence clauses* may be employed. This device typically runs like this: this statutory order shall have effect 'as if enacted in this Act' or that confirmation by the minister 'shall be conclusive evidence that the requirements of the Act have been complied with, and that the order has been duly made and is within the powers of the Act'. These clauses are meant to exclude judicial review of ministerial decisions and by-laws which have been made previously.

The courts have tried constantly to grapple with the problems of review and its limits. In Singapore, it would appear that as far back as 1978, the High Court adopted a generous view of its supervisory

---

[93] [1957] 1 QB 574, at 586.
[94] ibid, at 583.
[95] [1981] 1 AC 363.

powers in the face of ouster clauses. *In Re Application by Yee Yut Ee*,[96] the High Court had to consider the effect of section 46 of the Industrial Relations Act[97] which read:

> Subject to the provisions of this Act an award shall be final and conclusive, and no award or decision or order of a Court or the President or a referee shall be challenged, appealed against, reviewed, quashed, or called in question in any court and shall not be subject to certiorari, prohibition, mandamus or injunction in any court on any account.

Justice Choor Singh held that this clause did not preclude the High Court from exercising its jurisdiction to issue *certiorari* to the Industrial Arbitration Court to quash its decision if the tribunal:

> [W]as improperly constituted, or if it lacked or exceeded jurisdiction, or failed to comply with essential preliminaries, or if a conviction or order had been procured by fraud or collusion, or where there has been a breach of the rules of natural justice.[98]

Chief Justice Chan Sek Keong, in an extra-judicial speech, provocatively and rhetorically asked a group of law students if Singapore should follow English law 'and abolish the distinction between jurisdictional and non-jurisdictional errors of law'. His view was that it was misleading to believe that 'all errors of law, whether jurisdictional or non-jurisdictional, are amenable to judicial review' because in England, Parliament was supreme. However in the case of Singapore,

> [t]he answer may not lie in English principles of administrative law, but in Art 93 of our Constitution. I do not wish to suggest an answer but will provide an academic argument ... that an ouster clause may be inconsistent with Art 93 of the Constitution, which vests the judicial power of Singapore in the Supreme Court. If this argument is correct (and it has not been tested in a court of law), it would follow that the supervisory jurisdiction of the courts cannot be ousted, and therefore there is no need for our courts to draw the distinction between jurisdictional and non-jurisdictional errors of law.[99]

---

[96] [1977–1978] SLR(R) 490.

[97] Ordinance 20 of 1960.

[98] ibid, at 494–95.

[99] Chan Sek Keong, 'Judicial Review: From Angst to Empathy' (2010) 22 *Singapore Academy of Law Journal* 469, at 475–76.

C. Laches

Laches refers to an unreasonable delay or negligence in pursuing a right or claim, especially if it is an equitable one. Laches can occur when the aggrieved party is statutorily barred by being out of time, or where they have waited far too long to bring their case before the courts. Since laches proceeds on the equitable maxim *vigilantibus non dormientibus jura subveniunt*, meaning 'the laws aid those who are vigilant, and not those who sleep upon their rights', in cases where the position of the parties have changed substantially it would be inequitable for the court to have jurisdiction to entertain the suit. In the words of the Court of Appeal in a recent case:

> Laches is a doctrine of equity. It is properly invoked where essentially there has been a substantial lapse of time coupled with circumstances where it would be practically unjust to give a remedy either because the party has by his conduct done that which might fairly be regarded as equivalent to a waiver thereof; or, where by his conduct and neglect he had, though perhaps not waiving that remedy, yet put the other party in a situation in which it would not be reasonable to place him, if the remedy were afterwards to be asserted.[100]

D. Judgments of Superior Courts

In the exercise of its supervisory jurisdiction, the High Court pronounces on the validity of decisions of inferior or subordinate tribunals. It has no power to exercise its supervisory jurisdiction on a superior court or even one of co-ordinate or equal jurisdiction, such as the Court of Appeal or a High Court. This question arose in the case of *Marplan Pte Ltd v Attorney-General*,[101] where the applicant sought leave for judicial review to quash the decision of the High Court in respect of an appeal from the District Court. Justice Andrew Ang held that as the High Court was part of the Supreme Court and a superior court of record, no judicial review would lie against it for that would be 'tantamount to saying that the superior court of Singapore can exercise

---

[100]   *eSys Technologies Pte Ltd v nTan Corporate Advisory Pte Ltd* [2013] SGCA 27, at para 46.
[101]   [2013] 3 SLR 201.

supervisory jurisdiction over itself'. This, Ang J, added, 'makes non-sense of the word 'supervisory'.[102]

E. *Res Judicata*

Where a court has given a final decision in a case, it cannot re-opened, and the decision cannot be challenged on the matter decided on. This principle applies only where the parties are the same, the issue is the same, and the method of raising the question before the court has pre-viously been considered. Once a case has been authoritatively decided, it would be unfair and unjust to re-open it, since this could lead to end-less litigation. There would also be great uncertainty in the law if cases could be heard and reheard over and over again. However, the Court of Appeal in Singapore has recognised that the doctrine of *res judicata* should not apply in cases where

> the court itself has made such an egregious mistake that grave injustice to one or more of the parties concerned would result if the court's erroneous decision were to form the basis of an estoppel against the aggrieved party or parties.[103]

IX. PUBLIC LAW REMEDIES

Section 18(2), read with the First Schedule of the Singapore Supreme Court of Judicature Act sets out the High Court's prerogative powers. The Court may 'issue to any person or authority any direction, order or writ for the enforcement of any right conferred by any written law or for any other purpose' including: mandatory orders (*mandamus*), prohib-iting orders (prohibition), quashing orders (*certiorari*) and an order for the review of detention (*habeas corpus*). These prerogative writs consti-tute the public law remedies available to litigants. In addition to these prescribed remedies, the court may also issue private law remedies of injunctions and declarations. The use of these remedies was succinctly

---

[102] ibid, at 208.

[103] *Lee Tat Development Pte Ltd v Management Corporation Strata Title Plan No 301* [2009] 1 SLR(R) 875, at 921 (Court of Appeal).

summarised by Justice Philip Pillai in *Vellama d/o Marie Muthu v Attorney-General* as follows:

> The English common law courts devised special remedies known as pre-rogative orders for judicial review. These prerogative orders are special in the sense that these are public law remedies available only against public authorities. The four principal prerogative orders are: certiorari, prohibition, mandamus and the writ of habeas corpus. In Singapore, these orders are now known as the 'Quashing Order', 'Prohibiting Order', 'Mandatory Order', and the 'Order for Review of Detention' respectively. ...
>
> In Singapore, applications for first three prerogative orders must be made under Order 53 of the Rules of Court and are heard in two stages. At the first stage, the applicant must apply and obtain the leave of court to proceed. The court will not grant leave to proceed unless certain threshold conditions are met. The reason for requiring leave to proceed is to sieve out frivolous and hopeless applications at an early stage. It is ordinarily only if the threshold conditions for leave are met that the court will grant leave to proceed to the second stage and hear the application in open court. At the second stage, the applicant will have to establish his case in law and the court may, in its discretion, grant him a remedy.
>
> Quite apart from judicial review, declarations may be sought under O 15 r 16 of the Rules of Court to determine the constitutionality of ordinary legislation and constitutional questions. In contrast to judicial review applications, applications for declarations under O 15 r 16 do not require leave of the court but must meet certain other conditions.[104]

X. DOCTRINE OF PROSPECTIVE OVERRULING

If a statute (or part of it) is declared unconstitutional, that portion of the legislation becomes void (see Article 5). When a statute is declared void, it is *ab initio* (ie from the outset) and the effect is as if this statute never existed in the first place. This presents us a problem. Certain statutes may have stood for many years before being declared unconstitutional. Many individuals, lawmakers and administrators would have relied on the impugned provision and ordered their activities accordingly. To circumvent the problem of retrospectively reversing a whole

---

[104] [2012] 4 SLR 698, at 704.

series of acts and decisions, the doctrine of prospective overruling was developed by the United States Supreme Court in *Linkletter v Walker*[105] and accepted in Singapore in the Court of Appeal case of *PP v Manogaran s/o R Ramu*,[106] where Chief Justice Yong Pung How held:

> By judicial overruling of a previous decision, new law may be pronounced for the first time. The rule of law requires adherence to the maxim *ignorantia juris neminem excusat*: ignorance of the law excuses no one. However, if a person organizes his affairs in accordance with an existing judicial pronouncement about the state of the law, his actions should not be impugned retrospectively by a subsequent judicial pronouncement which changes the state of the law, without his having been afforded an opportunity to reorganize his affairs. This seeks to protect his reasonable and legitimate expectations that he did not act in contravention of the law.

XI. CONCLUSION

The judiciary is the only branch of government that is not elected. Yet, it plays a crucial part in interpreting the law and controlling the other two branches. This irony is often referred to as the 'counter-majoritarian' difficulty: Can it be right for a non-elected body to put the brakes on the actions of those who have the general support of the population?

Majoritarianism is a desirable but sometimes dangerous thing for the rights of the minority can be imperilled by the actions of the masses. It is the judiciary, through its interpretation of the law, which ensures that this does not happen. It is a very delicate and difficult business. Courts that are seen as being overly political or activist have been taken to task by the government. This was what happened to the Malaysian judiciary in the 1988 when several of the country's most senior judges, including Lord President Salleh Abas, were removed for what the executive characterised as 'judicial misconduct'.[107]

---

[105] 381 US 618 (1965).

[106] [1997] 1 SLR 22.

[107] On the Malaysian judicial crisis, see A Harding, 'The 1988 Constitutional Crisis in Malaysia' (1990) 39 *International & Comparative Law Quarterly* 57; FA Trindade, 'The Removal of the Malaysian Judges' (1990) 106 *Law Quarterly Review* 51; and V Sinnadurai, 'The 1988 Judiciary Crisis and Its Aftermath' in AJ Harding & HP Lee (eds), *Constitutional Landmarks in Malaysia: The First 50 Years, 1957–2007* (Kuala Lumpur, LexisNexis, 2007).

To ensure the courts can do their work properly, constitutional protection is given to them to maintain their independence. However, in Singapore, two innovations, which were introduced at a time when it was extremely difficult to attract top lawyers to the Bench—Judicial Commissioners and supernumerary or contract judges—stand out as stark exceptions to these measures to maintain judicial independence. These two schemes were necessary for their time, but with the dramatic rise in judicial salaries that have made Singapore's judges the highest paid in the world, it is now time to do away with these two provisions. Keeping judges beyond retirement age is not healthy but the current retirement age of 65 years for judges is early, by international standards. For example, there is no retirement age of judges in America and in England, judges retire at the age of 75. Perhaps it is also time to raise the retirement age of judges from 65 years to either 70 or 75 years. By raising the retirement age of judges and getting rid of Judicial Commissioners and supernumerary judges, Singapore can go further in strengthening its already formidable judiciary with a track record of excellence and efficiency.

FURTHER READING

K Blöchlinger, '*Primus Inter Pares*: Is the Singapore Judiciary First among Equals? (2000) 9 *Pacific Rim Law and Policy Journal* 591.

Chan Sek Keong, 'Judicial Review: From Angst to Empathy' (2010) 22 *Singapore Academy of Law Journal* 469.

AJ Harding, 'The 1988 Constitutional Crisis in Malaysia' (1990) 39 *International & Comparative Law Quarterly* 57.

Ng Peng Hong, 'Judicial Reform in Singapore: Reducing Backlogs and Court Delays' in M Rowat, WH Malik & M Dakolia (eds), *Judicial Reform in Latin America and the Caribbean: Proceedings of a World Bank Conference*, World Bank Technical Paper No 280 (Washington DC, World Bank, 1995) 127–33.

FT Seow, *Beyond Suspicion? The Singapore Judiciary* (New Haven, Yale University Southeast Asia Studies, 2006).

FA Trindade, 'The Removal of the Malaysian Judges' (1990) 106 *Law Quarterly Review* 51.

WEBSITES

http://app.supremecourt.gov.sg/default.aspx?pgID=1 (official website of Singapore's Supreme Court)

https://app.statecourts.gov.sg/subcourts/index.aspx (official website of the State Courts of Singapore)

https://app.syariahcourt.gov.sg/syariah/front-end/Home.aspx (official website of the Syariah Court of Singapore)

8

Fundamental Rights

———◆———

Introduction – The Rendel Constitution – The Reid Commission
in Malaya – Entrenching Rights in Post-Independence
Singapore – The Right to Property in Singapore – Preventive
Detention – Fundamental Liberties under Singapore's
Constitution – Interpreting Fundamental Liberties

I. INTRODUCTION

A BILL OF rights was included in Singapore's Constitution
only when it became a constituent state of the Federation of
Malaysia in 1963. Prior to its independence from Britain, the
matter of rights did not figure significantly in local debates or discourse.
Indeed, the early European settlers—swirling in their own superiority—
were totally against the granting of any kind of rights to locals. In a
letter to the Editor of the *Pinang Gazette* in 1869, a writer, who simply
signed off as 'An European' wrote:

> Let the Chinese be taught a lesson once and for all which they ought to
> have received long ago that they must either obey our laws, or be punished
> by sheer force.... Like slave emancipation bestowing English constitutional
> rights upon Asiatics, is a beautiful conception were it not practically absurd.
> To give Asiatics the constitutional privileges of ourselves is casting pearls
> before swine. They were never born for them and it will take centuries before
> they can appreciate them. Had India been ruled by English constitutional law
> none of us would be here today.[1]

While this may well have been the attitude of the average European
settler or sojourner, it was not the attitude of the courts. For example,
Chief Justice Sir Peter Benson Maxwell, speaking in the Legislative

---

[1] 'The Penang Riots' *The Straits Times* 7 Aug 1869, at 1.

Council debate on the Dangerous Societies Bill in 1870, prefaced his objection to aspects of the legislation with the following words:

> I feel it is my duty, with the strong respect I hold for constitutional principles, not to sit at this table and allow these principles to be violated without my protest, unless a necessity be proved for such violation.[2]

The Chief Justice—who up until the late-1880s was a member of the Legislative Council—objected to the bill giving the executive almost unfettered power to the police to kill fleeing rioters, and to the executive to banish aliens and naturalised subjects whose removal appeared to the Governor to be necessary for public safety. As the Second Charter of Justice 1826 mandated the Court of Judicature to decide cases according to 'justice and right', the principles of the common law—including the liberties of British subjects—were presumed by the Court to apply to the Straits Settlements as well. For example, the writ of *habeas corpus* was considered part and parcel of the received law of England,[3] as was the Bill of Rights 1688.[4]

Interestingly, it was the Straits Chinese, who professed themselves loyal British subjects, who first broached the matter of their constitutional rights. The Straits Chinese British Association, which was established in 1900 by some of the most prominent Chinese leaders and businessmen in Singapore, had as one key object of its Constitution, the safeguarding of 'the constitutional rights of British subjects for the Straits Born Chinese who are British subjects'.[5] This was probably drafted and included by its Secretary, Song Ong Siang, the first local-born Chinese to qualify as a lawyer.

In 1940, as war raged in Europe, another important Straits Chinese leader, Tan Cheng Lock, made a radio broadcast entitled, 'Straits Chinese Heart & Soul with Britain' in which he said:

> The principle is established in the governance of the British Empire that British liberty and British constitutional rights are not the exclusive patrimony

---

[2] 'Shorthand Report of the Legislative Council' *Straits Times Overland Journal* 1 Jul 1870, at 5.

[3] See *R v Willans* [1858] Kyshe 4; *In re Sheriffa Hameeda, An Infant* [1867] Kyshe 3; and *In Re Ex-Sultan Abdullah* [1877] Kyshe 3.

[4] See *In the Matter of the Petition of the Straits Steamship Company Limited v The Attorney-General* [1933] SSLR 11.

[5] 'Proposed "Straits Chinese British Association"' *The Singapore Free Press* 19 Jun 1900, at 3.

and privilege of the inhabitants of Great Britain and their descendants at home and overseas, but they rightfully belong to all under the British flag, who are equal to the responsibilities entailed by them.[6]

These exhortations were all made in the context of a colonial state, where there was no explicit guarantee of rights of any sort. The common law was presumed to provide the basis for rights protection for all British subjects.

II. THE RENDEL CONSTITUTION

In 1953, Singapore's first constitutional commission was appointed under the chairmanship of Sir George Rendel. The Commission held 37 meetings (including 2 public meetings) between November 1953 and February 1954. Memoranda from 39 individuals, institutions and associations were received. Many of these asked the Commission to recommend the inclusion 'of provisions designed to designed to ensure the rights of minorities and of the individual, and to preserve such principles as that of freedom of the Press, freedom of speech, independence of the broadcasting system, etc'.[7] In particular, the Commission's attention was drawn to the fact that the 1947 Ceylon Constitution provided that no law shall (a) make persons of any community or religion liable to disabilities or restrictions to which persons of other communities or religions are not made liable; or (b) confer on persons of any community or religion any privilege or advantage which is not conferred on persons of other communities or religions.[8]

While the Commission was 'deeply concerned that these rights and freedoms' were safeguarded and preserved, it refrained from making such specific recommendations since the constitution being proposed fell short of an independence constitution, and as such, 'the reserved and veto powers of the Governor should constitute a sufficient safeguard against any arbitrary or unjustified curtailment of the rights of

---

[6] 'Straits Chinese Heart & Soul with Britain: Life Under Nazi Tyranny Not Worth Living' *The Singapore Free Press* 30 Mar 1940, at 6.
[7] *Report of the Constitutional Commission* (Singapore, Government Printer, 1954), at para 165.
[8] ibid, at para 166.

minorities or the freedom of the Press'.[9] The Commission further added that the Governor was required to reserve assent to any bill that was discriminatory, or which evoked 'serious opposition by any racial, religious or other community, and which in the opinion of the Governor is likely to involve oppression or unfairness to any such community'.[10] The Commission was thus content to leave the protection of rights to the 'good sense, fair-mindedness ... and responsibility of the legislative and administrative authorities of the State' and in the last resort, the reserve powers of the Governor.[11] These qualities, thought the Commission, were 'necessary prerequisites of the success of any new constitution which may be adopted and which, if they do not exist already, cannot be produced by any recommendations' it cared to make.[12]

The Rendel Constitution came into operation in February 1955 and the first real general election in Singapore was held in April 1955. In the meantime, the decolonisation process in the Federation of Malaya was proceeding apace and would profoundly impact Singapore's own constitutional growth in the coming years. Debates on fundamental liberties in the Federation were to become very important for Singapore in the coming years. Indeed, when Singapore finally obtained her independence from Britain in 1963, Singapore joined the Federation of Malaysia as a constituent state. At that point, the liberties guaranteed under the Federal Constitution applied automatically to Singapore.

III. THE REID COMMISSION IN MALAYA

In July 1955, the Alliance[13] won 51 of the 52 seats in the first ever Federation of Malaya elections. Constitutional talks between the Alliance leaders and Great Britain followed, and this led ultimately

---

[9] ibid, at para 167.

[10] ibid. See also section 7, Instructions Passed under the Royal Sign Manual and Signet to the Governor and Commander-in-Chief of the Colony of Singapore, No S73, 24 Feb 1955.

[11] ibid, at para 168.

[12] ibid.

[13] The Alliance was a coalition of the three leading communally based political parties in Malaya: the United Malays Nationalist Organisation (UMNO); the Malayan Chinese Association (MCA) and the Malayan Indian Congress (MIC).

to the independence of the Federation in 1957. At the constitutional conference held in London between January and February 1956, it was proposed that an independent commission be appointed to devise a constitution for the soon-to-be independent Federation. A commission of five members was appointed, under the chairmanship of Lord William Reid, a prominent Lord of Appeal in Ordinary.[14]

The Commission—whose other members were Sir William McKell, former Governor-General of Australia; Sir Ivor Jennings, the noted constitutional law scholar; Justice Abdul Hamid, High Court Judge from West Pakistan; and Justice B Malik, former Chief Justice of the Allahabad High Court—held over 40 meetings and consulted with a wide range of individuals, institutions and associations in finalising its recommendation.

In the matter of human rights, the Reid Commission based much of its deliberations on the Alliance's Memorandum of 27 September 1956.[15] Among the 'fundamental rights normally enjoyed by free peoples' the Alliance wanted entrenched in the Constitution were the freedom of 'speech and expression', 'assembly' and 'worship'. Also to be included were the 'freedom from want' and 'freedom from fear'.[16]

In addition, the Alliance wanted a list of 14 fundamental rights to be written into the Constitution: (1) equality before the law; (2) protection of life and personal property; (3) freedom from arrest and detention except according to law; (4) protection against retrospective offences and punishment; (5) freedom of speech and expression, assembly and association; (6) freedom of worship, faith and belief; (7) freedom to acquire, hold and dispose of property; (8) protection against confiscation of property except according to the law and due compensation; (9) protection against slavery and forced labour; (10) freedom to engage in trade and in the professions; (11) protection of children in employment of a hazardous nature; (12) freedom to profess, practise and propagate any religion, and to establish and maintain religious institutions; (13) protection of the languages and culture of all races, and of their schools

---

[14] On the establishment and composition of the Commission and the roles played by the respective members, see JM Fernando, *The Making of the Malayan Constitution* (Kuala Lumpur, MBRAS, 2002), at 99–115.

[15] *Memorandum to the Reid Commission* (Kuala Lumpur, Alliance, 1956).

[16] ibid, at 10.

and cultural institutions; and (14) protection of the legitimate interests and rights of minorities.[17]

Because of the Alliance's overwhelming victory in the 1955 General Election, these representations were taken to represent the will of the people and discussions on the framing of the Constitution proceeded along this trajectory. The Reid Commission took a pragmatic and legalistic approach to the framing of fundamental rights in the Federal Constitution:

> A Federal constitution defines and guarantees the rights of the Federation and the States: it is usual and in our opinion right that it should also define and guarantee certain fundamental individual rights which are general regarded as essential conditions for a free and democratic way of life. The rights which we recommend should be defined and guaranteed are all firmly established now throughout Malaya and it may seem unnecessary to give them special protection in the Constitution.... The guarantee afforded by the Constitution is the supremacy of the Law and the power and duty of the Courts to enforce these rights and to annul any attempt to subvert any of them whether by legislative or administrative action or otherwise. It was suggested to us that there should also be written into the Constitution certain principles or aims of policy which could not be enforced by the Courts. We do not accept this suggestion. Any guarantee with regard to such matters would be illusory because it would be unenforceable in law and would have to be in such general terms as to give no real security.... Our recommendations afford means of redress, readily available to any individual, against unlawful infringements of personal liberty in any of its aspects.[18]

The Commission proceeded to recommend the inclusion of nine provisions which formed the bedrock of the fundamental liberties provisions of the Federal Constitution, all of which more or less mirrored the proposals put forward by the Alliance in their 1956 Memorandum. Although there were 14 proposals, several of them dealt with the same subject—such as land acquisition and the right to property—and these were reduced to nine articles under Part II of the Constitution. The articles proposed by the Reid Commission became Articles 5 to 13 in Part II of the Federal Constitution when Malaya became independent in 1957.

---

[17] ibid, app, at 21.

[18] *Report of the Federation of Malaya Constitutional Commission* (Rome, Food and Agriculture Organisation of the United Nations, 1957), at 70.

These same provisions applied automatically to Singapore when it became a constituent state of the Federation of Malaysia in 1963.

IV. ENTRENCHING RIGHTS IN POST-INDEPENDENCE SINGAPORE

A. A Patchwork Constitution

When Singapore left the Federation of Singapore on 9 August 1965, it was left with the task of crafting its own constitution. Despite many promises that the new constitution was ready and would be put before Parliament and the people, no such document was publicly available.[19] Instead, the temporary constitution was adopted by Parliament on 22 December 1965 and remained the only operational constitution Singapore had until it was consolidated in 1980. This document was actually a conglomeration of three separate documents: (a) the Constitution of the State of Singapore 1963; (b) the Republic of Singapore Independence Act 1965 (RSIA);[20] and (c) portions of the Malaysian Federal Constitution imported through the RSIA.[21] Because of the near to identical wording of the fundamental liberties provisions in both the Singapore and Malaysian Constitutions, the courts have read each other's judicial decisions with great interest and treated them as being of a high persuasive value. As such, many cases from Malaysia will be cited in the following chapters to show how the Malaysian courts have interpreted the relevant provisions.

Under the RSIA, certain provisions of the Malaysian Federal Constitution were to be made applicable to Singapore. Section 6 of the RSIA provided that the provisions of the Constitution of Malaysia, other than those set out in section 6(3), 'shall continue in force in Singapore subject to such modifications, adaptations and qualifications

---

[19] See 'A Team of Experts to Draft Singapore Charter' *The Straits Times* 11 Sep 1965, at 20; 'Singapore's Constitution for Parliament soon' *The Straits Times* 4 Oct 1965, at 10; 'Singapore Constitution' *The Straits Times* 16 Dec 1967, at 13; 'Draft Constitution to be out soon' *The Straits Times* 16 May 1968, at 4.

[20] Act No 9 of 1965.

[21] Most of the imported provisions pertain to the fundamental liberties provisions which are federal matters and were missing in the state constitution.

and exceptions as may be necessary to bring them into conformity with the independent status of Singapore upon separation from Malaysia'. Section 6(3) specifically excluded Article 13 of the Constitution of Malaysia because of the impending passage of the Land Acquisition Bill. This was one of the most important pieces of legislation that the PAP Government was anxious to pass so that it could proceed with its industrialisation and public housing programmes.

V. THE RIGHT TO PROPERTY IN SINGAPORE

A. The Land Acquisition Problem

Singapore's first land acquisition law was passed in 1920[22] and subsequently amended in 1946 and 1955. However, the powers of compulsory acquisition were limited and the government was compelled to pay market prices for property to be acquired. The government's main concern was with the adequacy and fairness of compensation rather than on coercive action. In 1955, internationally renowned Australian land valuer, Dr JFN Murray was commissioned to 'ascertain the most practicable means of controlling land prices, and to draft legislation which would ensure that, in future, community-created values would be retained by all the people of the Colony'.[23] In this report, Murray opined that legislative intervention was necessary to avert 'disastrous increases in land values'.[24] The resulting Land Acquisition (Temporary Provisions) Ordinance pegged the market value of land at 22 April 1955. Murray also argued that compulsory acquisition of land 'should be resorted to only when all possibility of obtaining land by agreement with an owner had ended, either because he was unwilling to sell or consistently asked too high a price'.[25]

When the PAP Government came to power in 1959, it was determined to amend the Land Acquisition Ordinance. In July 1963, the Land

---

[22] Straits Settlements Acquisition of Land for Public Purposes Ordinance 1920, Act No XXIII of 1920.

[23] See Colony of Singapore, *A Report on Control of Land Prices, Valuation and Compulsory Acquisition of Land* (Singapore, Government Printing Office, 1954).

[24] ibid, at 10, para 15.

[25] ibid, at 4.

Acquisition (Temporary Provisions) Bill was introduced in the Singapore Legislative Assembly to peg the value of land to be acquired for public purposes to that prevailing on 1 January 1961. It was blocked and lapsed. On 10 June 1964, the Land Acquisition (Amendment No 2) Bill was introduced in the Singapore Legislative Assembly. Speaking at the Second Reading of the bill, Prime Minister Lee Kuan Yew outlined two broad principles guiding the government in amending the land acquisition law: (a) that no private landowner should benefit from development which had taken place at public expense; and (b) that the price paid on the acquisition for public purposes should not be higher than what the land would have been worth had the government not contemplated development generally in the area. Public development should not, he said, benefit the landowners but 'benefit the community at large'.[26]

At the same time, the government introduced the Foreshores (Amendment) Bill, which was aimed at 'eliminating the elaborate and lengthy procedure in connection with foreshore reclamation and in the assessment of claims for compensation in respect of such foreshore reclamation'.[27] The main provision in this bill sought to repeal section 7 of the Foreshores Ordinance such that there

> shall be no compensation as of right in respect of any land or any interest therein alleged to have been injuriously affected whether on account of loss of sea frontage or for any other reason by the execution of such reclamation works.[28]

The object of these two bills was to 'ensure, albeit imperfectly, that the increase in value of land, because of the increase in population and in development, should not lead to unjust or windfall gains by private landowners and speculators'.[29]

B. Constitutional Difficulties

The Land Acquisition (Amendment) Bill was sent to select committee in 1964 but had to be withdrawn on the advice of the State

---

[26] *Singapore Legislative Assembly Debates Official Reports* 10 June 1964, vol 23, col 25.
[27] See speech of Prime Minister Lee Kuan Yew, ibid, at col 31.
[28] ibid. The Foreshores (Amendment) Ordinance No 2 of 1964.
[29] See speech of Prime Minister Lee Kuan Yew (n 26) at col 33.

Advocate-General's Chambers. In his statement before the Legislative Assembly on 16 June 1965, Law Minister EW Barker said:

> The State Advocate-General's Chambers have looked into these matters and have advised that, in order to remove any doubts on the validity of this new legislation, it will be necessary for the Malaysian Parliament to exempt such a Bill from the operation of Article 13 of the Constitution …
>
> Representation will be made to the Central Government for such an exemption provision to be passed in Parliament in order that these projects can be carried out in Singapore without any uncertainty about the constitutional validity of the formula for compensation.[30]

The constitutional right to property had been enacted as Article 13 of the Constitution of the Federation of Malaya. The article was derived from a similar provision in the Indian Constitution and automatically applied to Singapore when Singapore became part of the Federation of Malaysia. However, as noted above, Article 13 was deliberately left out of the Constitution when Singapore seceded from the Federation in 1965. Law Minister EW Barker explained the rationale as follows:

> Clause 13—we have specifically set out to exclude. The reason is quite simple. This Constitution was drawn up by five eminent jurists from five of the major Commonwealth countries for the old Federation of Malaya. It is, in form, modelled upon a similar provision in the Constitution of the Republic of India. Since the passage of that section in the Indian Constitution, amendments have had to be introduced because land reforms were not possible, if the strict tenor of the words were to be complied with. In other words, in clause 2, once we spell out that no law shall provide for the compulsory acquisition or use of property without adequate compensation, we open the door for litigation and ultimately for adjudication by the Court on what is or is not adequate compensation.
>
> … It very often happens, as it did in the case of the development of the Jurong industrial site, that when public funds have been expended in considerable amounts for the development of roads, services, harbours, the adjacent land appreciates in value. And when it became necessary to acquire parts of the adjacent land for future expansion of the estate itself or for ancillary services such as schools, hospitals, and so on, we had to pay the owner under our present acquisition laws the enhanced value of the land, a

---

[30] *Singapore Legislative Assembly Debates Official Reports*, 16 June 1965, vol 23, col 812.

value to which he himself had contributed nothing and which was, in fact, created wholly by the expenditure of State funds.... Whilst we were still in Malaysia, we had sought to get Article 13 excluded in its application to us, but, in the nature of things, these matters either took a very long time for any decision to be made or for some reason or other no decision was made. Now the jurisdiction again reverts to this House and it is our intention that the Land Acquisition Bill shall be proceeded with and Article 13 excluded.[31]

C. The Land Acquisition Act 1966[32]

On 21 April 1966, the Land Acquisition Bill was introduced in the newly constituted Singapore Parliament. At the Second Reading, on 22 June 1966, Law Minister EW Barker once again explained that the passage of the bill had been 'delayed because of constitutional difficulties'.[33] The bill was sent to select committee, passed on 26 October 1966 and became operational from 17 June 1967.[34] The most potent portion of the Act is section 5 which stipulates that the three grounds upon which land can be acquired by the state are: (a) for any public purpose; (b) by any person, corporation or statutory board, for any work or an undertaking which, in the opinion of the Minister, is of public benefit or of public utility or in the public interest; or (c) for any residential, commercial or industrial purposes.

Beyond the Land Acquisition Act, several other statutory bodies in Singapore have been conferred compulsory acquisition powers. Among them are the three bodies responsible for a substantial part of Singapore's infrastructural development—the Housing and Development Board, the Jurong Town Corporation and the Urban

---

[31] *Singapore Parliamentary Debates Official Reports*, 22 Dec 1965, vol 24, cols 435–36.

[32] See generally, TTB Koh, 'The Law of Compulsory Land Acquisition in Singapore' (1967) 2 *Malaya Law Journal* ix; WJM Ricquier, 'Compulsory Purchase in Singapore' in T Kotaka & DL Callies (eds), *Taking Land: Compulsory Purchase and Regulation in Asian-Pacific Countries* (Honolulu, University of Hawaii Press, 2002), at 263–85; N Khublall, *Compulsory Land Acquisition—Singapore and Malaysia*, 2nd edn (Singapore, Butterworths Asia, 1994); and Tan Sook Yee, *Principles of Singapore Land Law*, 2nd edn (Singapore, Butterworths Asia, 2001), at 638–49.

[33] *Singapore Legislative Assembly Debates Official Reports*, 22 June 1966, vol 25, col 133.

[34] For a commentary on this Act, see Koh, 'The Law of Compulsory Land Acquisition in Singapore' (n 32).

Redevelopment Authority (URA).[35] The overall national interest, which required vast tracts of land to be reclaimed and developed for industrial use, was crystallised in the passing of the Land Acquisition Act and providing various other statutory bodies with powers of compulsory acquisition.[36] The dramatic transformation of the Jurong Industrial Estate and the Housing and Development Board's world-famous public housing programme are often used to rebut criticism over the constitutional exclusion of individual property rights.

Even in instances when litigants were minded to challenge whether compulsory acquisition has been for a 'public purpose', the courts have been reluctant to encroach on the government's role in defining state economic imperatives. For example, the High Court ruled in *Galstaun v Attorney-General* that:

> The Government is the proper authority for deciding what a public purpose is. When the Government declares that a certain purpose is a public purpose, it must be presumed that the Government is in possession of facts which include the Government to declare that the purpose is a public purpose.[37]

In *Basco Enterprises Pte Ltd v Soh Siang Wai*,[38] the appellants challenged an acquisition by the government on the grounds that the URA had acquired the premises improperly and that the acquisition was for an improper purpose since it acquired the charming colonial building (Stamford Court) at 1973 prices and resold it on the open market, thereby making a substantial profit. The Court of Appeal held that there was no evidence that the purpose of acquisition was for the making of profit.

---

[35] These statutory authorities were established under the Housing and Development Act (Ordinance 11 of 1959) in 1959, the Jurong Town Corporation Act in 1968 (Act 5 of 1968) and the Urban Redevelopment Authority Act in 1973 (Act 65 of 1973) respectively. Other legislation in which powers of compulsory acquisition have been provided for include the: Planning Act, Economic Development Board Act, Public Utilities Act, Telecommunication Authority of Singapore Act, Controlled Premises (Special Provisions) Act, Railways Act, Preservation of Monuments Act and Local Government Integration Act. Most of the powers of acquisition originally given to these statutory authorities were removed in 1989. Indeed several of these statutes have since been repealed.

[36] Act 41 of 1966, currently Cap 152, Statutes of the Republic of Singapore, 1985 rev edn.

[37] See *Galstaun v Attorney-General* [1981] 1 MLJ 9, at 10, per FA Chua J.

[38] [1990] 1 MLJ 193.

VI. PREVENTIVE DETENTION

A. Background to Executive Detention in Singapore

Lee Kuan Yew's consolidation of power within his own party in the early-1960s was made possible by the existence and implementation of two draconian and powerful security laws: the Preservation of Public Security Ordinance (PPSO) and the Internal Security Act 1960. Both these laws provided for preventive detention of suspected subversives and communists. Individuals could be detained—without trial—for up to two years at a time by the government for suspected left-wing or communist activity.

Both Singapore and Malaysia derive their preventive detention legislation from the same source. Such legislation originated as part of the war powers of the British colonial executive, and eventually became a common weapon of the colonial administration. It was first introduced into Malaysia (then the Federated States of Malaya) by the Emergency Enactment 1930.[39] The early legislation was used mainly to deal with the subversive activities of the South Seas (*Nanyang*) Communist Party in Singapore and the Malayan Communist Party (MCP) in Malaya[40] who were committed to the overthrow of the British Government by force. The British battle against communism and the MCP in particular resumed in 1948 when a state of emergency was proclaimed and the MCP outlawed.[41] Under this Proclamation of Emergency, emergency regulations were passed to deal with the communists, but these regulations had to be reviewed and re-issued every few months. Since the Emergency was meant to be a temporary state of affairs, the rationale for this continuous review and re-enactment of regulations was evident.

The first attempt to put these preventive detention laws on a more permanent footing occurred in Singapore when the Legislative Council passed the PPSO on 21 October 1955.[42] The PPSO was based on

---

[39] See s 3(2)(b), Federated Malay States Gazette 1930 vol XXII.

[40] See Rais Yatim's excellent 'Detention Without Trial Under the Internal Security Act 1960: The Necessity for its Abolition' (1996) XXV No 2 INSAF 21, at 28. The author states that the South Seas Communist Party was formed in 1928 while the MCP was formed in 1930.

[41] On the Malayan Emergency generally, see R Clutterbuck, *Conflict and Violence in Malaysia and Singapore* (Singapore, Graham Brash, 1984).

[42] The PPSO was passed on 21 Sep 1955 as Ordinance 25 of 1955.

Indian, Pakistani and Burmese precedents. Section 3 gave the Chief Secretary the power to direct that a person be detained for a period not exceeding two years if the Governor-in-Council was satisfied that the detention was necessary to prevent that person from acting in a manner which was prejudicial to the security of Malaya, the maintenance of public order or the maintenance of essential services.[43] Significantly, the PPSO gave the final decision on whether a person should be detained to a panel of three judges.[44] The 1955 Rendel Constitution did not include a bill of rights. As such, no fundamental liberties were guaranteed under this essentially colonial constitution and no constitutional issues were raised when the PPSO was passed.

The Emergency in Malaya was only lifted in 1960, and the ISA,[45] which remains the centrepiece of all preventive legislation, was enacted by the then Federation of Malaya Government on 22 June 1960 to make possible the cessation of the 1948 Emergency on 31 July 1960. The Malayan ISA of 1960 was subsequently imported into Singapore when Singapore became part of the Federation of Malaysia on 16 September 1963. Under the Malaysia Act 1963,[46] all provisions of the Malayan ISA (with the exception of sections 8(1) and 8(2)) applied to Singapore. At the same time, sections 4 to 15 of the PPSO were repealed.[47] Later, a number of amendments were made to the ISA as it applied to Singapore; the net result being that the legislation in both states were practically word-for-word the same.[48] With the application of the Malayan Internal Security Act (ISA) to Singapore in 1963, the discretion to detain a person under the ISA moved completely to the President or the Minister of Home Affairs. In the meantime, When Singapore left the Federation in August 1965, the ISA continued to apply to Singapore by virtue of section 13(1) of the RSIA.[49] It was subsequently reprinted as Cap 115 of the 1970 Revised Edition of the Singapore Statutes.[50] In addition to the ISA, several other pieces of legislation provide for administrative detention. Notable among

---

[43] See PPSO, s 3.
[44] See PPSO, ss 5(4), 6 and 7.
[45] Federation of Malaya Act No 18 of 1960.
[46] Federation of Malaya Act No 23 of 1963.
[47] See LN 231/63.
[48] See LN 271/63, LN 334/64; and LN 335/64.
[49] Act No 9 of 1965.
[50] Currently Cap 142, Singapore Statutes, 1985 rev edn.

these are the Criminal Law (Temporary Provisions) Act (CLTPA),[51] the Infectious Diseases Act,[52] the Misuse of Drugs Act[53] and the Mental Health (Care and Treatment) Act.[54]

In 1956, the Lim Yew Hock Government detained some of the PAP's most important left-wing trade union leaders, including Lim Chin Siong, CV Devan Nair, Fong Swee Suan, James Puthucheary, and Sandy Woodhull. Their detention was made possible under the PPSO, and this enabled Lee's moderate faction to secure control of the party's leadership and to keep the left-wing leaders out of the PAP's Central Executive Committee. However, after the PAP won the 1959 General Elections, Lee Kuan Yew made it a condition of his taking office that the PAP's detained members be released. The released leaders were given a heroes' welcome and then promptly appointed to positions within government where they could do little harm and where they had no real power. Lim Chin Siong, for example, was appointed Political Secretary to Finance Minister Goh Keng Swee while Fong Swee Suan was Political Secretary to the Minister for Labour and Law.

While the left-wing leaders were unable to do much damage to the ministries to which they were attached, they continued to foment disaffection within the labour movement. The rift within the PAP became increasingly apparent and the party teetered on the brink of collapse. It took the issue of merger with the Federation of Malaya, and the British Borneo territories of Sabah and Sarawak to form the Federation of Malaysia that forced the dissensions into the open. In July 1961, 13 PAP Assemblymen were expelled from the party for abstaining on a vote of confidence in the government. They then established a new political party, the Barisan Sosialis (Socialist Front), with Lee Siew Choh as chairman and Lim Chin Siong as secretary-general.

In the battle leading up to merger with Malaysia in 1963, the Barisan pulled out all the stops. Tunku Abdul Rahman, Prime Minister of Malaya and soon-to-be Prime Minister of Malaysia, was greatly alarmed by the pro-communist and radical stance adopted by the Barisan. As the PAP's majority in the Legislative Assembly was whittled down to just one vote, the Tunku decided to act. In February 1963, the Internal

---

[51] Ordinance 26 of 1955, currently Cap 67, Singapore Statutes.
[52] Act 21 of 1976, currently Cap 137, Singapore Statutes.
[53] Act 5 of 1973, currently Cap 185, Singapore Statutes.
[54] Act 21 of 2008, currently Cap 178A, Singapore Statutes.

Security Council[55] approved Operation Coldstore, a joint Malayan-Singapore police operation that resulted in the arrest of 107 left-wing political leaders, trade unionists and supporters. These included practically the whole of the Barisan's Central Executive Committee. The arrests came as a relief to the PAP who went on to win 37 of the 51 seats in the general election that followed in September that year. That same month, Singapore became part of the new Federation of Malaysia and with the staunchly anti-communist Tunku in charge of the central government, the PAP was able to rebuild its mass support base without the need to fight a rearguard action against the pro-communists and radical left.

By 1968, when elections were required to be called under the Constitution, the Barisan was a decimated force. Its decision to abandon Parliament to take its struggle into the streets was perhaps its biggest political mistake for it left the PAP with hegemonic control over the entire political arena. With no opposition to challenge it, the PAP Government was able to put in place all the economic programmes and strategies it desired.

From a legal perspective, the PAP Government allowed the ISA to remain on the statute book after independence in 1965. Indeed, it continued to use it against suspected subversives and communists in the years to come. This was made possible by the inclusion of Article 9(6) of the Constitution which provides that any law 'in force before the commencement of this Constitution which authorises the arrest and detention of any person in the interests of public safety, peace and good order' shall not be invalid by anything in Article 9, which provides that 'No person shall be deprived of his life or liberty save in accordance with law'. The presence of this draconian law and the PAP Government's willingness to use it has acted as a major deterrent against anyone wishing to challenge the government's power other than in a general election.

---

[55] The Council was a panel proposed by the British to consider all matters relating to Singapore's internal security. It comprised the British High Commissioner, and two members nominated by the British, three Singapore representatives, including the Prime Minister, and one member nominated by the Federation of Malaya Government.

B. The Wee Chong Jin Commission

After a patchwork Constitution was cobbled together after Singapore seceded from the Federation, Parliament appointed a Constitutional Commission headed by the Chief Justice, Wee Chong Jin, to study how minority interests could be safeguarded.[56] Even though the terms of reference of the Commission[57] were limited to considering representations on the rights of racial, linguistic and religious minorities and how provisions for their protection through entrenchment in the Constitution could be effected, the Commission's report went far beyond that.

The Commission issued its report in 1966 and made a number of important recommendations.[58] It recommended that the constitutional provisions relating to 11 fundamental liberties, the judiciary, the legislature, general elections, minority rights and the special position of Malays, and the amendment procedures themselves, be entrenched. This was to be done by making these provisions amendable only if the amendment secures a vote of two-thirds majority in Parliament and two-thirds majority at a national referendum.[59]

The Commission further recommended the reintroduction of a modified clause to guarantee the right to property. In its report, the Commission stated that in view of the fact that all written constitutions guaranteed the right to property and 'one of the human rights proclaimed under the Universal Declaration of Human Rights by the General Assembly of the United Nations on 10 December 1948, is the right of an individual not to be arbitrarily deprived of his property'[60] a similar provision should be included in Singapore's Constitution. It was, the Commission continued, 'necessary, sound and wise and in the best

---

[56] Members of the Commission were: Wee Chong Jin CJ (chairman), AP Rajah (vice-chairman), CFJ Ess, MJ Namazie, CC Tan, SHD Elias, Syed Esa bin Syed Hassan Almenoar, G Abisheganaden, Graham Starforth Hill, Abdul Manaf Ghows, Kirpal Singh and S Narayanaswamy (secretary).

[57] See *Singapore Parliamentary Debates Official Reports* 22 Dec 1965, vol 24, cols 429–30.

[58] *Report of the Constitutional Commission 1966* (Singapore, Government Printer, 1966).

[59] ibid, at paras 78 and 81.

[60] ibid, at para 41.

interests of the people of Singapore ... that its Constitution should recognise and proclaim this fundamental right'.[61]

While the Commission did not recommend re-introducing Article 13 of the Constitution of Malaysia, it considered it imperative that 'a just and fair balance must be struck between the public interest on the one hand and private ownership on the other' and that this was best achieved through a new article in the Constitution providing as follows:

> 14(1) No person shall be deprived of property save in accordance with law.
>
> (2) No law shall provide for the compulsory acquisition or use of property except for a public purpose or a purpose useful or beneficial to the public and except upon just terms.

The Commission's recommendations were received by Parliament in December 1966 and the government squarely rejected this particular recommendation. Speaking before the House, Law Minister EW Barker said:

> The Government would accept this Article but for the words at the end, namely, 'and except upon just terms'.
>
> Members may be aware that we have, at various times while within Malaysia, sought to amend Article 13 of the Malaysian Constitution in its application to Singapore. The intention was to follow the provisions in the Indian Constitution so that any law providing for the compulsory acquisition of property shall be valid so long as that law provides for compensation and that such a law shall not be questioned in court as to the adequacy of the compensation. The new Land Acquisition Act, which has been passed by this House and will be brought into force shortly, provides for the setting up of a Lands Appeals Board and it is not considered desirable that the intentions of that legislation should be stifled by landowners being able to raise constitutional issues when disputes over the quantum of compensation arise.[62]

VII. FUNDAMENTAL LIBERTIES UNDER SINGAPORE'S CONSTITUTION

The 'Fundamental Liberties' provision is in Part IV of the Constitution. Its eight articles contain guarantees on: (a) life and liberty; (b) prohibition

---

[61] ibid, at para 42.
[62] *Singapore Parliamentary Debates Official Reports* 21 Dec 1966, vol 25, cols 1053–54.

of slavery and forced labour; (c) protection against retrospective criminal laws and repeated trials; (d) equality and equal protection of the law; (e) prohibition against banishment and freedom of movement; (f) freedom of speech, assembly and association; (g) freedom of religion; and (h) rights in respect of education. In the remainder of this chapter and the next, we consider how these various liberties and rights have been articulated and limited by the courts. As we noted above, this Part of the Constitution was adopted (almost word-for-word) from the Federation of Malaysia Constitution 1957 under the RSIA.

The framers of the Constitution obviously felt some liberties to be more important than others. Some of them are absolute (for example, Article 10(1) which states that 'No person may be held in slavery'), while others are qualified (for example, the exceptions to equality under Article 12); or protect only citizens (for example freedom of speech, association and assembly under Article 14). When looking at the continued applicability of the provisions of Part II of the Federal Constitution of Malaysia, the Wee Chong Jin Commission considered it 'wise, desirable and practical, having regard to the past, the present and the future, to preserve the common destiny of the peoples of Singapore and Malaysia' not to 'depart, except where we think it is necessary and desirable, from the form and substance of similar provisions in the Malaysian Constitution'.[63]

The Commission recommended that the

> best and most appropriate way of safeguarding the rights of the racial, linguistic and religious minorities ... would be specially to entrench in the Constitution the fundamental rights of both the individual and the citizen ... as well as all those provisions of the Constitution which we consider essential for the protection of those rights.[64]

The manner of entrenchment, the Commission added, was to make the fundamental liberties provisions amendable only 'by a two-thirds majority of the electors on the electoral roll at a referendum'.[65] These recommendations for entrenchment of fundamental rights were rejected by Parliament, especially since the amendment process for the State Constitution of Singapore 1963 had been changed just the year before.

---

[63] ibid, at para 14.
[64] *Report of the Constitutional Commission 1966* (n 58), at para 11.
[65] ibid, at para 18.

In December 1965, Parliament passed the Constitution of Singapore Amendment Act,[66] and made it retrospective to 9 August 1965. This Act changed the procedure required for constitutional amendment: the two-thirds parliamentary majority was abolished and only a simple majority was required for an amendment to the Constitution. The reason for this change in the amendment process was the PAP's fear that should it require to effect a constitutional amendment, it may not command the necessary two-thirds majority in the legislature to do so. The two-thirds majority for constitutional amendments was only restored in 1979.

Another effort to entrench the Part IV provisions in the Constitution came by way of the changes that created the elected presidency in 1991. Under Article 5(2A)—which has not yet been brought into force—any bill seeking to amend any provision in Part IV of the Constitution, must be approved by the President, acting in his personal discretion. If the President does not approve the amendment, the amendment can only be effected if it is supported by two-thirds of the total number of votes cast in a national referendum. This 'protection' of Part IV fundamental liberties depends greatly on the President, and does not automatically devolve to the people, as proposed by the Wee Commission. There is thus nothing to stop the President from colluding with Parliament to destroy any of the constitutional rights under Part IV, short of a revolution to throw either of them out.

In relation to the protection of minorities in Singapore—the central pillar of the Commission's terms of reference—the Commission took the view that

> a person, whether he is a citizen or not, who belongs to a racial or a linguistic or a religious minority in Singapore will have all his rights as a member of such racial or linguistic or religious minority adequately safeguarded if his fundamental rights as an individual, and as a citizen if he is one, are entrenched in the Constitution, and if those fundamental rights are enforceable by the Courts ... we do not propose, although it has been suggested that we should, to recommend any provision in the Constitution specifying, enumerating or defining the races, languages and religions which fall within the category of the racial, linguistic or religious minorities in Singapore.[67]

---

[66] Act No 8 of 1965.
[67] *Report of the Constitutional Commission 1966* (n 58), at paras 12–13.

The Wee Commission further recommended that a non-elected advisory body—which it called the Council of State—be established to safeguard minority rights and interests. Under its proposal, the Council would be appointed by the President, acting in his discretion, and in consultation with the Prime Minister, a group of 'able, mature citizens irrespective of race, colour or creed who have attained eminence or responsible positions in their respective walks of life but who are not members of any political party'.[68] It would be the responsibility of this Council to 'focus the attention of the public on any matter originating from Parliament which may adversely affect the interests of any minority group' and provide 'an additional check on new legislation ... on matters which might affect the minorities'.[69] And where there was no responsible or effective opposition in Parliament, the Council would put forward 'constructive and well-informed criticism or amendments of measures proposed in Parliament'.[70]

This proposal was accepted in principle and created as the Presidential Council in 1969. It was later renamed the Presidential Council of Minority Rights in 1973. When finally created, the Council comprised 21 members: a chairman appointed for 3 years; 10 permanent members appointed for life; and 10 other members appointed for a period of 3 years.[71] The Council has two functions: the general function to 'consider and report on such matters affecting persons of any racial or religious community in Singapore' referred to it by Parliament or the government; and the specific function to draw to Parliament's attention, 'any Bill or to any subsidiary legislation if that Bill or subsidiary legislation is, in the opinion of the Council, a differentiating measure'.[72] Under Article 78 of the Constitution, all bills passed by Parliament must be sent to the Council for consideration. The Council has 30 days to report on the bill, stating to Parliament whether it contains a 'differentiating' or discriminatory measure. If the Council issues an adverse report, Parliament may revise the bill, and then re-submit it to the Council, or else override the Council's report by a two-thirds

---

[68] ibid, at para 16.
[69] ibid.
[70] ibid.
[71] Constitution of the Republic of Singapore, Art 69.
[72] ibid, Art 77.

majority of votes. Meetings of the Council are in private, and to date, the Council has never issued any adverse report.

VIII. INTERPRETING FUNDAMENTAL LIBERTIES

As the Reid Commission noted, the entrenchment of fundamental rights in the Constitution benefits from the 'guarantee afforded by the Constitution' as 'the supreme Law and the power and duty of the Courts to enforce these rights and to annul any attempt to subvert any of them'.[73] Courts are thus called upon to interpret the Constitution in their efforts to construe the extent of the liberties protected. What then is the approach of the Singapore judiciary to constitutional interpretation? Two key questions arise in this process:

a. Should Singapore's Constitution be interpreted in its own terms or with reference to other similar constitutions?

b. Should the fundamental liberties provisions be interpreted more generously vis-à-vis other constitutional provisions?

A. Westminster Constitutions

Our short excursus into Singapore's constitutional history in chapter one clearly shows the Westminster lineage of its constitution. Like so many other constitutions drafted by the British in the last days of empire, Singapore's Constitution bears the imprint of the Westminster model: parliamentary democracy premised on a two-party system; fusion of membership in the executive and legislative branches with the Cabinet being drawn from Members of Parliament; the Prime Minister as head of government, and a titular head of state. How relevant is this background to the interpretation of the Constitution?

The importance of constitutional models was first discussed locally in the Malaysian case of *Loh Kooi Choon v Government of Malaysia*,[74] where the Federal Court considered the constitutionality of an amendment to the Constitution which had the effect of exempting provisions of the

---

[73] *Report of the Federation of Malaya Constitutional Commission* (n 18), at 70, para 161.
[74] [1977] 2 MLJ 187.

Restricted Residence Enactment from the application of Article 5(4) of the Federal Constitution. In the course of its judgment, the Federal Court held, citing the Privy Council case of *Hinds v The Queen*,[75] that in 'constitutions based on the Westminster model, in particular the provisions dealing with fundamental rights … impose a fetter upon the exercise by the legislature of the plenitude of its legislative power' until altered by a constitutional amendment. This was essentially a positivist reading of the amendment power and nothing turned on whether the constitution being interpreted was of the Westminster variety or not.

However, the important Privy Council decision of *Ong Ah Chuan v Public Prosecutor*[76] was to provide useful pointers in constitutional interpretation. In this case, the Privy Council had occasion to consider the meaning of the word 'law' under the fundamental liberties provisions of the Singapore Constitution and observed that while Singapore's rights provisions are almost identical with those of the Federal Constitution of Malaysia, they 'differ considerably in their language from and are much less compendious and detailed than those to be found in Part III of the Constitution of India under the heading "Fundamental Rights"' and 'differ even more widely from' the American Bill of Rights.'[77] This being the case, decisions of the Supreme Courts of India and the United States 'are of little help in construing provisions of the Constitution of Singapore or other modern Commonwealth constitutions which follow broadly the Westminster model'.[78] Repeating what it said in the *Minister of Home Affairs & Anor v Fisher & Anor* (1980), the Privy Council held:

> [T]hat the way to interpret a constitution on the Westminster model is to treat it not as if it were an Act of Parliament but 'as sui generis, calling for principles of interpretation of its own, suitable to its character … without necessary acceptance of all the presumptions that are relevant to legislation of private law'.[79]

And in applying these precepts to the case before it, the Privy Council held that in constitutions

> founded on the Westminster model and particularly in that part of it that purports to assure to all individual citizens the continued enjoyment of

---

[75] [1977] AC 195 (Privy Council, on appeal from Jamaica).
[76] [1980–1981] SLR 48.
[77] ibid, at 60–61.
[78] ibid, at 61.
[79] ibid.

fundamental liberties or rights, references to 'law' in such contexts as 'in accordance with law', 'equality before the law', 'protection of the law' and the like, in their Lordships' view, refer to a system of law which incorporates those fundamental rules of natural justice that had formed part and parcel of the common law of England that was in operation in Singapore at the commencement of the Constitution.[80]

These key passages in *Ong Ah Chuan* have been cited and re-cited in many cases that followed. But exactly how useful is the character or structure of Westminster constitutions in interpreting Singapore's home-grown variety? For a start, the Singapore courts have held that as the Singapore Constitution is based on the Westminster mode, it 'adopts and codifies most, if not all, of the laws, customs and conventions and practices of the British constitutional and parliamentary system'.[81]

The character of Westminster constitutionalism has been most successfully invoked when the courts were considering the nature of relationships between the various branches of government. One of the earliest uses of the doctrine in this connection was in the case of *Cheong Seok Leng v PP*,[82] where the High Court considered whether the test developed by the High Court of Australia[83] 'to differentiate between a legislative and an executive or administrative act' was applicable to Singapore. Chan Sek Keong J (as he then was) held that as Singapore's Constitution 'is also based on the doctrine of separation of powers (as modified to accommodate the Westminster model of parliamentary government)', the test was indeed applicable.[84] In *Law Society of Singapore v Tan Guat Neo Phyllis*,[85] the High Court (sitting as a bench of three), considered the nature of the prosecutorial power and discretion and observed that:

> In Singapore, the Constitution establishes a form of parliamentary government (based on the Westminster model) based on the separation of the legislative, executive and judicial powers. Each arm of the government

---

[80] ibid, at 61–62.

[81] *Jeyaretnam Joshua Benjamin v Attorney-General* [1987] SLR(R) 472, at 475 (High Court).

[82] [1988] 1 SLR(R) 530.

[83] *The Commonwealth v Grunseit* (1943) 67 CLR 58, per Latham CJ, at 82–83.

[84] [1988] 1 SLR(R) 530, at 543.

[85] [2008] 2 SLR(R) 239.

operates independently of the other and each should not interfere with the functions of the other. As each of them is limited in its authority and power by the Constitution itself, it is necessary that there should exist a means whereby each arm may be prevented from acting beyond its constitutional powers. Under the Constitution, the means adopted and recognised by all three arms of government is the judicial power of the court to review the legality of legislative and executive acts and declare them unconstitutional and of no legal effect if they contravene the provisions of the Constitution. The modifications to the Constitution that established the office and powers of the elected President do not affect this feature of the Constitution. However, the Constitution also expressly provides for the separation of the judicial power from the prosecutorial power. The express separation of the two powers is relevant to the role of the court in relation to the exercise of the prosecutorial power.[86]

In *Public Prosecutor v Manogaran s/o R Ramu*,[87] the Court of Appeal was asked to consider whether the word 'law' in Article 2 of the Constitution included judicial pronouncements, interpretations and statutory provisions that created criminal liability. The Court cited *Ong Ah Chuan* and held that constitutional provisions 'should be liberally construed to advance their intent and prevent their circumvention' and that Article 2 was indeed drafted sufficiently widely to include judicial interpretations of the Constitution. In *Yong Vui Kong v Attorney-General*,[88] the Court of Appeal was asked to decide on the extent of the President's discretionary powers under Article 22P. The Court invoked the Westminster model and held that

a ceremonial Head of State who: (a) must act in accordance with the advice of the Cabinet in the discharge of his functions; and (b) has no discretionary powers except those expressly conferred on him by the Constitution. In our local context, Art 22P is not a provision which expressly confers discretionary powers on the President.[89]

Finally, in considering the nature of the separation of powers under the Constitution in *Mohammad Faizal bin Sabtu v Public Prosecutor*,[90] Chan Sek Keong CJ offered the most detailed exposition of the relevance of the

---

[86] ibid, at 310.
[87] [1996] 3 SLR(R) 390.
[88] [2011] 2 SLR 1189.
[89] ibid, at 1208–09.
[90] [2012] 4 SLR 947.

Westminster model of constitutionalism in Singapore. The case concerned the constitutionality of section 33A(1)(a) of the Misuse of Drugs Act, which provided for mandatory punishment for repeat drug offenders. The Westminster system of government, opined the learned Chief Justice, was predicated on the distribution of the state's sovereign powers between the parliamentary, executive and judicial branches of government. There are, however, two key differences between the 'pure' Westminster system as practised by Britain and that of Singapore. First, Singapore's written constitution is supreme, whereas Parliament is supreme in the UK. Second, while judicial power is vested in the UK courts under the common law or by statute, it is vested in the courts under a constitutional provision— Article 93—and is thus 'co-equal in constitutional status with the legislative power and the executive power'.[91]

B. The Interpretation of Rights in Light of International Legal Instruments

Singapore is not a party to either of the two big human rights treaties— the International Covenant on Civil and Political Rights and the International Covenant on Economic, Social and Cultural Rights—but is a party to some others, like the Convention on the Elimination of All Forms of Discrimination Against Women (CEDAW), the Convention on the Rights of the Child (CRC), and most recently, the Convention on the Rights of Persons with Disabilities. As a state, Singapore adopts a dualist view of international law and no treaties are self-executing.[92] All treaty obligations must be transformed through the enactment of local law to be effective. In *The 'Sahand' and Other Applications*, the High Court held that it would be contrary to Article 38 of the Constitution to hold that treaties concluded by the executive branch of government were directly incorporated into domestic law:[93]

> By virtue of Art 38 of the Constitution ... the legislative power of Singapore is vested in the Legislature. It would be contrary to Art 38 to hold that treaties concluded by the Executive on behalf of Singapore are directly incorporated into Singapore law, because this would, in effect, confer upon

---

[91]   ibid, at 958.
[92]   See *Public Prosecutor v Tan Cheng Yew & Anor Appeal* [2013] 1 SLR 1095, at 1116.
[93]   [2011] 2 SLR 1093.

the Executive the power to legislate through its power to make treaties. Accordingly, in order for a treaty to be implemented in Singapore law, its provisions must be enacted by the Legislature or by the Executive pursuant to authority delegated by the Legislature. In so far as a treaty is not implemented by primary or subsidiary legislation, it does not create independent rights, obligations, powers, or duties.[94]

In recent years, there have been several attempts to read into the Constitution rights other than those explicitly provided by the Constitution by reference to human rights ostensibly embodied in customary international law. Customary international law—if proven—applies to Singapore except where 'it is inconsistent with the domestic law'.[95] A rule of customary international law must 'be clearly and firmly established before its adoption by the courts'.[96] In *Public Prosecutor v Nguyen Tuong Van*,[97] the High Court was asked to consider if terms of the Vienna Convention on Consular Relations 1963 applied to Singapore even though Singapore was not a party to the Convention. Justice Kan Ting Chiu held that the Convention was a 'key instrument in the regulation and conduct of consular activities' and observed that at least 167 countries were parties to the Convention, and as Singapore held itself 'out as a responsible member of the international community' and conformed 'with the prevailing norms of the conduct between states', its terms applied.[98] However, when the Court of Appeal was asked—in the same case on appeal—to consider if the mandatory death penalty violated a customary rule of international law, it held that there was 'simply not sufficient State practice to justify' a finding that it violated customary international law.[99]

C. The 'Four Walls' Doctrine and Beyond

The 'four walls' doctrine of constitutional interpretation[100] was first articulated locally in the Malaysian Federal Court decision of *Government*

---

[94] ibid, at 1107.
[95] *Public Prosecutor v Nguyen Tuong Van* [2004] 2 SLR(R) 328 (High Court).
[96] *Nguyen Tuong Van v Public Prosecutor* [2005] 1 SLR(R) 103 (Court of Appeal).
[97] [2004] 2 SLR(R) 328.
[98] ibid, at 345–46.
[99] *Nguyen Tuong Van v Public Prosecutor* [2005] 1 SLR(R) 103, at 127–28.
[100] See generally, Li-ann Thio, 'Beyond the "Four Walls" in an Age of Transnational Judicial Conversations: Civil Liberties, Rights Theories, and Constitutional Adjudication in Malaysia and Singapore' (2006) 19 *Columbia Journal of Asian Law* 428.

of State of Kelantan v Government of the Federation of Malaya,[101] in which Lord President Thompson stated that 'the Constitution is primarily to be interpreted within its own four walls and not in the light of analogies drawn from other countries such as Great Britain, the United States of America or Australia'.[102] Thompson LP made this observation in the light of a passage in the Privy Council decision of *Adegbenro v Akintola*[103] which emphasised the primacy of the constitutional text as opposed to constitutional practice:

> [I]t is in the end the wording of the Constitution itself that is to be interpreted and applied, and this wording can never be overridden by the extraneous principles of other Constitutions which are not explicitly incorporated in the formulae that have been chosen as the frame of this Constitution.[104]

This observation was elevated to doctrine by the Singapore High Court when Chief Justice Yong Pung How repeated and affirmed Thompson LP's words in *Chan Hiang Leng Colin & Ors v Public Prosecutor*.[105] This approach to constitutional interpretation prima facie rejects the utility of foreign judgments in interpreting and understanding the provisions in Singapore's Constitution. In application, this can be almost perfunctory. For example, in *Chan Hiang Leng Colin & Ors v Public Prosecutor*, the High Court rejected several American decisions and international legal instruments on religious freedom 'without reasons, other than a bare assertion of "difference"'.[106] Over the years, the application of the 'four walls' doctrine has become more nuanced. In *Chee Siok Chin v Public Prosecutor*[107] for example, Justice VK Rajah—while extolling the merits of the 'four walls' approach—seriously examined and distinguished foreign judgments cited by counsel. This same approach was adopted by the Court of Appeal in subsequent cases like *Review*

---

[101] [1963] MLJ 355.
[102] ibid.
[103] [1963] 3 WLR 63 (on appeal from Western Nigeria).
[104] ibid, at 73.
[105] [1994] 3 SLR(R) 209, at 231. This approach was further affirmed by the High Court in *Taw Cheng Kong v Public Prosecutor* [1998] 1 SLR(R) 78; and by the Court of Appeal in *Nappalli Peter Williams v Institute of Technical Education* [1999] 2 SLR(R) 529.
[106] See Thio Li-ann, *A Treatise on Singapore Constitutional Law* (Singapore, Academy Publishing, 2012), at 562.
[107] [2006] 1 SLR(R) 582.

Publishing v Lee Hsien Loong,[108] *Yong Vui Kong v Public Prosecutor*[109] and *Shadrake Alan v Attorney General.*[110]

One of the big problems of such a restricted 'four walls' approach is that if the courts are discouraged from looking askance for constitutional meaning, then they must necessarily look inwards to the Constitution and to what it allows Parliament to do. Notwithstanding the limits placed on constitutional amendment, Parliament still has a wide latitude to change the law and to pass laws that may be patently unfair. For example, there is no constitutional provision that will allow the Singapore courts to strike down any law that provides for extremely severe penalties for minor infractions. So, Parliament may technically pass a law to imprison for 20 years, a person guilty of illegal parking. So long as procedures for amending the Constitution and passing statutes are scrupulously observed, these types of draconian measures will pass muster.

This may be exacerbated by the fact that courts will not challenge the probity of Parliament's intent. Take Article 12—which provides that '[a]ll persons are equal before the law'—for example. In interpreting this provision, the courts have adopted the 'reasonable classification' test, which essentially provides that that so long as there is a reasonable nexus between the class of persons discriminated against and the legislative object, the law is valid. This problem was drawn into sharp relief in two cases—*Tan Eng Hong v Attorney-General*[111] and *Lim Meng Suang & Anor v Attorney-General*[112]—involving the constitutionality of section 377A of the Penal Code, which makes it a crime for any 'male person' to commit 'any act of gross indecency with another male person'. The applicants in these cases argued that section 377A was unconstitutional in that it discriminated against male homosexuals. The High Court, applying the two-step 'reasonable classification' test, held that section 377A was constitutional since: (a) male homosexuals constituted a clear, definable and rational class; and (b) it was clear from the legislative history of section 377A that Parliament had clearly intended to criminalise

[108] [2010] 1 SLR 52.
[109] [2011] 2 SLR 189.
[110] [2011] 3 SLR 778.
[111] [2013] 4 SLR 1059.
[112] [2013] 3 SLR 118.

the 'grossly indecent acts; of male homosexuals'.[113] Both cases are on appeal before the Court of Appeal as this volume goes to press.

D.   Balancing of Rights: Between State and Individual

One of the primary challenges for any court interpreting constitutional rights is how to strike the right balance between the rights of individuals and the imperatives of state. Singapore courts have traditionally adopted a 'purposive approach' to constitutional interpretation. Section 9A(1) of the Interpretation Act provides that in interpreting any provision of written law, 'an interpretation that would promote the purpose or object underlying the written law ... shall be preferred to an interpretation that would not promote that purpose or object'.[114] This purposive approach was sanctioned and applied in *Constitutional Reference No 1 of 1995*, where it was held that it is 'well established and not disputed by either parties that a purposive interpretation should be adopted in interpreting the Constitution to give effect to the intent and will of Parliament'.[115]

The purposive approach thus requires the court to ascertain the will of Parliament and then determine how the words or provisions in question ought to be interpreted in light of the Constitution. In making such a determination, the court may rely on any material forming part of the record that may shed light on Parliament's intent. This appears to be a fairly straightforward exercise but problems arise the moment the court is called upon to weigh the competing interests of the individual and the state. A recent example of this balancing occurred in the case of *Chee Siok Chin v Minister of Home Affairs & Anor*.[116] The three applicants and another person staged a 'peaceful protest' outside the Central Provident Fund Building. The police arrived and told them to disperse as they were creating a public nuisance. The protestors surrendered their placards and protest T-shirts and commenced an action against the

---

[113]   ibid, at 145–57.
[114]   See generally, *Public Prosecutor v Low Kok Heng* [2007] 4 SLR(R) 183.
[115]   ibid, at 814.
[116]   [2006] 1 SLR(R) 582.

Minister for Home Affairs for a violation of their Article 14(1) right to freedom of expression.

In the course of its judgment, the High Court had to consider whether the applicants' Article 14(1) rights had been legitimately restricted by virtue of Article 14(2)(a), which empowered Parliament to impose restrictions that 'it considers necessary or expedient in the interest of' the security of Singapore or public order. The High Court held that the words 'necessary or expedient' in Article 14(2) of the Constitution conferred on Parliament 'an extremely wide discretionary power and remit that permits a multifarious and multifaceted approach towards achieving any or the purposes specified in Article 14(2) of the Constitution'.[117] 'The touchstone of constitutionality', held the Court, was 'whether the impugned legislation can be fairly considered "necessary or expedient" for any of the purposes' under Article 14(2) and all that 'needs to be established is a nexus between the object of the impugned law and one of the permissible objects stipulated in Art 14(2) of the Constitution'. The government could, under its 'wide legislative remit', take a 'prophylactic approach in the maintenance of public order'.[118] There can be 'no questioning of whether the legislation is "reasonable"'.[119] This judgment demonstrates the wide berth given to state authorities in their curtailment of fundamental liberties.

It can thus be seen that Singapore courts have seen their roles primarily as watchdogs rather than as bloodhounds. In protecting human rights and fundamental liberties, the courts often proceed on the assumption that Singapore has a good and honest government run by persons of integrity and good faith. This assumption sets a high bar for those who allege bad faith or mala fides on the part of the state. This difficulty is exacerbated by the fact that in many laws, the executive is afforded wide discretionary powers.

[117] ibid, at 602.
[118] ibid, at 603.
[119] ibid, at 602.

FURTHER READING

HE Groves, 'Fundamental Liberties in the Constitution of the Federation of Malaysia' in M Suffian, HP Lee and FA Trindade (eds), *The Constitution of Malaysia: Its Development, 1957–1977* (Kuala Lumpur, Oxford University Press, 1978).

AJ Harding, 'Property Rights under the Malaysian Constitution' in FA Trindade & HP Lee (eds), *The Constitution of Malaysia: Further Perspectives and Developments: Essays in Honour of Tun Mohamed Suffian* (Singapore, Oxford University Press, 1986).

RH Hickling, 'Law and Liberty in Singapore' (1979) 21 *Malaya Law Review* 1.

N Khublall, *Compulsory Land Acquisition—Singapore and Malaysia*, 2nd edn (Singapore, Butterworths Asia, 1994).

TTB Koh, 'The Law of Compulsory Land Acquisition in Singapore' (1967) 2 *Malaya Law Journal* ix.

WJM Ricquier, 'Compulsory Purchase in Singapore' in T Kotaka & DL Callies (eds), *Taking Land: Compulsory Purchase and Regulation in Asian-Pacific Countries* (Honolulu, University of Hawaii Press, 2002) 263–85.

LA Sheridan, 'Constitutional Protection of Property' (1962) 28 *Malaya Law Journal* lxv, lxxiii, lxxxix, cv, cxxv, cxli.

Tan Sook Yee, *Principles of Singapore Land Law*, 2nd edn (Singapore, Butterworths Asia, 2001), at 638–49.

Thio Li-ann, 'An "i" for an "I" Singapore's Communitarian Model of Constitutional Adjudication' (1997) 27 *Hong Kong Law Journal* 152.

———, 'Trends in Constitutional Interpretation: Oppugning Ong, Awakening Arumugam' [1997] *Singapore Journal of Legal Studies* 240.

———, 'Beyond the "Four Walls" in an Age of Transnational Judicial Conversations: Civil Liberties, Rights Theories, and Constitutional Adjudication in Malaysia and Singapore' (2006) 19 *Columbia Journal of Asian Law* 428.

———, 'Protecting Rights' in Thio Li-ann & KYL Tan (eds), *Evolution of a Revolution: Forty Years of the Singapore Constitution* (London, Routledge-Curzon, 2009) 193–233.

AK Thiruvengadam, 'Comparative Law and Constitutional Interpretation in Singapore: Insights from Constitutional Theory' in Thio Li-ann & KYL Tan (eds), *Evolution of a Revolution: Forty Years of the Singapore Constitution* (London, RoutledgeCurzon, 2009) 114–52.

9

Conclusion

———◆◆◆———

Three Leitmofits – Regime Dominance – Economic Growth and Development – Management of Ethnicity and Religious Diversity – Conclusion

I. THREE LEITMOTIFS

THE EVOLUTION OF Singapore's Constitution from the end of the Second World War to the present day is unique in many ways. Unlike many former British colonies, Singapore has progressed and prospered without abandoning the established constitutional order. The Westminster model of constitutionalism was, to a large extent, maintained and altered to fit the prevailing needs. Legal continuity was maintained and notwithstanding some of its illiberal facets, the Singapore Constitution retains its primacy and legitimacy among the people of Singapore. It may not be as revered a document as the American Constitution, for example, but it nevertheless continues to form the basic framework for social, economic and political advancement. Its initial flexibility in the post-independence era allowed the government to make sweeping reforms in all spheres. Success, apparently, breeds success. Changes and amendments to the constitutional structure were in many respects self-legitimising since the government's economic and political policies were on the whole remarkably successful. In a basically immigrant society where material well-being has traditionally been valued above legal rights, even the most fundamental changes to the Constitution are easily tolerated.

The key to legitimacy in constitutional law and politics is undoubtedly the ability of the government to forge a consensus with its people. It is crucial that the electorate supports the government's agenda for action based on the agreed constitutional framework. Ideals, aspirations and political values are not etched in stone and do not transcend the generations. They are dynamic in nature and with each generation, a new consensus must be reached. In Singapore, the Constitution has thus far been seen as a basic framework of social and economic progress. The Constitution of Singapore, unlike the American Constitution, is not based on the Lockean philosophy of limited government, which stresses control and checks on government. Instead, it is a pragmatic document that provides a springboard for governmental action. It is an instrument that promotes change, but which at the same time assures the populace of a large measure of stability. Singapore's constitutional growth and development can best be understood by reference to three overlapping themes: regime dominance; economic development and growth; and the management of ethnicity and religion. We consider these in greater detail below.

II. REGIME DOMINANCE

A. Power and Governance

Central to the People's Action Party (PAP) Government's programme of action in its 1959 election campaign was the promise to bring economic growth through industrialisation and the development of key sectors of the economy.[1] At a special party congress at the Singapore Badminton Stadium on 25 April 1959, party chairman Toh Chin Chye read out the Central Executive Committee's proposed five-year plan 'for the transformation of a feudalistic and conservative outlook to a progressive socialist outlook, and so prepare the preliminary groundwork for a future socialist society'.[2] Specifically, the PAP promised to industrialise Singapore's economy, develop the agricultural and fisheries sectors, train personnel for construction work, improve workers' welfare, improve education, streamline state administration, improve the health of the people and empower women.[3]

---

[1] See generally, KYL Tan, 'Economic Development and the Prospects for Constitutionalism' in A Chin & A Choi (eds), *Law, Social Sciences And Public Policy: Towards A Unified Framework* (Singapore, Singapore University Press, 1998).

[2] 'Five-year PAP plan for S'pore' *The Straits Times* 26 Apr 1959, at 1.

[3] ibid.

It was clear that if the PAP were to keep its election promises, it had to first acquire the wherewithal to do so. The surest way was to win big and to establish a strong central government with control over all levers of power. This was to prove much harder in practice than in theory. Even though the PAP won the 1959 elections handsomely, its hold on power was tenuous. Internal divisions within the party between the moderate group led by Lee Kuan Yew and the radical left-wing group headed by Lim Chin Siong were soon to tear the party apart. Indeed, it was the issue of merger with the Federation of Malaya that brought the rift out into the open and led to a massive defection of PAP members to form the Barisan Sosialis (Socialist Front) in 1961. The two erstwhile bedfellows battled to represent the 'political left' outside the Malayan Communist Party.

B. Consolidating Party and State

The battle for supremacy within the PAP has been well documented elsewhere.[4] As was previously discussed in chapter eight, the consolidation of power by Lee's moderate wing was made possible the PAP's use of the two key preventive detention laws: Preservation of Public Security Ordinance (PPSO)[5] and the Internal Security Act 1960.[6] This enabled the PAP to defeat a decimated Barisan Sosialis to win the 1963 general election. The Barisan's decision to abandon Parliament in 1966 and boycott the 1968 general election allowed the PAP to exert hegemonic control over Singapore politics. Having secured the Party's survival, it was necessary for the PAP to ensure that the Singapore state could survive. Various constitutional amendments were effected towards this end. In particular, Part III of the Constitution, which guarantees the sovereignty of the state, was inserted in 1972. This amendment ensured that should Singaporeans wish to surrender Singapore's sovereignty or control over its armed and police forces, this

---

[4] See esp, J Drysdale, *Singapore: Struggle for Success* (Singapore, Times Books, 1984); D Bloodworth, *The Tiger & the Trojan Horse* (Singapore, Times Books International, 1986); and S Yap, R Lim & Leong Weng Kam, *Men in White: The Untold Story of Singapore's Ruling Political Party* (Singapore, Straits Times Press, 2009).

[5] Ordinance 25 of 1955.

[6] Act 18 of 1960 (Federation of Malaya).

could only be done if two-thirds of the voters agree to do so during a national referendum. At the same time, national security and public order became serious trumps vis-à-vis individual rights. The Jehovah's Witnesses were banned as an organisation in 1972 on the grounds that their members refuse to serve compulsory military service (mandatory for all male citizens and permanent residents). Constitutional challenges to this ban—on grounds that it violated rights to religious freedom—were rejected by the Court of Appeal.[7]

C. Regime Hegemony

By 1968, when elections were required to be called under the Constitution, the Barisan was a decimated force. Its decision to abandon Parliament in 1966 to take its struggle into the streets was perhaps its biggest political mistake as it left the PAP with hegemonic control over the entire political arena. With no opposition to challenge them, the PAP Government was able to put in place all the economic programmes and strategies it desired. There was also nothing to prevent the PAP from amending the Constitution in any way it wanted.

The PAP Government allowed the ISA to remain on the statute books after independence in 1965. Indeed, they continued to use it against suspected subversives and communists in the years to come. Interestingly, no constitutional challenge was lodged against the validity of the ISA between 1965 and 1978 when Parliament amended the Constitution to insert what is now Article 9(6),[8] which provides that 'any law 'in force before the commencement of this Constitution which authorizes the arrest and detention of any person in the interests of public safety, peace and good order' shall not be invalid by anything in Article 9(1) of the Constitution, which provides that 'No person shall be deprived of his life or liberty save in accordance with law'. The presence of this draconian law and the PAP Government's willingness to use it has acted as a major deterrent against anyone wishing to challenge the government's power other than in a general election.

---

[7] See *Chan Hiang Leng Colin & Ors v Minister for Information and the Arts* [1995] 3 SLR 644; *Chan Hiang Leng Colin & Ors v Public Prosecutor* [1994] 3 SLR 662.

[8] Republic of Singapore Constitution (Amendment) Act, Act 5 of 1978.

Even though it has won every single election handsomely since 1959, the PAP began worrying about the possibility of a 'freak result', especially after it lost the Anson by-election in 1981. This then triggered the significant changes to Singapore's parliamentary system which we discussed in chapter three—the Non-Constituency MP Scheme, the Group Representation Scheme, the Nominated MP Scheme—as well as the elected presidency scheme discussed in chapter six. These changes were prompted by the fear of what might happen to Singapore should the PAP be voted out and power vest in politicians they saw as being lesser than themselves.

III. ECONOMIC GROWTH AND DEVELOPMENT[9]

A. Striving for Economic Legitimacy

Even though the PAP Government benefited immensely from the arrests under Operation Coldstore, it could not hope to rule by force alone. In any case, military power remained in the hands of the British and Singapore did not even have its own standing army until 1968. What the PAP Government needed to do was to gain what Friedrich calls 'performance legitimacy' through the delivery of economic promises and goods.[10] It understood quite early on that rights, freedom and limited government mean very little to people living on the verge of starvation. Neither does it mean much to those who see their standards of living falling day by day. Therefore, unless a government—whether legally or constitutionally legitimate or not—confronts and deals with basic issues such as food, housing, job opportunities and education, its legitimacy will quickly evaporate.

---

[9] See generally, C Carter, *Eyes on the Prize: Law and Economic Development in Singapore* (The Hague, Kluwer, 2002); and KYL Tan, 'Economic Development and the Prospects for Constitutionalism' in Chin & Choi (eds), *Law, Social Sciences And Public Policy: Towards A Unified Framework* (n 1) 187–206; and KYL Tan, 'Economic Development and Human Rights in East Asia: Legal Reforms in Singapore and Taiwan' in J Bauer & DA Bell (eds), *The East Asian Challenge For Human Rights* (Cambridge, Cambridge University Press, 1999) 264–84.

[10] CJ Friedrich, *Limited Government: A Comparison* (New Jersey, Prentice-Hall, 1974), at 114.

B. The Prevailing Economic Milieu

The basis for Singapore economic development, noted Huff, was 'and for most of its history has remained—geography'.[11] Between 1819 and 1868, Singapore emerged as the main British trading post in Southeast Asia largely because of its geographical location. Even so, it was a modest trading settlement until the opening of the Suez Canal in 1869 and the rapid increase in world demand for primary produce like tin and rubber catapulted Singapore into a major international trading centre.[12] From then on, Singapore's trade exploded:

> Between 1871/73 and 1900/02 Singapore's trade (imports + exports) increased more than sixfold from an annual average of $67 million to $431 million. A second phase of growth began after 1910, and by 1925/27 trade had expanded a further fourfold to reach a pre-World War II apex of $1,832 million. These are current-dollar figures, but they indicate rapid real growth for Singapore's trade sector—and thus for its highly trade-dependent economy as a whole … real trade growth averaged 3.3% between 1870 and 1937, representing a doubling in volume every 22 years.[13]

The Japanese Occupation (1942–45) put paid to this spectacular growth. When the British returned to the island in 1945, they found an economy shattered by war, and the British Military Administration (1945–46), a martial-law administration, did little to stem the black marketeering and corruption that had become endemic. What greeted the British on their return in 1946 was an impoverished population disenchanted and disillusioned by Britain's inability to defend Singapore—the 'Malta of the East'. Even so, the years between 1946 and 1953 saw quick economic growth that saw Singapore recover economically significantly from the devastation of the Japanese Occupation. This recovery did not percolate down to the bulk of the population and below this veneer of prosperity lurked a hotbed of communist activity, trade union radicalism and militant student activism that became increasingly problematic by the 1950s.

Communists and their sympathisers had infiltrated most of the trade unions. From 1954 to 1965, labour stoppages, strikes and riots—the

---

[11] See WG Huff, *The Economic Growth of Singapore: Trade and Development in the Twentieth Century* (Cambridge, Cambridge University Press, 1994), at 7.

[12] ibid, at 8.

[13] ibid, at 11–12.

stock in trade weapons of nationalist movements—were commonplace. Between 1954 and 1963, a total of 2,866,355 man-days were lost as a result of 697 strikes involving 183,022 workers.[14] While unemployment in 1957 was running at about 5 per cent—about the same as during its pre-War period—there was widespread poverty.[15] It was estimated that 19 per cent of households and 25 per cent of individuals lived below the poverty line.[16] At the same time, the birth rate grew an average of 4.4 per cent annually between 1947 and 1957—the highest known in the world.[17] Thus, when the PAP Government took office in 1959, it became imperative for it to address the population's economic concerns as a matter of priority. Recalling those early days, Goh Keng Swee— Singapore's first Finance Minister and chief economic architect— remarked:

> [W]hen we took office in June 1959 ... the setting could hardly have been less auspicious ... There were extensive acts of violence, largely communist-inspired, in the course of this anti-imperialist struggle. Apart from acts of terror on individuals, such as the execution of recalcitrant trade union and student leaders by underground terror gangs, three large-scale riots occurred between May 1954 and October 1956. Seventeen people lost their lives and seventy-eight were seriously injured. In addition, acts of arson caused serious loss of property.[18]

The '*laissez-faire* policies of the colonial era', thought Goh, 'led Singapore to a dead end with little economic growth, massive unemployment, wretched housing and inadequate education'. If the PAP was to fulfil its election promises, it '*had* to try a more activist and interventionist approach'.[19] Over the next 50 years, the state thus became the key engine driving Singapore's economic growth. The fact that Singapore has been, since 1963, a polity dominated by a single political party—the PAP—is significant in understanding the story of its

---

[14] These figures were gleaned from Huff, ibid, at 295.
[15] See Goh Keng Swee, *A Social Survey of Singapore: A Preliminary Study of Some Aspects of Social Conditions in the Municipal Area of Singapore* (Singapore, Dept of Social Welfare, 1947).
[16] Huff, *The Economic Growth of Singapore* (n 11), at 291.
[17] ibid, at 292.
[18] Goh Keng Swee, 'A Socialist Economist that Works' in CV Devan Nair (ed), *Socialism That Works ... The Singapore Way* (Singapore, Federal Publications, 1976) 77–85, at 77.
[19] ibid, at 84.

economic success. The PAP Government saw its principal source of legitimacy in economic terms.

Writing in 1960, one of Singapore's pioneering economists, Professor Lim Tay Boh worried that 'the pressure of unbalanced nationalism, political extremism and ignorance may lead to the adoption of measures which will wreck the structure of Singapore's economy'.[20] He opined that the government's success in implementing its economic programme depended on three factors: (a) the extent it was able to mobilise the country's financial resources for investment in capital formation; (b) the availability of skilled administrative and technical personnel; and (c) the leadership of the politicians, civil servants and business and community leaders.[21]

C. The Power to Succeed

While independence was realised through merger with Malaysia in 1963, Singapore seceded after two tumultuous years in the Federation. At that point, no one thought that Singapore could survive economically on its own. Having independence thrust upon it, the Singapore Government was now faced with the daunting task of securing an economic future for the island. As noted earlier, the main strategy for economic development was massive industrialisation and a diversification of the country's economic portfolio.

To do this, it was essential to centralise a great deal of the state's resources and power in the hands of the government through legislation. The PAP's growth strategy was based on three objectives: first, the achieve a society where all citizens could earn a decent living, and this involved the provision of public housing; second, to provide jobs for all; and third, to give workers rising incomes and improved standards of living over the years. These three aims could only be achieved 'through continuous and rapid economic growth'.[22] Growth was to be achieved through the development of human resources and economic

---

[20] Lim Tay Boh, *The Development of Singapore's Economy* (Singapore, Eastern Universities Press, 1960), at 22.
[21] ibid, at 30.
[22] ibid, at 80–81.

infrastructure.[23] In practical terms, this meant the provision of accessible schooling and adequate technical training for the citizens and workforce, and providing 'an environment favourable to investment in employment-creating and output-raising industries'.[24] As Goh Keng Swee never stopped arguing, mere infrastructural development was insufficient. The government 'had to involve itself in direct ownership and control of many industrial, financial and commercial enterprises' and undertake 'risk-taking ventures in partnership with the private sector'.[25] As economist Lawrence Krause noted, the government no longer confined itself to 'traditional economic pursuits and the building of infrastructure, but instead began to enter into activities that were or could have been the domain of private enterprise' there being 'no ideological barrier preventing the government from entering any economic activity'.[26]

As discussed in chapter eight, one of the first things the post-independence government did was to omit the constitutional right to hold property from the new constitution. The government also used legislation to create statutory bodies such as the Economic Development Board[27] and the Jurong Town Corporation,[28] which would be highly financed and relatively autonomous in their operations but at the same time governed by rules and guidelines established by the government. These bodies were the main instruments through which the economic transformation of Singapore would be effected. The approach of the administration was to accomplish the process of economic development through statutory boards,[29] government departments, public corporations and government companies.

---

[23] ibid, at 81–82.

[24] ibid, at 82.

[25] ibid, at 83.

[26] See LB Krause, 'The Government as Entrepreneur' in K Singh Sandhu & P Wheatley (eds), *Management of Success: The Moulding of Modern Singapore* (Singapore, Institute of Southeast Asian Studies, 1989) 436, at 438–39.

[27] Established under the Economic Development Board Act, Ordinance 21 of 1961.

[28] Established under the Jurong Town Corporation Act, Act 5 of 1968.

[29] On the roles and functions of statutory boards in Singapore, see JST Quah, 'Statutory Boards' in JST Quah, Chan Heng Chee & Seah Chee Meow (eds), *The Government and Politics of Singapore* (Singapore, Oxford University Press, 1985) 120–45.

The key feature of enabling legislation was to give these corporations wide charters and to use privative clauses to minimise the delays which might be caused by legal challenges in court. The reported cases indicate a relatively small volume of legal challenge and dispute resolution through the courts in comparison with the size and scale of activity undertaken by these agencies. Public efficiency and goal-driven public administration were apparently valued more highly than delays and individual rights. In this respect, social justice has a paramount pride of place over individual rights, this being justified on grounds of group survival.

D. Constitutional and Legal Regime of Public Enterprises

One of the most significant characteristics of Singapore's post-independence development has been the substantial role played by statutory boards and government-linked companies.[30] Statutory boards such as the Housing and Development Board, the Public Utilities Board and the Singapore Tourist Promotion Board (now the Singapore Tourism Board) were instrumental in developing Singapore's economic and social infrastructure[31] in a way that few states can. Instead of resorting to centralised state planning, the Singapore Government chose to utilise the legal vehicle of the statutory board and the ordinary corporation—a creation of the British colonial government—as the main instrument of social and economic transformation.

The statutory board is an autonomous government agency established by an act of Parliament with specific purposes, rights and powers. It is separate from the government and is not staffed by civil servants. Neither does it enjoy the legal privileges and immunities of government departments. The main difference is its greater autonomy and flexibility. A Cabinet minister, representing Parliament, oversees the statutory

---

[30] See L Low, 'Public Enterprise in Singapore' in You Poh Seng & Lim Chong Yah (eds), *Singapore: Twenty-five Years of Development* (Singapore, Nan Yang Xing Zhou Lianhe Zaobao, 1984) 253–87; and L Low, *The Political Economy of Privatization in Singapore: Analysis, Interpretation and Evaluation* (Singapore, McGraw-Hill, 1991), at 43–71.

[31] LB Krause, 'The Government as an Entrepreneur' in LB Krause, Koh Ai Tee & Lee Tsao Yuan, *The Singapore Economy Reconsidered* (Singapore, Institute of Southeast Asian Studies, 1987) 107–127, at 112.

board's activities. Constitutionally, this is provided for under Article 30 which empowers the Prime Minister to 'charge any Minister with responsibility for any department or subject'.[32] A Board of Directors manages each statutory board and its members are typically senior civil servants, businessmen, professionals or trade union officials.

The starting point for the state's extensive participation in the Singapore economy is the premise that in a free-market economy—even one with socialist pretensions—the government should not and cannot become involved in every aspect of the economy. This would lead to inefficiencies and create a bloated leviathan of a government sector. At the same time, the Singapore Government knew that the state could not sit back and hope for the forces of demand and supply to bring about an alignment of forces that would create the necessary infrastructure for development. As Pillai noted, there are several reasons for the creation of state enterprises, 'reflecting a series of events and perceived needs in which the state has taken a pioneering and dominant role'.[33]

The first group of public enterprises and statutory boards simply carried on functions historically undertaken by the British colonial government such as public housing (Housing and Development Board), public utilities (Public Utilities Board) and port operations (Port of Singapore Authority). The second group of public corporations were created after independence and were typically single-purpose in nature, created to perform very specific functions. These included central banking (Monetary Authority of Singapore), tourism promotion (Singapore Tourist Promotion Board and Sentosa Development Corporation) or regulating public lotteries (Singapore Totalisator Board). The third group of state enterprise have been evident in strategic sectors such as in shipping (Neptune Orient Lines), petroleum (Singapore Petroleum Company) and defence (Sheng-Li Holdings). The fourth group of public enterprises were created to demonstrate the government's confidence in the viability of a pioneer industry such as shipbuilding and insurance. State enterprise in the company form helps rationalise the

---

[32] Constitution of the Republic of Singapore, Art 30(1)(a).
[33] See PN Pillai, *State Enterprise in Singapore: Legal Importation and Development* (Singapore, Singapore University Press, 1983), at 75.

state's activity within the whole administrative system and to lower cost overheads by entry into the commercial market as well.[34]

E. Economic Development and State Power

The PAP's economic strategy obviously worked. Between 1960 and 1990, the economy grew rapidly, with trade as its main engine of growth. There were, however, three developments that set this phase of development apart from the earlier periods. First, the economy was much more diversified with the manufacturing and financial and business services sectors leading the charge. Second, much growth came from public enterprises and multi-national corporations, and third, the government's activist hand in planning and spearheading economic growth was far more pronounced than in any other period in its history.[35] In this period, the Gross Domestic Product (GDP) grew by an average of 8.7 per cent annually.[36]

The state proved to be the ideal apparatus for economic intervention for two reasons. First, two key characteristics of modern states make them powerful engines for effecting economic changes: universal *membership* of states (unlike in private economic organisations), and the state's powers of compulsion which are generally unavailable to private economic organisations.[37] These two unique characteristics enable the state to play a pivotal role in planning, regulating and charting the course of economic development within its own boundaries. Second, the widespread application of the ideas of John Maynard Keynes literally made it mandatory for modern states to intervene in economic matters. The positive reaction to Keynesian economics following the Great Depression of the 1930s[38] in the industrialised West triggered off a wave of interventionist policies by governments throughout the world.

---

[34] ibid, at 70–75.

[35] Huff, *The Economic Growth of Singapore* (n 11), at 299.

[36] ibid, at 14.

[37] JE Stiglitz, 'On the Economic Role of the State' in A Heertje (ed), *The Economic Role of the State* (London, Basil Blackwell, 1989) 11, at 21.

[38] See M Weir & T Skocpol, 'State Structures and the Possibilities for "Keynesian" Responses to the Great Depression in Sweden, Britain and the United States' in PB Evans, D Rueschemeyer & T Skocpol (eds), *Bringing the State Back In* (Cambridge, Cambridge University Press, 1985), at 107.

The success of supply-side economics provided the impetus needed for governments to abandon their hitherto *laissez-faire* attitudes towards the marketplace and its actors.

F. Disciplining Labour

In a celebratory pamphlet published in 1991, the Economic Development Board stated that the three main prerequisites for sustained economic growth were: (a) gaining the people's support and acceptance; (b) establishing a comprehensive legal system; and (c) developing the infrastructure.[39] In this context, the gaining of the people's support meant disciplining the trade unions, while the comprehensive legal system was one that set out 'the principles governing the conduct of business activities … and helps immeasurably to gain investor's confidence'.[40] Reflecting on that early period of Singapore's political economy, Goh Keng Swee remarked:

The greatest difficulty we faced was in industrial relations. How to break the vicious cycle of trade union militancy and poor economic performance? We were fortunate that part of the solution was contributed by the Malaysian Government during the two years of merger, when we were a constituent state.

Most of the militant trade unions were under the control of the underground Communist Party of Malaya and operated under the leadership of open United Front leaders. As trade union activities were legal, it was not possible for the Singapore Government to arrest them. Nor was it of any use to plead with them to moderate their activities in the national interest.[41]

To counter the radical left-wing's dominance of the labour movement, the PAP Government turned to the law.[42] One of the first things it

---

[39] See *Economic Development of Singapore, 1960–1991* (Singapore, Economic Development Board, 1992), at 4–6.

[40] ibid at 6.

[41] Goh Keng Swee, 'Transformation of Singapore's Economy, 1960–1985' in L Low (ed), *Wealth of East Asian Nations* (Singapore, Marshall Cavendish Academic, 2004) 23–33, at 26.

[42] On trade unions and Singapore labour law generally, see C Gamba, *The Origins of Trade Unionism in Malaya: A Study in Colonial Labour Unrest* (Singapore, Eastern Universities Press, 1962); A Josey, *Industrial Relations: Labour Laws in a Developing Singapore* (Singapore, Federal Publications, 1976); and Chew Soon Beng, *Trade Unionism in Singapore* (Singapore, McGraw-Hill, 1991).

did after coming to power in 1959 was to introduce the Trade Unions (Amendment) Bill. Under the bill, the Registrar of Trade Unions was empowered to refuse registration of any trade union. Appeals against the Registrar's decision lay to the Minister for Labour whose decision was final. With these powers firmly in hand, the PAP Government then disbanded and deregistered numerous small splinter unions.

By way of background, the first major conglomerate of trade unions, the Singapore Trades Union Congress (STUC), was founded by VK Nair and Lim Yew Hock in May 1951. Lim was its first president. The STUC was closely affiliated with the Labour Front political party and one of its largest affiliates was the 40,000 strong Federation of Services Unions (FSU). In 1955, the left-wing Singapore General Employees' Union (SGEU) held secret talks with the STUC to determine how to build a united trade union front that led to a further affiliation of 29 other radical unions associated with the left-wing, pro-communist unions. With the fusion of these unions, it became the largest conglomerate of unions in Singapore and it was dominated by left-wing politicians and unionists. In 1959, after the PAP swept to power, it amended the Trade Union Ordinance, giving the Registrar powers to deregister unions deemed to be acting against workers' interests. To bring the unions under its control, the government deregistered many anti-government unions and affiliated them with the STUC.

In 1960, the government introduced the Trade Unions Bill to further tighten its hold on the labour movement and to create a unified trade union body. Under the bill, all unions seeking registration had to have a minimum of 250 members, belong to one of the 13 categories enumerated in the law, and be affiliated to an 'association of unions' (in this case the Trades Union Congress). However, the bill was ultimately allowed to lapse when relations between the left-wing union leaders and the PAP crumbled. By this time, it was clearly not in the PAP's interests to have a strong unified labour movement moving against its economic imperatives.

In 1961, the STUC itself was proscribed by the government and deregistered. The conflict within the PAP between the moderates and the left-wing faction over merger with Malaya and the abolition of the Internal Security Council led to the establishment of the opposition Barisan Sosialis. This also split the STUC into the pro-PAP National Trades Union Congress (NTUC), led by CV Devan Nair, and the Singapore Association of Trade Unions (SATU), which had the support of the SGEU, the Singapore Bus Workers' Union (SBWU) and the Singapore Business Houses Employees' Union (SBHEU). The NTUC quickly became the leading trade union organisation, largely because of its effectiveness and government support.

The government accused SATU of instigating 77 strikes between August and December 1961 and maintained a close watch on the Association. On 25 August 1963, the SATU unions and the Singapore Chinese Chamber of Commerce organised a mass rally to press the Japanese for compensation for wartime atrocities. When Prime Minister Lee Kuan Yew attempted to speak at the rally, he was booed off the stage. Three days later, the Registrar of Trade Unions asked seven SATU unions, including the SGEU, SBWU and SBHEU why their registration should not be cancelled for displaying anti-Malaysian banners and placards at the rally, activities that were deemed communist United Front activities. In October 1963, these unions were deregistered and 50 branches of deregistered SATU unions left to join the NTUC.

Following Operation Coldstore which resulted in the massive detention of all the top pro-Barisan union leaders, the power of the unions was broken. By the time of Singapore's independence in 1965, the PAP Government 'did not have to deal with a union movement that was substantially divided ideologically and which included a radical union with its own parent political party'.[43]

Three other major changes to labour legislation completed the PAP Government's efforts to tame the trade unions. The first was the Trade Unions (Amendment) Bill introduced on 24 June 1967. It amended the Trade Unions Ordinance and provided that employees of any statutory board—or body specified by the Minister for Labour—could not be a member or any union unless that union's membership was restricted only to the employees of that board or body. This change was targeted at reducing the influence of the Amalgamated Union of Public Employees (AUPE), which was the largest common union organisation of public employees. Shortly after the bill's enactment, the Minister for Labour directed employees of three statutory boards—the Singapore Telephone Board, the Housing and Development Board and the Public Utilities Board—to leave the AUPE and form their own separate unions. As far as the PAP Government was concerned, the rights of

---

[43] R Vasil, 'Trade Unions' in Singh Sandhu & Wheatley (eds), *Management of Success: The Moulding of Modern Singapore* (n 26) 144–70, at 154.

workers and unions were subjugated to the imperatives of economic development:

> To them, compulsions of economic advancement and racial harmony made it imperative that the government control all instruments and centres of power, and as a corollary that no foci of power, such as unions and business and industry, be allowed to become too strong.[44]

The next two important pieces of legislation to be passed by the PAP Government were the Employment Act and the Industrial Relations (Amendment) Act of 1968. This omnibus Employment Act clearly defined and established the rights and obligations of employers and employees. The blurred line between management and labour was now very clearly drawn. Certain matters, most notably promotions, internal transfers, recruitment of staff, retrenchment, dismissal or reinstatement of staff and allocation of duties or assignments were now clearly within the management's purview and could no longer constitute the basis of a trade dispute or part of a collective-bargaining process or agreement. With these changes, the unions' role was restricted to issues such as wages, work benefits and some aspects of employment conditions. They had no further role in determining issues such as promotions, transfers, recruitment, retrenchment, dismissal or allocation of duties. Following the amendments in 1968, the Industrial Relations Act now required that all disputes go to arbitration before the Industrial Arbitration Court (IAC). The IAC was established in October 1960 to deal with industrial matters concerning employer-employee relations and the settlement of trade disputes. A second IAC was constituted in 1962 but this ceased functioning in 1970 with the decline in the number of cases brought before the tribunal.

With these legal measures, the PAP Government successfully brought labour under control. In the coming years, it would move towards a tripartite association between the party, employers and labour. In 1968, the PAP even nominated six NTUC Central Committee members as candidates in the general elections. On 19 November 1969, the NTUC held a major seminar on the theme of 'Modernisation of the Labour Movement', which involved all the major political leaders in Singapore. The seminar laid the foundation 'for a close relationship between the union movement and the PAP Government, which eventually developed

---

[44] ibid, at 157.

into what came to be called the "PAP-NTUC symbiotic relationship".[45] This relationship was cultivated and forged over the next decade with the help of CV Devan Nair's leadership of the NTUC. In June 1980, the Central Committee of the NTUC approved an institutional arrangement devised by Devan Nair to include the NTUC secretary-general in Cabinet meetings. As noted in chapter five, the NTUC's Secretary General Lim Chee Onn was appointed Minister without Portfolio in the government on 15 September 1980.

IV. MANAGEMENT OF ETHNICITY AND RELIGIOUS DIVERSITY

A. Strategies

Singapore's particular ethnic mix, reinforced by its great religious diversity, has made it a potentially unstable and politically volatile state. Tactically, there are two ways this issue can be dealt with. The first is simply to suppress differences and assimilate the minorities into the majority as has been done by states like Thailand and Indonesia. The other is to reinforce these cleavages further by establishing ethnically based political parties and aggregating their elites in some kind of consociational troika as has been done in Malaysia. The PAP chose a third way. It acknowledged equality of all groups by ensuring that no laws would discriminate against any group, but also made great efforts to provide public assistance to disadvantaged groups and communities to help level the playing field.

Singapore's constitutional response to multi-culturalism has been based on multi-racialism. This is not surprising especially since much of the racial tension in the past has been between the dominant Chinese community and the indigenous, but by-now minority, Malay community. This traditional segmental cleavage[46] is further heightened by the fact that a further segmental cleavage of religion serves to deepen this rift. Couple that with the geo-political situation of Singapore in Southeast Asia (see preceding chapters) and the situation is doubly volatile.

---

[45] ibid, at 160.

[46] See generally, A Lijphart, *Democracy in Plural Societies: A Comparative Exploration* (New Haven, Yale University Press, 1977).

The innovations that have revised Singapore's Westminster-based Constitution are unique experiments in maintaining stability and order in a pluralistic society, and must be seen in that light. Thus far, much of Singapore's multi-racial policy has been made possible by reducing the currency of race and by ensuring some kind of semiotic representation of multi-racialism through the Constitution and in turn through the state's various legal institutions. The stability that Singapore has achieved through its government's policies has also helped in no small measure to keep the situation well under control. Ultimately, the process of forging a more lasting and permanent multi-racial and multi-cultural polity will take generations, and a great deal of education.

B. The Wee Chong Jin Commission's Recommendations

The establishment of the Wee Chong Jin Constitutional Commission in 1965 was just the first step in this direction. Earlier, in an informal way, multi-ethnicity in the political leadership was introduced by Chief Minister David Marshall when he formed a multi-racial Cabinet in 1955 which comprised a Jew, a Malay, a European, an Indian, an Eurasian and two Chinese. Marshall's choice set a high bar in inter-ethnic relations but this was not legally formalised. The next Chief Minister could well have chosen an all-Chinese cabinet without breaching any laws. This was what made the Wee Chong Jin Commission's work so important. Eschewing a racial approach to managing ethnic difference, the Commission recommended entrenching the judiciary and fundamental liberties in the Constitution, and proposed a Council of State to ensure that no legislation would discriminate against racial, any linguistic or religious minority in Singapore. This recommendation was accepted and implemented as the Presidential Council for Minority Rights.

C. Malay Interests

From its formation in 1948, citizens of the Federation of Malaya accepted Malay dominance as part of the constitutional bargain. The Chinese, Indians and other minorities accepted that Malays would be privileged above everyone else and that political power was to be in the hands of Malays. While this was not the case in Singapore, the issue of Malay rights became extremely sensitive at the time when the Federation of Malaysia was being formed. The ethnic-based United Malays Nationalist Organisation argued that the Malays in Singapore should have the same rights as those of their counterparts in the Malay states.

The first serious attempt to embed some kind of protection for the special position of the Malays was made in the run-up to the 1956 Constitutional Talks in London when Chief Minister David Marshall submitted a memorandum which contained a clause that contains many of the words with which we are now fairly familiar. Paragraph 8(8) of this document provides:

> That it shall be the duty of the Government of Singapore at all times to protect the political, economic, social and cultural interests of the Malays, Eurasians and other minorities domiciled in Singapore. It should also be the deliberate and conscious policy of the Government of Singapore at all times to recognise the special position of the Malays, who are the indigenous people of the Island and are most in need of assistance, and within the framework of the general good of Singapore, to support, foster and promote their political, economic, social and cultural interests, and the Malay language.[47]

These words were affirmed by the British Government during the Constitutional Talks of 1957 and enacted in the preamble of the 1958 Order-in-Council (or Constitution) almost verbatim. The only changes made were to the clause 'at all times to protect the political, economic, social and cultural interests of the Malays, Eurasians and other minorities domiciled in Singapore', which was changed to 'it shall be the responsibility of the Government of Singapore constantly to care for the interests of racial and religious minorities in Singapore'.[48] It is important to point out that at this time, these duties, which were imposed on the Singapore Government, were only directory and not mandatory. A preamble of a Constitution does not have the force of law that other provisions of the document do. As such, they are treated very much as directive principles of state, rather than constitutional guarantees.

---

[47] See 'Heads of Agreement' as appended to the Memorandum to Colonial Government, *Report of the All-Party Constitutional Conference*, 1956, at para 8(8).
[48] See Singapore (Constitution) Order-in-Council 1958, SI 1956 of 1958.

As Federation with Malaya became ever more a reality, this preamble took on a different complexion. It became necessary to entrench these provisions in the Constitution proper and this is where some problems with Malaysia arose. The Singapore Government was anxious that any constitutional guarantee of Malay rights should not carry with it an obligation to reserve places in the public service for Malays as was the practice in Malaya. Indeed, it was provided in the Agreement relating to Malays[49] that:

> No discriminatory provision shall invalidate any law relating to Malay rights but ... there shall be no reservation for Malays in accordance with Article 153 of positions in the public service to be filled by recruitment in Singapore, or of permits or licences for the operation of any trade of business in Singapore.[50]

When Singapore became part of the Federation in 1963, the new State Constitution included a new Article 89, which provides as follows:

89(1)   It shall be the responsibility of the Government constantly to care for the interests of the racial and religious minorities in Singapore.

89(2)   The Government shall exercise its functions in such manner as to recognise the special position of the Malays, who are the indigenous people of Singapore, and accordingly it shall be the responsibility of the Government to protect, safeguard, support, foster and promote their political, educational, religious, economic, social and cultural interest and the Malay language.

The current Article 152 is word-for-word the same as the old Article 89; it has simply been renumbered.

Article 152 has never been invoked, challenged or questioned in a court of law. As such, its impact, if any, has been largely psychological rather than legal. From a constitutional perspective, it is doubtful whether a literal reading of the document imposes on the Singapore Government the duty to protect Malay rights as such. Indeed, nowhere are the words 'right' or 'rights' used throughout the article; only the word 'interests'. Nonetheless, the inclusion of this provision signifies a conscious attempt to entrench and honour the Malays as the indigenous people of the land through the state's most important legal document. It also requires the government to safeguard and protect

---

[49] Cmd 22, 1963.
[50] ibid, at para 68.

their economic, social, cultural and linguistic interests. Unlike the Malaysians who have opted for affirmative action in favour of Malays, the Singapore Government has interpreted its constitutional duty as providing opportunities for Malays to compete on equal terms with the rest of the population by providing assistance wherever needed. This has largely been the field of education, where, until recently, free education up to university level was one of the cornerstones of the government's policy.

One major criticism of this approach has been that the idea of promoting Malay interests is totally at odds with the government's policy of meritocracy, which it pursues aggressively. On the other hand, a number of better-educated Malays feel that Article 152 is no longer needed and should be removed. Leaving Article 152 in the Constitution serves only to cultivate a 'crutch mentality' and give credence to the claim that Malays, no matter how talented, succeeded on account of their race alone.

D. Group Representation Constituencies

The Group Representation Constituency (GRC) scheme, which we discussed in some detail in chapter three is the latest effort to institutionalise multi-ethnicity by ensuring that a 'balanced slate of candidates' are elected into Parliament. However, with the twinning of the GRC scheme with Town Council scheme, the GRC became, from 1988, a useful regime dominance tool for the PAP Government as opposition parties had problems finding suitable candidates to stand in the ever-enlarged GRC wards, and could not unseat incumbent PAP teams helmed by instantly recognised high-profile Cabinet ministers. It was not till 2011 that this particular hegemony was broken when the PAP lost the five-member Aljunied GRC to the Workers' Party.

V. CONCLUSION

The Singapore Government's intervention in its economy is well known and accepted. It was made possible by placing the state at the centre of power. Its constitutional and legal framework was structured and augmented to serve the overriding imperative of economic development and in this regard, the government's success has been spectacular. Not only has it gained the economic legitimacy it sought in the 1960s, it has created a non-ideological political system that has engendered little political opposition. Singapore is a textbook example of a 'soft authoritarian' state, a kind of benevolent dictatorship. The PAP Government makes no apologies for this, nor has it baulked at the need to pay the necessary price. S Rajaratnam, Singapore's long-time Foreign Minister noted:

> These countries which are now judged as affluent, as advanced, were lucky in that they embarked on modernization and industrialization when there were no trade unions and no parliament. Modernisation in most of these countries was pushed through by dictators, autocratic monarchs or elites who were not dependent on the popular vote. So they could extract the price for modernization, sometimes an inhuman price for modernization, knowing full well that there were no trade unions or parliament to call them to account.[51]

The soft authoritarian state is highly centralised and powerful. It makes all key political, social and economic decisions and the general population live relatively happily under this all-knowing leadership. They are politically and socially stable and have performed remarkably well in terms of economic development. Politicians and economists, desperate for solutions to Third World problems have become fascinated by the phenomenon of the Four Little Dragons of Asia—South Korea, Taiwan, Hong Kong and Singapore. Linking economic progress to their respective governmental systems and political culture, some scholars have argued that having a form of government with massive powers and a culture which subjugates individual freedom to the wider interest might be the best way to secure economic growth and a better life.

The idea of a soft authoritarian state runs counter to everything a constitutional lawyer holds dear. The ideas of the separation of powers, limited government and fundamental rights appear to be cast to the wind. But in the light of what we have discussed above, do the lessons of Singapore point the way to future constitutional development or regression? Governments must first accumulate enough power to govern. Only then can they begin to put into motion their economic plans and reforms. The form of government suitable to this kind of

---

[51] Speech of Foreign Affairs Minister & Minister for Culture, S Rajaratnam *Singapore Parliament Report of Official Debates* 9 May 1968, Vol 27, col 337.

transformation is, unfortunately, the very antithesis of the western liberal democratic constitutional model advocated by much of the western world.

Singapore's Constitution has been shaped by practicality and workability—as seen through the eyes of the ruling PAP. The Constitution was constantly amended and new institutions were created to deal with immediate problems. Most of the constitutional innovations resulted from anticipated problems that the PAP sought to deal with in a pre-emptive way. The Group Representation Constituency and the elected presidency are two classic examples of these pre-emptive manoeuvres. When creating these new institutions, basic constitutional principles were sometimes side-stepped. For example, when the shortage of Supreme Court judges reached crisis stage, the government did not worry too much about the principles governing judicial independence when it introduced contract judges and Judicial Commissioners, especially since neither had security of tenure.

In the early post-independence years, the government was anxious to ensure that it had enough authority to proceed with its ambitious economic programme. The PAP knew that legitimacy flowed from performance and its hold on power would be secure if it delivered on its election promises and on the economic goods. However, the consolidation and aggregation of power also means the removal of constitutional fetters. As Singapore matures into its 50th year as a republic, the winds of change may well be blowing again. Following the 2011 General Election, when the ruling PAP lost its first GRC in Aljunied, there is serious soul searching within the party. What if it loses a few more GRCs in the next election? It may well be time to consider having an upper chamber or returning most seats to single-member wards. The 2011 presidential election also got everyone thinking. Is there any point in having an elected president with no real mandate from the people? Will it not be too easy to side-step the President, especially since Article 5(2A) is not yet in force.

Governments who ignore the connections between economic development and constitutionalism do so at their own peril. Will soft authoritarianism rule the day? But whether their peoples will continue to live happily under their respective forms of government is a big question that remains unanswered in Singapore. In the long run, when economic success comes to be taken for granted, and where the bulk of the people have satisfied their most important needs, greater demands will be made for a more liberal constitution and form of government. The highest levels of needs, according to Maslow are the 'self-actualising' needs or 'the desire to become more and more what one idiosyncratically is, to become everything that one is capable of becoming'.[52] When people of Singapore reach this level of needs, there will be a corresponding cry for less government and more freedom.

---

[52] A Maslow, *Motivation and Personality*, 2nd edn (New York, Harper & Row, 1970), at 46.

Index